PRODUCTION, MULTI-SECTORAL GROWTH AND PLANNING

Essays in Memory of Leif Johansen

CONTRIBUTIONS
TO
ECONOMIC ANALYSIS

154

Honorary Editor:
J. TINBERGEN

Editors:
D. W. JORGENSON
J. WAELBROECK

NORTH-HOLLAND
AMSTERDAM · NEW YORK · OXFORD

PRODUCTION, MULTI-SECTORAL GROWTH AND PLANNING

Essays in Memory of Leif Johansen

Edited by:

Finn R. FØRSUND

Department of Economics
University of Oslo
Oslo, Norway

Michael HOEL

Department of Economics
University of Oslo
Oslo, Norway

and

Svein LONGVA

Central Bureau of Statistics of Norway
Oslo, Norway

1985

NORTH-HOLLAND
AMSTERDAM · NEW YORK · OXFORD

ISBN: 0 444 87838 6

Publishers:
ELSEVIER SCIENCE PUBLISHERS B.V.
P.O. Box 1991
1000 BZ Amsterdam
The Netherlands

Sole distributors for the U.S.A. and Canada:
ELSEVIER SCIENCE PUBLISHING COMPANY, INC.
52 Vanderbilt Avenue
New York, N.Y. 10017
U.S.A.

PRINTED IN THE NETHERLANDS

Introduction to the series

This series consists of a number of hitherto unpublished studies, which are introduced by the editors in the belief that they represent fresh contributions to economic science.

The term 'economic analysis' as used in the title of the series has been adopted because it covers both the activities of the theoretical economist and the research worker.

Although the analytical methods used by the various contributors are not the same, they are nevertheless conditioned by the common origin of their studies, namely theoretical problems encountered in practical reserch. Since for this reason, business cycle research and national accounting, research work on behalf of economic policy, and problems of planning are the main sources of the subjects dealt with, they necessarily determine the manner of approach adopted by the authors. Their methods tend to be 'practical' in the sense of not being too far remote from application to actual economic conditions. In addition they are quantitative rather than qualitative.

It is the hope of the editors that the publication of these studies will help to stimulate the exchange of scientific information and to reinforce international cooperation in the field of economics.

The Editors

EDITORS' PREFACE

Professor Leif Johansen's contributions to economic science are well documented in his articles and essays for economic journals, symposium volumes, and Festschrifts recently published by North-Holland (<u>Collected Works of Leif Johansen</u>, Vol. I and Vol. II, North-Holland, 1985).

When initiating the idea of such a collection, Professor Dale W. Jorgenson also suggested a memorial volume by associates and others that would include papers devoted to research topics directly inspired by Leif Johansen. In the present volume this idea is realised. Three topics are covered: production theory, multisectoral growth models, and planning. The papers presented were either under work at the time of Leif Johansen's death or prepared especially for this volume. They do not, of course, exhaust the list of topics or papers inspired by Johansen's research.

The introductory paper by R.M. Solow (to some extent built upon his memorial article in The Scandinavian Journal of Economics, Vol. 85 (4), 1983, 445-456) gives an overview of Leif Johansen's contribution to the three topics. In particular, Solow discusses Johansen's pioneering contribution to the putty-clay production concept, his introduction of the first successfully implemented applied general equilibrium growth model without fixed-coefficient input assumptions, and his important influence on models adopted for use in practical applications within economic planning.

Johansen's development of the production function concept had its roots in his seminal article of 1959 on putty-clay models in an economic growth context. Inputs are substitutable when production capacity is created, but once a plant is built inputs are required in fixed proportions. Empirical applications of Leif Johansen's production function framework are provided in the paper by F.R. Førsund, L. Hjalmarsson and Ø. Eitrheim, and in the paper by J. Muysken. In the former the short-run industry production function concept is utilised to make an intercountry comparison of cement production in the Nordic countries. Various aspects of structural change over a twenty year period are clearly illustrated by examining the developments of the short-run functions.

While the cement production study is based on discrete data, J. Muysken in his paper sets out to estimate continuous capacity distributions. The characteristics of the short-run industry production function are implicitly given by the continuous capacity distribution. Muysken fits a beta function to represent the capacity distribution of the Swedish dairy industry.

A. Seierstad in his contribution elaborates a more general theoretical approach to the short-run production function. Allowing the form of the capacity distribution to be of any type (discrete, continuous, or a mixture), a survey of results is presented related to properties of the capacity distribution, the industry (or macro) short-run production function, and the profit function. A more detailed mathematical exposition based on the theory of zonoid of moments, and which includes proofs of results concerning the one-to-one relationship between the capacity distribution and the macro profit function, is also given.

When production functions exhibit putty-clay technology and investment decisions are made with respect to production capacity, information about future prices and demands are needed. K.O. Moene pursues the impact of fluctuations and uncertainties on the profit-maximising choice of ex ante factor proportions. He concludes that due to uncertainty, even under risk neutrality the production technique of a private firm can be too labour intensive if labour can be made redundant without cost.

The introduction of putty-clay technologies into multisectoral growth models was strongly recommended in one of Leif Johansen's last papers. F.R. Førsund and E.S. Jansen pursue this theme in their contribution. They look into the possibilities and difficulties one encounters when trying to implement Leif Johansen's production function approach of ex ante and ex post micro functions and his industry short-run function into a multisector model of the national economy.

The most influential contribution of Leif Johansen is the multisectoral growth model, MSG, first presented in his doctoral thesis of 1960. Within the structure of a multisectoral growth model for the entire economy, MSG makes the basic Walrasian general equilibrium model operational for macroeconomic forecasting and planning purposes. The allocation of labour and capital between production sectors is determined by the interplay of profit-maximising producers and utility-maximising consumers in competitive markets. L. Bergman gives a survey of applications and extensions of this model outside of Norway.

One type of MSG-extension mentioned by Bergman and in the spirit of the Leif Johansen paper mentioned above, is followed up by H. Persson. He establishes the existence of solutions to a model of the MSG-type characterised by sectoral ex ante production functions with substitution possibilities and by dated vintages of capital exhibiting fixed coefficients ex post.

The MSG-model has been used as a tool for long-term planning and forecasting in Norway for more than two decades. It has been revised and extended several times since the early sixties. S. Longva, L. Lorentsen, and Ø. Olsen present the latest version of the MSG-model, MSG-4, in actual use in Norway. Compared with earlier versions, this fourth generation of the model includes a much more general representation of the neo-classical theory of production, a greater number of alternative assumptions concerning the capital market, and a more explicit treatment of the interaction between the economy and energy production and utilisation. In addition, econometric methods have been applied to a greater extent in assessing model parameters. Empirical characteristics of three MSG-4 versions are provided to illustrate the functioning of the model.

From an inside view, P. Schreiner and K.A. Larsen present the history of the MSG-model in the development of Norwegian planning, and by their narrative give us a vivid picture of the entire process of Norwegian economic planning. O. Bjerkholt and S. Tveitereid elaborate on one recent application of the MSG-model within Norwegian long-term planning; namely the preparation of the so-called "Perspective Analysis" for the Norwegian economy during the period 1980 to 2000.

Norway's increasing dependency on oil income has accentuated the need to practically model uncertainty in economic planning models. I. Aslaksen and O. Bjerkholt outline an approach to optimal planning procedures for an economy dependent on assets with stochastic returns. The starting point is an adaption of some ideas put forward by Leif Johansen on parametric certainty equivalence procedures. These procedures are used both for solving the dynamic stochastic optimisation model and for deriving revealed preferences from recent projections of the Norwegian economy.

The manuscripts have all been processed with the new word processor equipment at The Department of Economics. We want to thank all the persons involved in this effort, especially Mrs Gro Winsnes and Randi Borgen for not giving in to an alienating technology and for overcoming numerous teething problems with the word processor and its malfunctioning

software programme.   We also want to thank Mrs Inger-Johanne Kroksjø
and Mrs Ester Larsen (Central Bureau of Statistics) for drawing magnifi-
cent figures, and Bruce Wolman for reading carefully all the manuscripts,
weeding out the worst misuses of English, and improving upon the exposition.

Finn R. Førsund
University of Oslo

Michael Hoel
University of Oslo

Svein Longva
Central Bureau of Statistics of Norway

CONTENTS

Contents   xiii

Production, Multi-Sectoral Growth and Planning
F.R. Førsund, M. Hoel, and S. Longva (Editors)
© Elsevier Science Publishers B.V. (North-Holland), 1985

LEIF JOHANSEN'S CONTRIBUTIONS TO THE THEORY OF PRODUCTION, PLANNING, AND MULTISECTORAL GROWTH

Robert M. Solow

Massachusetts Institute of Technology

1. Production theory

What is the role of the theory of.production in the broad enterprise of analytical economics? We need an answer to that question before we can begin to evaluate the contribution of Leif Johansen and those who have been inspired by him, as illustrated by the papers included in this memorial volume. I take it for granted that the theory of production, pure and applied, is not intended to provide an <u>exact</u> description of technological processes. Some degree of abstraction — not always the same degree of abstraction — is always to be expected. The economic theory of production is not a substitute for chemical engineering. To tell the truth, not even the engineer's description of a production process is likely to be literally exact.

The economist does not usually want a description of production for its own sake. It is an instrumentality, a means rather than an end. The most obvious use for a model of production is that of an indispensable step toward an understanding of a producing unit's supply responses. This is, of course, most obvious in the case of a profit-seeking firm. The position and the elasticity of its supply curve depends on the firm's technological possibilities, given input prices, and any legal, conventional or other constraints it observes. The supply behavior of the firm depends in key ways on the substitutability of inputs and outputs for one another, and on the nature of returns to scale. And those are precisely the aspects of technology that have been most thoroughly studied.

To traditionally trained economists, the profit-seeking firm is only the most familiar type of producing unit. But of course any kind of producing unit has characteristic supply responses, so long as it has the power to make input and output decisions and a coherent criterion according to which it makes decisions. The nature of those supply responses will depend on the choice criterion, but also on the technological possibilities actually available. In any social environment the student of supply must also be a student of production.

For exactly the same reasons, a producing unit's input requirements, its input-demand responses, will also depend on the technological alternatives it is able to exploit. In a capitalist economy, the demand for inputs is a major determinant of input prices and, therefore, of the (functional) distribution of income. Thus the study of income distribution is a somewhat broader purpose for which economic analysis needs a description of production processes. To be useful in this broader framework, the theory of production has to categorize inputs in such a way that they make sense both technologically and distributionally. This may sometimes require compromises. I think it has generally been the profession's belief that the demand side of factor markets is the more "important" side, in the sense that variations in input prices are more likely to reflect fluctuations in demand than fluctuations in supply. More recently, however, I suspect the supply side has assumed greater prominence in the study of input markets, especially labor inputs, and especially if the "supply side" is broadly interpreted to include various institutional features of the labor market that differentiate it sharply from the markets for material inputs.

Finally, and this is particularly important in the context of Leif Johansen's work, the theory and practice of economic planning requires some representation of current technological possibilities. And in addition the planner or student of planning needs some idea of changes in technology, whether they occur exogenously or as a result of decisions that are part of the plan itself. Qualitatively, this role for the economic analysis of production is not so different from the case of the single producing enterprise. It is mostly a matter of level of aggregation and breadth of scope. To the economist, however, the difference in scope highlights certain analytical differences.

It is important to realize that in all of these applications a representation of technology, if it is to be useful, can not limit itself to those technologically feasible outcomes that are actually realized and observed. In each of the three areas of application mentioned, the unrealized and unobserved possibilities matter just as much. This is hard to explain to noneconomists (and even to some economists, I have found).

The supply response of the firm is what it is precisely because it seems more desirable to the firm than any alternative that is technologically (and otherwise) feasible. The same is equally true of a producing unit's input-demand response. To the extent that input prices, and the distribution of income are market determined, the response of distribution to changes in the environment will depend on the elasticity of demand for factor inputs, and therefore on the nature of unobserved, but latently observable, production possibilities.

Most plainly of all, since the essence of planning is choice, a planner can not choose intelligently without some view of the range of feasible actions.

It is therefore not surprising that the theory of production has been a central topic in economics for a hundred years or more. This is not the place to sketch the history of that theory from Wicksteed to the present day. It is pertinent, however, that Johansen, when he came to the economic analysis of production, was working in a Norwegian tradition firmly established by the great Ragnar Frisch.

Frisch's work in production seems — to an outsider, at least — to have been motivated mainly by the application to planning. This shows itself in the attention he paid to descriptions of technology that could be adapted to mathematical programming methods. Johansen shared this orientation. His work on planning models made much use of the input-output description of production possibilities, often with interesting variations. Even his most original work in this field, the refinement of the capacity-distribution method, may have been stimulated by the likelihood that the smoother production function approach could prove to be optimistically misleading in the context of planning.

It is interesting and pleasant to see that some of the contributions to this part of the memorial volume pursue Johansen's deep and successful interest in the development of an analytical approach to production which is susceptible to rigorous aggregation at a level useful for industry-wide or economy-wide planning.

The book on production functions - subtitled "An Integration of Micro and Macro, Short Run and Long Run Aspects" - was published in 1972, but clearly has its roots in the putty-clay article of 1959. The connection is worth describing. In the spirit of the putty-clay model, inputs are substitutable when productive capacity is first created and capital committed. Depending on current and expected cost and demand conditions, and subject of course to technological constraints, a firm can build a plant of given capacity with a larger or smaller commitment of fixed factors, compensated by smaller or larger requirements for variable inputs during its operating lifetime. The particular mix of variable inputs can be chosen fairly freely, but is partially or completely predetermined at the time capacity is created. The simplest sharp embodiment of this idea allows fairly free substitutability ex ante among the fixed and variable inputs; but once a plant is built it requires variable inputs in fixed proportions and exhibits constant returns to scale up to a capacity, beyond which it can not exceed. That was the message of the 1959 paper.

The next step is the one analyzed in detail in the 1972 book. Within any industry there will exist an array of plants (or smaller productive units) built at various times in the past. The various choices of input proportions will have been made under different technological constraints, more recent capacity being more advanced, and also with different experience and expectations of the prices of variable inputs. The current short-run state of the industry is thus described by a k-variate capacity distribution if there are k variable inputs. This distribution shows how much capacity there is corresponding to each technologically feasible collection of input coefficients. Its total volume is the current capacity of the industry. If we assume that input requirements do not change as a plant ages, then the capacity distribution changes through time only as old capacity is retired and new capacity is built. Otherwise the situation is more complex.

Now consider a given instant. One can do two important exercises with this model. First, take as given the k+1 prices of output and the variable inputs. Only a certain easily calculable subset of the possible vectors of input coefficients is viable, in the sense that such a plant could break even or earn a positive profit at the given prices. The capacity associated with the viable plants represents the competitive supply of output at the given configuration of prices. By varying the prices, one calculates the supply function for the industry as a function of the prices of output and the variable inputs. It is easy to see that this supply function is generated by an efficient allocation of variable inputs to units of capacity. If it were possible to produce a given output with less of some variable inputs and no more of any of them than in the configuration given by the supply function, there would have to be idle capacity that can earn a profit, and that is excluded by construction.

This suggests the second exercise. Choose a level of output. Fix the input prices and find the output-price that generates a supply equal to the stipulated output. This will be possible if the stipulated output is not to large. Calculate the input requirements of the plants viable at the price configuration thus reached. Since the allocation of resources is efficient, this input-bundle represents a point on the isoquant for the level of output with which we started. Hold to the same level of output, try a different input-price configuration and find a second point on the same isoquant. By going on in this way one can in principle generate the complete isoquant, and then every isoquant, and thus the complete short-run production function. (For very high outputs, the range of possible variable-input-bundles will narrow; at the extreme, the largest output producible is the capacity of the industry, and since it requires that every plant be fully used, there is only a single bundle of variable inputs capable of producing it - the isoquant shrinks to a point.)

This idea of generating a production function by aggregating over elementary cells with a distribution of input-coefficients was originaly due to Houthakker. He proved the neat result that a modified Pareto-distribution of input-coefficients gives rise to a Cobb-Douglas production function when aggregated. There is related material in W.E.G. Salter's <u>Productivity and Technical Change</u> (1960). Johansen carries the analysis much further, with great patience, care, and ingenuity. I will give only one example. Any economist would be curious about the derivatives of the aggregate production function and their relation to the characteristics of the capacity distribution over the underlying micro-cells. On reflection, those derivatives must depend on the characteristics of the marginal cells (i.e. those just breaking even at the initial aggregate inputs and output) because small changes in output will occur through the activation or deactivation of marginal capacity. Johansen works out all the details and shows how the first- and second-order properties of the aggregated production function, including the elasticities of substitution between variable factors, can be written neatly in terms of the "statistical" properties - the means, variances and covariances - of the existing capacity distribution over the marginal cells. It is very satisfying.

It seems to me that this "distribution approach" to the vintage putty-clay model of production must be the right foundation for any serious theory of investment intended for application at something less than the highest level of aggregation. Think, for example, of the need to deal currently with the existing mix of capital equipment having varying

degrees of energy-efficiency and the complicated incentives set up by the
prospect of rising (or falling) energy prices. The model is hard to work
with, and that is probably why it has not been used much. (There was an
early application of the putty-clay apparatus to U.S. investment data by
Charles Bischoff, and I have the impression that this approach is favored
by the Dutch Planning Bureau.)

All those who wish to deal with this approach can learn from
Johansen's treatment of it. Apart from important details, they will learn
something about the way a certain sort of fine theorist works. I am thinking here of two characteristics. One is supremely important: it is the
constant check of common sense. It is always in his mind that the strict
assumptions of theory will not hold in practice: ex post input-coefficients
are not quite fixed; they do change a bit as capacity ages; the allocation
of variable factors to units of capacity may not be quite efficient. There
are marvelous theorists who are not troubled by such intrusions; Leif
Johansen was not one of them. The second characteristic is a kind of
playfulness, a willingness to try out special cases and specific assumptions in the hope that something interesting will turn up. In his case, it
often does. That can not be mere luck.

2. Multisectoral models and macroeconomic planning

I have not found it possible to summarize in any neat way Leif
Johansen's lifelong interest in the use of fairly aggregative - but still
multisectoral - long-term models as a guide to macroeconomic planning.
His main contributions to this subject are A Multi-Sectoral Study of
Economic Growth (1960) and the two volumes of Lectures on Macroeconomic
Planning (1977 and 1978). A good way to get the feel of his approach is a
fifty-page article "Explorations in long-term projections for the Norwegian
economy" written in collaboration with Håvard Alstadheim and Åsmund
Langsether and published in Economics of Planning, 1968. There are also
incidental items in English and no doubt much more material, published
and unpublished, in Norwegian.

The underlying model is in most respects an equilibrium construction.
For example it provides always enough consumer demand to maintain full
employment. This is a reasonable way to proceed in a model whose
purpose is to provide "a background and a framework for the continuous

flow of decisions which have to be taken with respect to those elements of the economy which are under more or less influence by the government, in addition to serving its purpose for providing a background for the general four-year programs." Equilibrium is presumed to be maintained by active policy, not by automatic forces. The structure of the model is a sort of hybrid. Interindustry flows of materials and services are governed by a fixed-coefficient input-output matrix. (Johansen described it as "disappointing" that he had not yet been able to introduce more technological flexibility here.) For capital and labor, however, each sector is given its own Cobb-Douglas production function, including an industry-specific exponential technological change factor. Thus, technological progress does not economize on flows of raw materials and intermediate goods.

Aggregate investment is allocated among sectors through rates of profit, but it is not assumed that the flow of investment equalizes the rate of profit across sectors. Instead there is a stationary structure of relative rates of profit by sector. Johansen regarded this assumption as a "weak link" in the model. He tested it by fitting an autoregressive model to the observed rates of return in sixteen separate manufacturing industries, 1950-1963. It was found that the convergence of relative rates of return to their estimated stationary levels was quite slow if it occurred at all. Johansen then made the interesting observation that in general the rate of return in "sheltered" industries was rising relative to that for "exposed" industries during the sample period. I do not know when that particular dichotomy entered discussion in Norway; I first heard about it in connection with the "Scandinavian model of inflation," some years later.

There is another interesting aspect of the empirical results that struck me on rereading the 1968 paper, but on which Johansen offered no comment. The direct price elasticities of demand are estimated for each sector using Ragnar Frisch's "complete scheme." (Income elasticities are taken over from the Central Bureau of Statistics.) The price elasticities are all very small: the largest (-0.4) is for electricity consumption and the largest among manufactured products is for the mechanical and electrotechnical industry (-0.3).

These few details are not meant even to give the flavor of the model. My goal is just to say something about Johansen the economist. What is striking in this part of his work is its pragmatic approach. There is always the discipline of a formal model in the background. It is too much to say that anything goes; but he was always willing to experiment, to relax an a priori constraint to see if doing so will improve the fit of a model to reality, and to listen to the data and their limitations, yet remain as sophisticated in conceptual approach as those limitations will allow. This pragmatic attitude is visible also in the Lectures on Macroeconomic Planning, which have that reassuring ability to suggest the controlling presence of analytical bones in the background, while allowing for the cushion of common sense in applying them to the everyday problems of the real economy.

References

Bischoff, C. (1971), "Business Investment in the 1970s: A Comparison of Models", Brookings Papers on Economy Activity 1, 13-63.

Houthakker, H.S. (1955-56), "The Pareto distribution and the Cobb-Douglas production function in activity analysis", The Review of Economic Studies 23, 27-31.

Johansen, L. (1959), "Substitution Versus Fixed Production Coefficients in the Theory of Economic Growth: A Synthesis", Econometrica 27, No. 2, 157-176.

Johansen, L. (1960), A Multi-Sectoral Study of Economic Growth, North-Holland Publishing Co., Amsterdam, 1960. (Second enlarged edition, 1974.)

Johansen, L. (1968), "Explorations in Long-Term Projections for the Norwegian Economy" (in collaboration with Håvard Alstadheim and Åsmund Langsether), Economics of Planning 8, No. 1-2, 70-117.

Johansen, L. (1972), Production Functions. An Integration of Micro and Macro, Short Run and Long Run Aspects, North-Holland Publishing Co., Amsterdam-London.

Johansen, L. (1977), Lectures on Macroeconomic Planning, 1. General Aspects, North-Holland Publishing Co., Amsterdam - New York - Oxford.

Johansen, L. (1978), Lectures on Macroeconomic Planning, 2. Centralization, Decentralization, Planning under Uncertainty, North-Holland Publishing Co., Amsterdam - New York - Oxford.

Salter, W.E.G. (1960), Productivity and Technical Change, Cambridge University Press, Cambridge.

Production, Multi-Sectoral Growth and Planning
F.R. Førsund, M. Hoel, and S. Longva (Editors)
© Elsevier Science Publishers B.V. (North-Holland), 1985

AN INTERCOUNTRY COMPARISON OF CEMENT PRODUCTION:
THE SHORT-RUN PRODUCTION FUNCTION APPROACH

Finn R. Førsund
University of Oslo

Lennart Hjalmarsson
University of Gothenburg

Øyvind Eitrheim
Norges Bank

1. Introduction

The production function is one of the fundamental concepts in economics. Yet, Leif Johansen begins his book on micro-macro, short-run
and long-run production functions (Johansen (1972)) by rightly pointing
out that econometric research, despite its growing sophistication, has
failed to produce firmly established knowledge. At the root of the
problem is the actual conceptualisation of the production function: "The
crudeness of the concept of the production function, as it is being used
in most econometric research, is accordingly out of proportion with the
sophistication of the theories and methods by which it is surrounded."
(Johansen (1972), p. 1)

The distinction between smooth <u>ex ante</u> substitution possibilities during
the actual construction of a production unit and limited <u>ex post</u> substitution possibilities is crucial to Johansen's approach of introducing a
production theory more suitable for establishing empirical results.

Leif Johansen expressed the hope that his production theory will be

This paper is based upon work within a project of structural analysis of
industry in the Nordic countries. The project has participants from
Norway, Sweden, and Finland, and has been supported financially by
The Nordic Economic Research Council and the Jan Wallander Research
Foundation.

helpful "as for suggesting new approaches for empirical work" (op.cit., p.2).

The present study is firmly based on the short-run production function concept for an industry. This concept rests on the assumption of vintage structure within an industry, i.e. that each unit in the industry, for example a plant or a subsection, is characterised by fixed production coefficients with respect to current inputs and the presence of fixed factors in the form of capital. The function is defined by maximising the industry's total production for given amounts of total inputs. This also means that the industry's total production costs are minimised for any factor-price ratio and any level of production, assuming that all production units face the same prices.

The purpose of this study is to compare the cement industries in the Nordic countries - Norway, Sweden, Denmark, and Finland - over the twenty year period 1960 to 1980 with respect to productivity development and nature of technical change by means of short-run industry functions.

Using a traditional average production function approach several papers have recently examined productivity growth at a rather aggregated sector level in an intercountry (USA - Japan) framework of more than two inputs (see Jorgenson (1978), Jorgenson and Nishimizu (1979), Christensen et al. (1981), Denny and Fuss (1983), and Norsworthy and Malmqvist (1983)). Some more conventional studies deal with comparisons between EEC countries and between the United Kingdom, the United States, and West-Germany (see de Jong (1981), Prais (1981), Bianchi et al. (1981) and Smith et al. (1982)). Comparisons at a more disaggregated level have also been done, e.g. between single firms and establishments of the same industry in different countries (see Panic (1976), Carlsson (1978), Rodas and Homberg (1980), and Pratten (1976a,b)). Of the above mentioned studies only Bianchi et al. (1981) and Carlsson (1978) cover the cement industry. Bianchi et al. study the structure of the cement industries in the EEC countries with special emphasis on regulation in a traditional industrial organisation framework, while Carlsson (1978) makes a very detailed comparison of productivity and choice of technology between the Swedish and the US cement industry.

There are several reasons why the cement industry is an interesting sector to study:

1.   Following the rising energy prices in the 1970s, the cement industry,

which is very fuel intensive, has drawn a great deal of attention. Thus, it is interesting to investigate the impact of the jumps in energy prices on the structure of the industry .

2. The industry expanded rapidly in the Nordic countries during the 1950s and 1960s due to the increase in construction. However, the construction boom came to a halt in the beginning or middle of the 1970s and the demand for cement decreased substantially while, at the same time, energy prices rose tremendously.

3. Capital equipment for this industry is produced by just a few international companies. The knowledge about available technologies and their characteristics are well known among the cement producers. It is reasonable to assume that all cement companies can choose from the same ex ante or choice of technique function when investments are made. This means that the main reasons for differences in productivity between countries should be differences in the development of relative prices, demand conditions, technical and managerial skill, and the effects of public regulations.

4. There were considerable differences between the Nordic countries in the level and development of the relative prices for this industry during the period under investigation.

5. During this period the industry in all Nordic countries except Denmark has to a great extent converted from one technology, wet kilns, to another technology, dry kilns.

6. Because of the high level of concentration, the industry is subject to some degree of public regulation.

The short-run industry production function approach based on microdata is an especially suitable method for the cement industry. The product is homogeneous, and the different production techniques are identifiable. Moreover, the various stages in the cement manufacturing process are distinct.

The long-run development of the cement industry is analysed on the basis of the shifts in the short-run function during the period. The short-run function shows the actual production possibilities of the industry and is changed by investments in new technologies and scrapping of old capacity. More specifically this production function approach may highlight the following points:

a)   Long-run substitution and bias in technical progress
b)   The development of unit costs due to technical progress
c)   Differences in productivity and technical efficiency between the coun-
     tries and the time path of these differences
d)   Differences in international competitiveness
e)   The dispersion of different technologies and their competitiveness in
     the industry at different relative prices.

We start off by providing an overview of the tools of analysis.   A
description of the cement process and the data we have obtained will then
be followed by a presentation of the empirical results.

2.   The construction of the short-run industry production function

When establishing a production unit on the basis of an ex ante production function, the full capacity values $\bar{x}$ of output x and $\bar{v}_j$ of the
current inputs v_j (j=1,...,n) are determined. As in Johansen (1972) we
assume the following limitational law to hold for the ex post function at the
micro level:

$$(1) \qquad x = \text{Min} \left[\frac{v_1}{\xi_1}, \ldots, \frac{v_n}{\xi_n}, \bar{x} \right]$$

where the input coefficients $\xi_j = \bar{v}_j / \bar{x}$ (j=1,...,n) are constant, i.e.
independent of the rate of capacity utilisation.

In the following we assume that all cement kilns are characterised by
the simple structure given in (1) with, of course, different production
capacities and different input coefficients.   (We shall return to the empirical basis for these assumptions in Section 4.)   The input coefficients,
ξ_j, are estimated by means of the observed coefficients.

The short-run industry function $X = F(V_1, \ldots, V_n)$ is obtained by
solving the following problem:

$$(2a) \qquad \underset{x^i}{\text{Max}} \ X = \sum_{i=1}^{N} x^i$$

subject to

(2b) $\sum\limits_{i=1}^{N} \xi_j^i \, x^i \leq V_j$, $j=1,\ldots,n$

(2c) $x^i \in [\,0, \bar{x}^i\,]$

where X denotes output and $V_1,\ldots,V_n$ current inputs for the industry
as a whole, and where $i=1,\ldots,N$ refers to plants with a capacity of $\bar{x}^i$.
Since, for our purpose, we are only interested in the economic region it
is natural to assume free disposal of input as expressed by Equation
(2b).

The necessary first-order conditions are:

$$(3) \qquad 1 - \sum_{j=1}^{n} q_j \, \xi_j^i \, \left\{\begin{matrix} \geq \\ < \end{matrix}\right\} \, 0 \text{ when } \dot{x}^i \in [0,\bar{x}^i] \quad \begin{matrix} x^i = \bar{x}^i \\[4pt] \\[4pt] x^i = 0 \end{matrix} \,, \quad i=1,\ldots,N.$$

The variables $q_1,\ldots,q_n$ are shadow prices of the current inputs in
terms of units of output per unit of input. It follows directly then that
$q_1,\ldots,q_n$ represent the marginal productivities of the inputs of the
industry function. Whether a production unit is to be in operation or not
is, according to (3), decided by current operating "costs" (dimension-
less), calculated at these shadow prices, being either lower than or
exceeding unity. This corresponds to utilising units with non-negative
quasi-rents. An equality sign in (3) defines the zero quasi-rent line in
the input-coefficient space, thus giving the boundary of utilisation of the
set of production units. When operation costs equal unity we have a
marginal production unit in the sense that it may, or may not be in operation in the optimal solution. For a more detailed exposition, see
Johansen (1972, pp. 13-19).

Since the short-run production function appears in a nonparametric
form, the question then is how the function should be represented. This
must, of course, depend on the use to which the function is to be put.
In order to analyse long-run technical progress and structural change,
we should have a complete representation of each isoquant of the set
found suitable for analysing the three aspects: factor bias, productivity
change, and change in substitution properties.

Due to the linear structure of the problem (2a-c), the isoquants will be
piece-wise linear in the two-factor case considered in the sequel. In

principle, the short-run function (2) can be derived by solving a number
of LP-problems. However, when the aim is to establish a reasonably interesting number of isoquants in order to reveal all the corners of the
piece-wise linear isoquants, solving the LP-problems (2a-c) is not a practical procedure.

If one is satisfied with the information provided by a limited number
of isoclines, these are readily obtained by a simple ranking of the micro
units according to unit production costs for given input prices. Such a
cost minimisation procedure is used by Johansen (1972), W. Hildenbrand
(1981), and K. Hildenbrand (1982).

For the two-factor case, our approach yields a complete description of
the isoquants by locating all the corner points geometrically, providing
the whole set of isoclines and, in addition, thus enabling us to provide a
full characterisation of the production function via marginal productivities,
marginal rates of substitution, elasticities of substitution, and elasticities
of scale. Even for problems with a large number of production units the
computation of isoquants is performed within a very reasonable amount of
computer time. (Although addressed to other apects of the short-run
function, this geometric approach was inspired by a memorandum of Seip
(1974).)

Briefly, the algorithm works in the following way (a complete description with examples is given in Førsund and Hjalmarsson (1984): The
boundaries of the substitution region are found by ranking the units
according to increasing input coefficients for each input separately. This
corresponds to a ranking of units according to unit costs when one input
at a time has a zero price. We know that the isoquant must be piece-wise
linear, downward sloping, convex to the origin, and minimising costs for
every factor-price ratio. The essential idea is to substitute production
units successively along the isoquant so that all the above mentioned
properties are fulfilled. This is achieved by the following geometric procedure: Starting from an arbitrarily chosen output level on the upper
boundary, the last unit entered on the boundary is partially utilised.
The problem is to find the next corner point on the isoquant. The algorithm, then, compares the slopes in the input coefficient space of the
connecting lines between the starting unit and all units. Thus two units
are always partially utilised along an isoquant segment.

In the case of increased utilisation of the starting unit, when moving
from the boundary along the isoquant segment, the first isoquant corner

point is reached either when the capacity of the starting unit is exhaust-
ed, or when the capacity utilisation of the decreasing unit reaches zero.
When the capacity utilisation of the starting unit decreases, the corner
point is reached when the utilisation of this unit reaches zero, or the utilisation of the increasing unit reaches 100 per cent. At each corner only
one unit is partly utilised.

The first segment can, at most, be vertical because the boundary
units are sorted according to increasing input coefficients of the input
that is increasing along the isoquant towards the lower boundary. The
actual length of the segment depends on the capacity of the activated
units.

The next step is to compare the angles of all other units in the input-
coefficient space with the partly activated unit at the previously found
corner point. The angle of the next line segment is then determined by
the unit giving the second-steepest angle compared to the angle of the
previous line segment, and so on, until the lower boundary is reached.

The successive angles in the input-coefficient space between the units
activated along the isoquant are the same as the slopes of the line
segments in the input space. Intuitively, this can be grasped by considering the shadow price interpretations of the dual variables (q_1 and
q_2).

3. The activity regions

In addition to representing the short-run function by a limited number of isoquants it may also be useful to portray the complete set of efficient combinations of the micro units. A highly stylised example is given
in Figure 1.

Let us return to Johansen's original formulation of the short-run
industry production function in the discrete case. It should be noted
that Johansen regarded discrete observations as the most realistic. The
continuous representation constituting the main part of his book was considered to be a practical approximation for the sake of convenience (see
Johansen (1972), p. 29). The short-run industry production function for
three units of production is shown in Figure 1.

Note that the utilisation of each unit is shown as a parallelogram.
Such a parallelogram is called an activity region. The attempt to general-

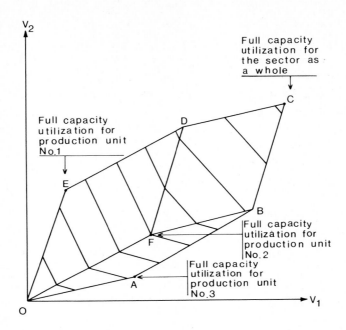

Fig. 1.   Short-run industry production function for three units
            V_i = total amount of input No. i

Source: Johansen (1972, Fig. 2.1, p. 17)

ise to an arbitrarily large set of units, even in the case of two inputs, did
not turn out to be entirely trivial.   Johansen mentions in passing that an
illustration such as Figure 1 may, of course, be generalised to more
units.   The complete solution to this problem is shown in Førsund and
Hjalmarsson (1984).

Starting at zero industry production and expanding this to full capacity utilisation the activity regions are formed by adding micro units in
accordance with the requirement that maximum industry output is obtained
at each point in the substitution region.   Each parallelogram is formed by
combining two units.   Within the parallelogram the utilisation rate is
between zero and one.   Each line segment of the parallelogram represents
the locus of isoquant corners.   Therefore, the activity regions
representation contains the complete set of all possible isoclines.

Such an activity region representation of the substitution region
allows you to follow each unit's utilisation as a function of the industry's

capacity utilisation.

In the two-factor case the actual construction of the activity regions follows the same algorithm used for the construction of isoquants. Starting at the upper boundary of the substitution region with the unit in use at the chosen point, the units which are to be combined with this one when moving along the strip to the lower boundary are simply found by inspecting the slopes of the connecting lines between this unit and all others. Negative slopes mean that these units are to be combined with the starting unit.

In Figure 2 the short-run production function for the Swedish cement

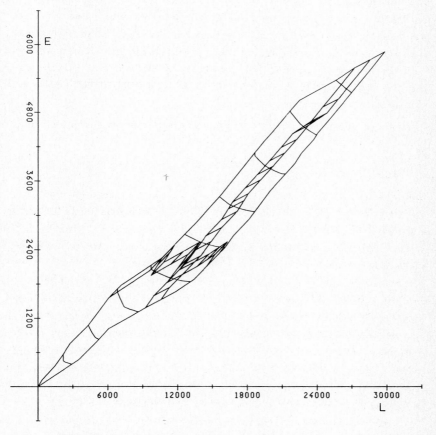

Fig. 2.   Utilisation strips.   Swedish Cement Industry 1974.   Isoquant distance 500 ktonnes

industry in 1974 is represented by a substitution region and a set of isoquants, and the utilisation of two units of production – in this case individual kilns.   The utilisation strip for each unit consists of a set of paral-
lelograms where the unit under consideration recurs in combination with
several other units.

Along the borders of the substitution region the units are utilised
according to a ranking of one input coefficient at a time.   In Figure 2, the
upper borderline shows a ranking according to increasing labour input
coefficients measured from the origin and outwards.   A unit with a completely different ranking according to the two types of inputs will have a
rather extended utilisation, as may be seen in the figure.   Here, the utilisation of one unit starts at about 35 per cent of the industry's total
capacity, and continues right up to a total production level of about 95
per cent of the industry's total production capacity.   The other unit has
approximately equal ranking numbers for both the two input coefficients.
But the utilisation strip is not parallel with the isoquants across the region of substitution, but zig-zags across within about 30 to 50 per cent
utilisation of total capacity.

4.   Data

In simple terms, the cement process consists in introducing dry or
wet limestone powder or chalk into one end of a long rotating pipe where
it is burnt and calcinated; the powder comes out at the other end of the
pipe in the form of "clinker."   The kiln, which is our production unit in
this analysis, is a long cylindrical steel pipe that rests on rollers.   It is
slightly inclined, and rotates slowly around its own axis at a rate of about
one rotation a minute.   It is lined with firebrick.

Our data comprises three production techniques.   In a wet kiln, the
limestone powder is mixed with water.   In a semi-dry kiln, the waste
gases from the heating in the pipe are used to evaporate some of the
water in the limestone powder before it is introduced into the kiln.   In a
dry kiln, the flour is dry before it enters the pipe.   Consequently, the
latter technique uses the least amount of energy.

The data have been collected for five-year periods from 1960 until
1980, including data on the energy consumption of each kiln.   For

Denmark it is only possible to get data on the plant level.   The energy
consumption is fairly closely tied to the nature of the capital equipment,
and fits quite well into the putty-clay assumption.   Note, however, that
the energy coefficient varies somewhat with the utilisation of production
capacity, i.e. it decreases with rising utilisation.   The labour input is not
as dependent on the kiln since it is tied to the plant as a whole, which
may comprise several kilns.   We have, nevertheless, opted for keeping
the kiln as our production unit, and for distributing labour to the kilns in
proportion to total production.   The energy sources are coal and oil,
which in our calculations have been converted to a common physical unit,
calories.   Labour input is measured in hours.   We have also obtained the
production capacity for each kiln.   The estimation of capacity varies
somewhat between countries.   Maxium daily capacity is defined in more or
less the same way, but there are national differences in the count of
annual operating hours.

   Table 1 shows production capacity, production, number of kilns in
use, type of technology, and the number of kilns taken into or out of
production in the previous five-year period.   The data for Denmark cover
the only surviving firm in 1984.   It's share of total production has
increased from 80 per cent in 1960 to 98 per cent in 1980.   We see that the
utilisation of capacity was consistently higher during the 1960s than
during the 1970s.   The particularly low capacity utilisation in Sweden in
1980 was due to the running in of a large new kiln, found in the column
"Taken into production."   Production capacity peaked in 1970 in Norway
and Sweden, and in 1975 in Denmark, while it continues to rise in
Finland.   Actual production reached a peak in Sweden in 1970, in Norway
in 1975, while it has continued to rise in Denmark and Finland.   Sweden
has experienced the sharpest reduction in the number of kilns in use.
Particularly wet kilns were taken out of use during the 1970s.   All newly
constructed kilns (except for Denmark and a single exception in Sweden)
are dry kilns.   In Denmark all kilns are wet due to the type of raw
material used (chalk).   In Finland, the wet kilns removed from production
(of which there were 7 in the period between 1975 and 1980) have not
been scrapped, but may still be put to use again if the market situation
changes.

   The development of factor prices is shown in Table 2.   During the
1960s, wage rates rose considerably more steeply than the price of energy, but with the first oil price leap in 1973 the situation was reversed.

Table 1. The cement industry in Norway, Finland, Sweden, and Denmark

Year	Capacity (ktonnes)	Production (ktonnes)	Capacity utilisation %	No. of existing kilns	No. of wet kilns	Taken into production	Taken out of production
						(in previous 5 years period)	
Norway							
1960	1155	1139	99	9	6	–	–
1965	1708	1484	87	9	6	3	3
1970	2759	2526	92	11	7	2	0
1975	2759	2599	94	11	7	0	0
1980	2422	2101	87	9	6	0	2
Sweden							
1960	2962	2797	94	20	17	–	–
1965	3744	3846	103*	23	18	4	2
1970	4967	3968	80	25	19	4	8
1975	4374	3415	78	19	12	2	11
1980	3827	2327	61	9	3	1	
Denmark							
1960	809	805	100	7	7	–	–
1965	1099	1013	92	8	8	1	0
1970	1493	1414	95	8	8	1	1
1975	2015	1833	91	7	7	2	3
1980	2015	1963	97	7	7	0	0
Finland							
1960	1125	997	85	9	9	–	–
1965	1605	1452	90	11	11	2	0
1970	2005	1681	84	13	10	2	0
1975	2415	1923	80	14	7	1	0
1980	2335 +	1569	67	9	2**	1	6 (2**)

*)   The number of operating hours this year exceeded the number of hours defining full capacity utilisation.

**)   Mothballed

+)   Including mothballed capacity

Table 2. Development of factor prices 1960–80 in each country's currency

Year	Wage rate**	Energy cost	Development of relative price (labour/energy)	
Norway*	NOK/hour	NOK/Gcal	Gcal/hour	Index
1961	7.8	8.3	0.9	1.0
1965	10.6	8.0	1.3	1.4
1970	15.9	7.7	2.1	2.2
1975	48.8	53.1	0.9	1.0
1980	69.4	82.6	0.8	0.9
Sweden	SEK/hour	SEK/Gcal	Gcal/hour	Index
1960	7.4	9.6	0.8	1.0
1965	11.1	8.3	1.3	1.7
1970	15.3	7.3	2.1	2.7
1974	26.5	31.7	0.8	1.1
1980	55.2	69.7	0.8	1.0
Denmark	DKK/hour	DKK/Gcal	Gcal/hour	Index
1960	6.2	8.8	0.7	1.0
1965	9.2	8.4	1.1	1.6
1970	16.6	8.3	2.0	2.8
1975	36.5	35.7	1.0	1.7
1980	62.5	50.9	1.2	1.7
Finland	FMK/hour	FMK/Gcal	Gcal/hour	Index
1960	2.8	4.7	0.6	1.0
1965	4.1	4.7	0.9	1.5
1970	6.6	6.8	1.0	1.6
1975	18.7	26.5	0.7	1.2
1980	29.2	41.2	0.7	1.2

*) For 1961–75 the figures refer to a single establishment; for 1980 to the average for the whole industry.

**) Including social insurance costs.

In all countries except Denmark the relative prices were about the same in 1980 as in 1960.   In Denmark, however, wage rates continued to rise relatively faster than energy prices during the latter half of the 1970s. Wage rates have increased by a factor of 7 for Sweden, 10 for Denmark and Finland; energy prices by factors of about 7 for Sweden, 10 for Norway, 6 for Denmark, and 9 for Finland.   The smaller increases in Sweden and Denmark are due to a switch from oil to coal during the latter part of the 1970s for Sweden and the first part of the 1970s for Denmark – a switch that had not yet taken place as of 1980 in Norway.   Finland has used mostly coal during the entire period.

5. Individual country analyses

    The development in each country of the short-run industry produc-tion functions for 1960, 1970, and 1980 are shown in Figures 3-6.   Each country has its own characteristics.   The analyses follow the questions introduced in Section 1 about the nature of technical change and produc-tivity development.

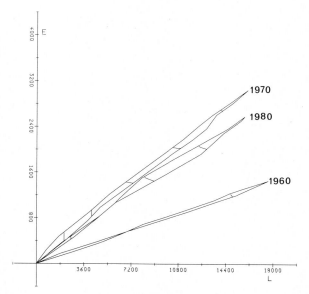

Fig. 3.   Short-run production functions for Norwegian Cement Industry
          1960-1970-1980. Isoquant distance 500 ktonnes

Norway

In the case of Norway we see from Figure 3 that the development from 1960 to 1970 was marked by a strong movement of the substitution region in the direction of the energy axis. In the 1970s we have a complete reversal. The 1980 industry production function has swung back towards the labour input axis. As far as the shape of the isoquants is concerned, we note that in the first-third of the capacity it is almost impossible to alter the total labour input. Following the same isoquant (the 500 ktonnes isoquant), we see that the technical progress from 1960 to 1970 turns into regress between 1970 and 1980. Productivity change is measured by changes in average unit costs of the variable inputs for constant prices

Table 3.a. Salter-measure, T, of technical progress. Norwegian cement industry 1960-1980. 1980 prices. $T = AC(t+1)/AC(t)$

| | OUTPUT LEVEL (ktonnes) | | | | | |
	FRONTIER	500	1000	1500	2000	2500
1965/1960	0.68	0.68	0.60			
1970/1965	0.49	0.49	0.48	0.47		
1975/1970	1.22	1.22	1.22	1.17	1.11	1.07
1980/1975	1.02	1.02	1.02	1.03	1.08	
1980/1960	0.42	0.42	0.35			

Table 3.b. Salter-measure, D, of factor-saving bias. Norwegian cement industry 1960-1980. 1980 prices. $D = (E(t+1)/L(t+1))/(E(t)/L(t))$

| | OUTPUT LEVEL (ktonnes) | | | | | |
	FRONTIER	500	1000	1500	2000	2500
1965/1960	1.40	1.31	1.38			
1970/1965	1.80	1.76	1.70	1.84		
1975/1970	0.85	0.85	0.85	0.85	0.90	0.92
1980/1975	1.03	1.03	1.05	1.04	0.95	
1980/1960	2.19	2.03	2.09			

(see Salter (1960), and Førsund and Hjalmarsson (1983)). Table 3 shows
the character of technical change and the degree of technical progress/
regress based on a particular isocline, namely the one corresponding to
the observed price ratio between labour and energy for Norway in 1980.
As we can see, technical progress was especially rapid between 1965 and
1970, but then changed to a marked regress between 1970 and 1975, continuing into a slight decline from 1975 to 1980. For the period as a whole
we can nevertheless see a not insignificant technical progress in the form
of reduced average costs per unit of production. Concerning the character of technical progress, we have found a marked labour-saving progress
in the 1960s. Although this changed to energy-saving technical progress
in the 1970s, the labour-saving progress dominated in the period as a
whole.

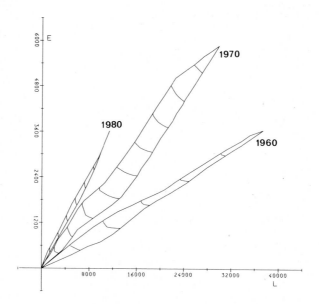

Fig.4.   Short-run production functions for Swedish Cement Industry
          1960-1970-1980. Isoquant distance 500 ktonnes

Sweden

The development in Sweden is shown in Fig. 4. Compared to Norway, there was a similar movement of the sustitution region towards the energy axis in the 1960s, but in Sweden this tendency continued to some extent into the 1970s. From the increasing slope of the isoquants we see that the kilns have become more equal with respect to input coefficients for labour. Table 4 provides some figures on the type of technical progress and on total technical progress measured by changes in average production costs. Table 4.a shows a steady technical progress throughout the period, reaching a low-point in the 1970s. Note that from 1975 to 1980, progress was clearly greater at the higher isoquant levels. This means that the average is about to catch up with "best practice". This phenomenon is noticable throughout the entire period. The development in

Table 4.a. Salter-measure, T, of technical progress. Swedish cement industry 1960-1980. 1980 prices. $T = AC(t+1)/AC(t)$

	OUTPUT LEVEL (ktonnes)								
	FRONTIER	500	1000	1500	2000	2500	3000	3500	4000
1965/1960	0.70	0.71	0.66	0.63	0.61	0.62			
1970/1965	0.65	0.64	0.63	0.65	0.68	0.68	0.67	0.67	
1975/1970	0.88	0.88	0.87	0.90	0.89	0.89	0.89	0.93	0.97
1980/1975	0.73	0.73	0.74	0.69	0.65	0.64	0.63	0.59	
1980/1960	0.29	0.29	0.27	0.25	0.24	0.24			

Table 4.b. Salter-measure, D, of factor-saving bias. Swedish cement industry 1960-1980. 1980 prices. $D = (E(t+1)/L(t+1))/(E(t)/L(t))$

	OUTPUT LEVEL (ktonnes)								
	FRONTIER	500	1000	1500	2000	2500	3000	3500	4000
1965/1960	1.49	1.48	1.51	1.58	1.68	1.57			
1970/1965	1.07	1.10	1.37	1.46	1.26	1.34	1.39	1.41	
1975/1970	1.01	0.99	0.91	1.01	1.04	1.04	1.06	0.99	0.90
1980/1975	1.92	1.88	1.50	1.35	1.49	1.44	1.37	1.45	
1980/1960	3.11	3.04	2.83	3.15	3.27	3.14			

Sweden is also characterised by labour-saving technical progress: it almost came to a halt during the first half of the 1970s, but gained momentum again during the latter half.

Denmark

Since the data are on a plant level, it has not been possible to distinguish between the input coefficients of the various kilns.   The substitution regions for 1960, 1970, and 1980 shown in Figure 5 then collapse into straight lines.   The development during the period between 1960 and 1970 was characterised by a strong movement of the substitution region towards the energy axis.   To a somewhat lesser extent this development continued in the 1970s.   In this respect the development of the Danish cement industry is very similar to that of Sweden.

The productivity changes and the nature of technical progress are easily grasped from following the same isoquant levels in Figure 5.   The

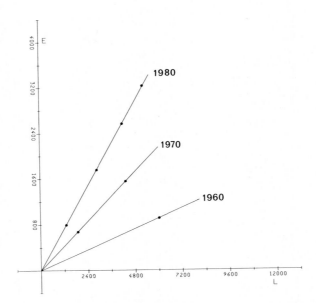

Fig. 5. Short-run production functions for Danish Cement Industry
1960-1970-1980. Isoquant distance 500 ktonnes

quantitative measures are shown in Table 5. The measures are, of course, the same for all output levels. The progress for the entire twenty-year period actually took place between 1965 and 1970, the first five-year period actually showing regress, while the other remained at more or less a standstill. As to the nature of technical change it is labour saving except for the first five-year period. The labour-saving bias is most significant for the period between 1965 and 1970 with marked technical progress.

Table 5.a. Salter-measure, T, of technical progress. Danish cement industry 1960-1980. 1980 prices. T = AC(t+1)/AC(t))

	ALL OUTPUT LEVELS
1965/1960	1.08
1970/1965	0.70
1975/1970	0.98
1980/1975	1.00
1980/1960	0.74

Table 5.b. Salter-measure, D, of factor-saving bias in Danish cement industry 1960-1980. 1980 prices.
D = (E(t+1)/L(t+1))/(E(t)/L(t))

	ALL OUTPUT LEVELS
1965/1960	0.97
1970/1965	2.43
1975/1970	1.45
1980/1975	1.18
1980/1960	4.04

Finland

The development of the short-run industry production function for
Finland follows a pattern which is quite different from the other countries
(see Fig. 6). Here we have only had a very slight movement towards the
energy axis. As shown in Table 6, there has been a steady technical

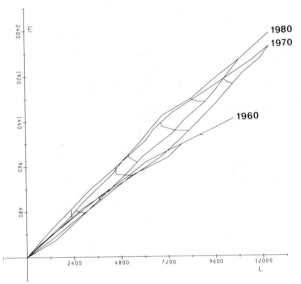

Fig. 6.   Short-run production functions for Finnish Cement
                 Industry 1960-1970-1980. Isoquant distance 500 ktonnes

Table 6.a.   Salter-measure, T, of technical progress. Finnish cement
                 industry 1960-1980. 1980 prices. T = AC(t+1)/AC(t)

	OUTPUT LEVEL (ktonnes)				
	FRONTIER	500	1000	1500	2000
1965/1960	0.74	0.72	0.62		
1970/1965	0.94	0.95	0.96	0.89	
1975/1970	0.91	0.90	0.88	0.83	0.77
1980/1975	1.00	1.00	0.99	0.99	1.07
1980/1960	0.64	0.61	0.52		

Table 6.b.   Salter-measure, D, of factor saving bias in Finnish cement
               industry 1960-1980. 1980 prices.
               $D = (E(t+1)/L(t+1))/(E(t)/L(t))$

| | OUTPUT LEVEL (ktonnes) | | | | |
	FRONTIER	500	1000	1500	2000
1965/1960	1.29	1.44	1.64		
1970/1965	0.88	0.80	0.85	0.95	
1975/1970	1.23	1.27	1.23	1.19	1.23
1980/1975	1.00	0.92	0.83	0.87	0.80
1980/1960	1.39	1.35	1.44		

progress measured by changes in average costs, apart from the last
period between 1975 and 1980 with no changes at all. The measures of
factor bias give a somewhat cyclical picture, starting with a labour-saving
bias in the first five-year period, then reversing to an energy-saving
bias in the next, reversing again to a labour-saving bias and ending up
with a weak energy-saving bias in the last period.

6. **Intercountry comparisons**

A comparison of the short-run industry production functions in the
individual countries is now made possible by combining the functions for
the same year. This is done in Figures 7, 8, and 9. We see that in 1960,
the regions of substitution for Denmark and Finland lie to the left of that
of Sweden, while that of Norway lies to the right. In 1970, the substitution regions come together. The slimmer substitution regions of Norway
and Finland are now inside that of Sweden, while that of Denmark has
moved to the left towards the energy axis. In 1980, the Danish and the
Swedish short-run industry production functions swing farther towards
the energy axis, while Finland and Norway are left behind - Norway has
even moved back towards the labour input axis.

Pooling the data sets permits us to study the competitiveness of the
Nordic countries' cement production due to technical differences in utilising current inputs. Although the Nordic countries do not actually com-
pete (e.g. due to high transportation costs and other reasons) the

Førsund et al.

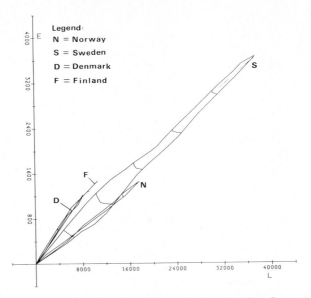

Fig. 7. Short-run production functions of the Nordic Cement Industries
1960. Isoquant distance 500 ktonnes

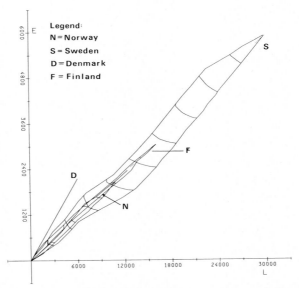

Fig. 8. Short-run production functions of the Nordic Cement Industries
1970. Isoquant distance 500 ktonnes

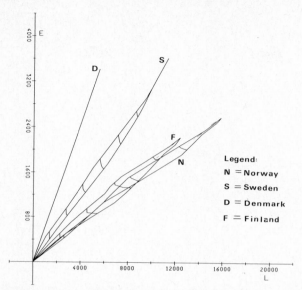

Fig. 9. Short-run production functions of the Nordic Cement Industries
1980. Isoquant distance 500 ktonnes

kind of normative analysis performed by pooling the data and then developing production and cost functions for this set still seems useful in a
comparative study.

By choosing the isocline that corresponds to the observed factor-price
ratio in Norway in 1980, we get a picture of technical efficiency by constructing the cost function for the entire data set for the years 1960, 1970
and 1980. This has been done in Figure 10. The graphs of the marginal
and average costs are drawn in full. As we go outwards along the ab-
scissa, the utilisation of the individual countries' kilns are labelled S for
Sweden, F for Finland, D for Denmark, and N for Norway. We see that in
1960, the most cost effective kilns are Finnish, then Norwegian, some
Swedish, etc., while in 1970 some of the Norwegian kilns are the most cost
effective. In 1980 all Swedish kilns come first, followed by some Finnish,
then some Norwegian, and so forth; finally ending with some Finnish and
some Norwegian. The Norwegian kilns in particular push up the graph of
marginal costs in 1980. The Danish kilns were at about average cost level
in 1960 and 1970, but with a deteriorating position in 1980 due to high
energy coefficients.

In order to check whether or not the impression we are given by the

34   Førsund et al.

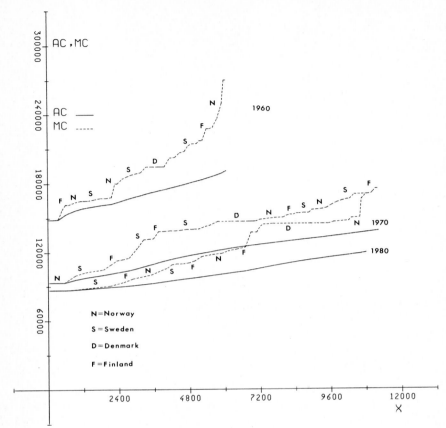

Fig.10. Variable Cost functions of the Nordic Cement industry. Pooled
        data 1960-1970-1980 in Norwegian 1980 prices.
        AC = average variable costs
        MC = marginal costs

variable cost functions is dependent upon the particular isocline we have
chosen, we shall look at how the several countries' kilns are utilised in
total cement production in the Nordic countries. Figures 11, 12, 13, and
14, show the utilisation pattern of the kilns within the pooled data set for
Finland in 1960, Norway in 1970, Denmark in 1970, and Sweden in 1980.

    We see that in 1960, a large proportion of the Finnish kilns have en-
tered the area by the energy input axis near the origin; they are, in
other words, labour efficient. However, utilisation strips for Finnish
kilns are found throughout most of the domain of the short-run function.
Strips of kilns go all the way up to about 80 per cent of total production

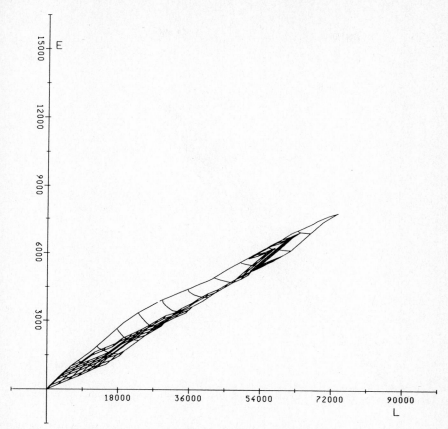

Fig.11. Partial utilisation strips of Finnish cement kilns within Nordic
        short-run function based on pooled data 1960. Isoquant distance
        500 ktonnes

capacity in the Nordic countries.

In 1970, some Norwegian kilns are included from the beginning. One
is the most efficient in terms of energy, and this and one other are also
very efficient as regards labour. These are dry kilns. The bulk of
the Norwegian kilns, however, are utilised in the second half of total
production capacity.

The Danish kilns are the most labour efficient in 1970 and 1980.
However, due to the very low relative energy efficiency the utilisation
strips follow a mostly longitudinal pattern, as seen in 1970 in Figure 13,
from the origin right up to about the level of 90 per cent of total Nordic

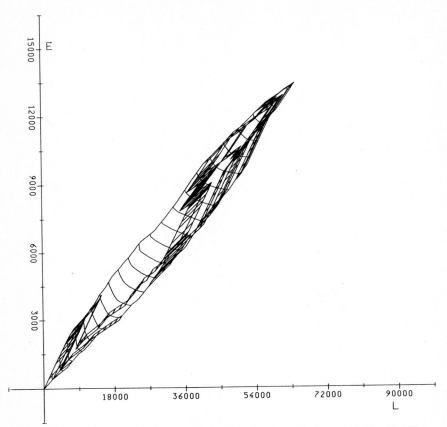

Fig.12. Partial utilisation strips of Norwegian cement kilns within Nordic
short-run function based on pooled data 1970. Isoquant distance
500 ktonnes

production. Such a utilisation pattern implies that the ranking along the
cost functions show especially high sensivity with respect to relative price
of energy and labour. With a higher relative price of labour than that
used in 1970 and 1980 in Figure 10, the Danish kilns would have entered
the cost functions at much lower levels of output. In 1980 the situation is
even more extreme, since the Danish kilns are now still most efficient as
regards labour, but least efficient as regards energy, i.e. the utilisation
strips span the entire substitution region.

In 1980 one Swedish kiln is the most energy efficient, with about 2/3
of the capacity being fairly energy efficient as well; at the same time all

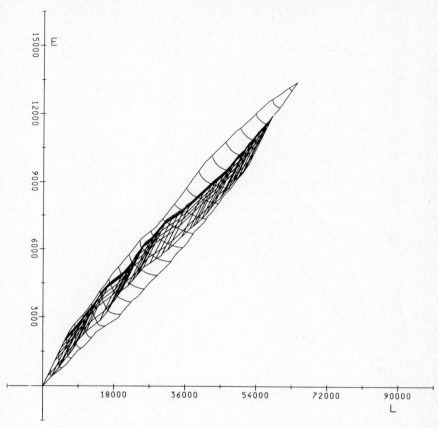

Fig. 13. Partial utilisation strips of Danish cement kilns within Nordic
short-run function based on pooled data 1970. Isoquant distance
500 ktonnes

Swedish kilns come next to the Danish ones with regard to labour efficiency. This results in quite a different utilisation pattern for the
Swedish kilns in 1980 than for Denmark shown in Figure 14. Entering the
upper boundary (labour input coefficient ranking) after the Danish kilns
the utilisation strips zig-zag downwards toward the lower boundary (energy input coefficient ranking). The bulk of Swedish capacity should be
fully utilised within about 1/3 of total Nordic production. The only substantial change possible in the cost ranking along the cost curves shown
in Figure 10 is for the Danish kilns to move ahead of Swedish capacity at
an extremely high relative price of labour.

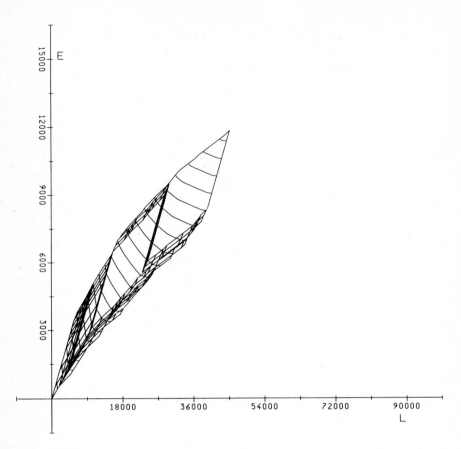

Fig. 14. Partial utilisation strips of Swedish cement kilns within Nordic
short-run function based on pooled data 1980. Isoquant distance
500 ktonnes

7. Tentative Conclusions

´The use of the short-run industry production function in a comparative analysis of an industry clearly brings out the differences in development. It is particularly the rate of labour-saving technical progress which
varies from country to country, and from period to period. Finland had

already moved far ahead in terms of rationalising labour by 1960. All
countries had difficulties during the 1970s, but Norway had the most.
Here, the development has gone in the direction of a more labour consuming technology. Of all the countries, Sweden has handled the problems of the 1970s most effectively. The continued progress in labour
productivity has been achieved thanks to the installment of large kilns,
and the scrapping of small ones. In Denmark there has been a standstill
as regards energy efficiency for the entire 20-year period, while labour
productivity has increased substantially, especially over a rather limited
period towards the end of the 1960s. Norwegian plants appear to have
pursued a different policy than their Nordic neighbours, possibly because
of government pressure to maintain the employment level. Moreover,
Sweden, Denmark, and Finland enjoy a marked factor-price advantage
over Norway, measured in the same currency unit. It is particularly
striking that Norway pays so much more for its energy than the others.
This is partly due to the other countries' use of coal, which Norway at
that time had not yet begun to use. Labour is also more costly in
Norway. When measuring variable costs in actual local prices shown in
Table 2 and comparing competetiveness due both to factor prices and
technical efficiency, Finland is in terms of labour and energy the cheapest
country in which to produce cement by a significant margain. Since the
technology is international, adding capital costs should not change this
picture; but raw material costs may differ substantially. They are especially cheap in Denmark.

References

Bianchi, P., Colenutt, D., and D. Gribbin (1981), "The cement industry.
    Studies in public and private control", in H.W. de Jong (ed.), The
    structure of the European Industry, Martinus Nijhoff Publishers,
    Rotterdam.

Carlsson, B., (1978), "Choice of Technology in the Cement Industry - A Comparison of the United States and Sweden", in B. Carlsson, G. Eliasson, and I. Nadiri (eds.), The Importance of Technology and the Permanence of Structure in Industrial Growth, The Industrial Institute of Economic and Social Research, Stockholm.

Denny, M. and Fuss, M. (1983), "A General Approach to Intertemporal and Interspatial Productivity Comparisons", Journal of Econometrics 23, No. 3, December.

Christensen, L.R., D. Cummings and D.W. Jorgensen (1981), "Relative productivity levels, An international comparison", European Economic Review 16,61-94.

Førsund, F.R. and Hjalmarsson (1983), "Technical progress and structural change in the Swedish cement industry 1955-1979", Econometrica 51, September, 1449-1467.

Førsund, F.R. and L. Hjalmarsson (1984), Analysis of industrial structure: A production function approach, Working Paper No. 135, The Industrial Institute for Economic and Social Research, Stockholm.

Førsund, F.R. and E. Jansen (1983), "Analysis of energy-intensive industries. The case of Norwegian aluminium production 1966-1978", in O. Bjerkholt, S. Longva, Ø. Olsen and S. Strøm (eds.), Analysis of Supply and Demand of Electricity in the Norwegian Economy, 221-259, SØS 53, Central Bureau of Statistics of Norway.

George, K.D. and T.S. Ward (1975), "The structure of industry in the EEC, An international comparison", Occasional Papers 43, Cambridge University Press.

Johansen, L. (1972), Production functions, North-Holland Publishing Company, Amsterdam-London.

de Jong, H.W. (ed.), (1981), The Structure of European Industry, Martinus Nijhoff Publishers, Rotterdam.

Jorgenson, D.W. (1978), "U.S. and Japanese economic growth, 1952-1974: An international comparison", The Economic Journal 88, 707-726.

Jorgenson, D.W. and M. Nishimizu (1979), "Sectoral differences in levels of technology: An international comparison between the United States and Japan 1955-1972", Discussion Paper, Harvard Institute of Economic Research.

Norsworthy, J.R. and Malmquist, D.H. (1983), "Input Measurement and Productivity Growth in Japanese and U.S. Manufacturing", The American Economic Review 73, No. 5, December, 947-967.

Panic, M. (ed.) (1976), "The UK and West German Manufacturing Industry 1954-72", NEDO monograph 5, London.

Prais, S.J. (1981), "Productivity and Industrial Structure", Social Research, Economic and Social Studies 33, Cambridge University Press, Cambridge.

Pratten, C.F. (1976a), "Labour productivity differentials within international companies", Occasional Papers 50, Cambridge University Press, Cambridge.

Pratten, C.F.(1976b), "A comparison of the performance of Swedish and U.K. companies", Occasional Papers 47, Cambridge University Press, Cambridge.

Rodas, S. and R. Homberg (1980), Produktivitet i verkstadsföretag. En jämförelse Finland-Sverige, Helsingfors.

Salter, W.E.G. (1960), Productivity and Technical Change, Cambridge University Press, Cambridge.

Seip, D. (1974), "A Geometrical Approach to Aggregation from Micro to Macro in Putty-Clay Aggregated Production Functions", Memorandum, 18 December, Department of Economics, University of Oslo.

Smith, A.D., Hitchens, D.M.W. and Davies, S.W. (1982), <u>International</u>
<u>Industrial Productivity. A Comparison of Britain, America and</u>
<u>Germany</u>, Cambridge University Press, Cambridge.

Production, Multi-Sectoral Growth and Planning
F.R. Førsund, M. Hoel, and S. Longva (Editors)
© Elsevier Science Publishers B.V. (North-Holland), 1985

ESTIMATION OF THE CAPACITY DISTRIBUTION OF AN INDUSTRY: THE SWEDISH DAIRY INDUSTRY 1964-1973

Joan Muysken
University of Limburg

1. Introduction

In his elucidative and inspiring book Production Functions, Leif Johansen introduced the capacity distribution of production units in an industry as a crucial concept for understanding the nature of the industry short-run aggregate production function. The existence of such a distribution enables one to aggregate the putty-clay production functions of the individual units in an elegant way. Assuming efficient behavior, the properties (for instance the form and parameters) of the capacity distribution of production units in the industry fully determine the properties (form and parameters) of the aggregate short-run production function of that industry. Hence, the characteristics of the short-run production function are implicitly given in the capacity distribution.

It can be worthwhile to explore and establish the properties of the capacity distribution, using data on individual production units in an industry. Illuminating examples are found in Johansen (1972, ch. 9) and Hildenbrand (1981). With respect to a further exploration of the capacity distribution, Johansen concluded that "in empirical work one would probably have to apply numerical methods which are not confined to cases which can be represented by nice mathematical formulas" (p. 51). Hildenbrand even went further, stating that "any assumption on the functional form of the 'capacity distribution' ... is quite artificial, in any case

The research for this paper started during a stay at the University of Oslo, spring 1981, and was completed during a stay at the State University of New York at Buffalo, with the financial support of the Netherlands Organization for the Advancement of Pure Research (ZWO). I am grateful to late Professor L. Johansen and Professor F.R. Førsund for their inspiring discussions on earlier versions, and to Professor N. Revankar and Drs. G. Joosten for their stimulating comments.

difficult to justify."   Hence, "there is no justifiable reason for the hope
that the distribution... has a simple parametric representation."[1]

A different opinion is found in Sato (1975) who considers it "important to determine its likely form from empirical data" (p.196) and devotes
a chapter to "illustrate how to fit a specific mathematical function to
distribution data of individual industries" (p.197). For analytical reasons
we sympathise with the last point of view: One should look for a functional form that fits the capacity distribution well and estimate its parameters. In that case the form and parameters of the aggregate production
function are implied[2] and the properties of the short-run production
function can be derived analytically.

The aim of this article is to discuss the estimation of the industry
capacity distribution for a given functional form. After a brief sketch of
the distribution approach in Section 2, this estimation is discussed in
general in Section 3.   When data on individual production units are available, the parameters of the distribution can be estimated by means of the
maximum likelihood method. However, this is hardly possible when data
are only available in grouped form, as is usually the case. In that case
the method of moments can be applied.

In Section 4 we analyse in more detail the estimation of a beta-capacity distribution. This analysis is applied to the case of the Swedish dairy
industry in Section 5. We find that the beta function shows a reasonable
fit to the observed capacity distribution of this industry. Moreover, the
estimation results do not differ very strongly between maximum likelihood
estimation on individual data on the one hand, and method-of-moments
estimation on the other. This is discussed further in the concluding
remarks of Section 6.

2.   The distribution approach

We assume that the production structure of an industry under consideration is of a putty-clay nature with only one variable input, labour.
Then each production unit in that industry will be characterised in the
short run by a fixed amount of capacity output, x, and a fixed labour
productivity, β. The labour productivity has a maximum value, β^o: no
production unit can produce more efficiently. A useful way of summarising

the conglomeration for production units in the industry is to use the concept of the capacity distribution. This is the distribution η of capacity output of the industry in terms of the labour productivities of the production unit (Johansen (1972), Sato (1975)). For this distribution

$$(1) \qquad \eta(\beta;\beta^o,\pi) > 0 \qquad \text{for } 0 < \beta < \beta^o$$

holds, where β^o and π represent its set of parameters. The distribution is defined in such a way that $\int_L^H \eta(\beta;\beta^o,\pi)d\beta$ gives the aggregate capacity output of all production units whose productivities lie in the interval $L < \beta < H$. Assuming profit-maximising behaviour at given prices, the aggregate short-run production function can be derived from the capacity distribution. Its form is

$$(2) \qquad \frac{Y}{C} = F(\frac{\beta^o V}{C};\pi)$$

where C stands for the aggregate capacity output of the industry, Y for its aggregate output, and V for its aggregate employment (Johansen (1972), Sato (1975)). Since there is a one-to-one correspondence between the capacity distribution and the production function (Seierstad (1982)), the characteristics of the short-run production function of the industry are implicitly given in the capacity distribution. A useful characteristic would be, for instance, that the function F be invariant over time. That is, shifts in the production function should reveal themselves only through changes in C and β^o. In order to derive the corresponding characteristics of the capacity distribution, we define the normalised capacity distribution as follows:

$$(3) \qquad \omega(\beta;\beta^o,\pi) = \frac{1}{C} \cdot \eta(\beta;\beta^o,\pi).$$

Since the integral of the capacity distribution, η, over its domain $0 < \beta < \beta^o$ is equal to C, the integral of the normalised capacity distribution, ω, over its domain is unity. Sato (1975, p.29) proves that the invariance of F implies that the normalised capacity distribution can be written as

$$(4) \qquad \omega(\beta;\beta^o,\pi) = \frac{1}{\beta^o} \cdot f(\frac{\beta}{\beta^o};\pi)$$

where f is invariant over time. As a consequence, the capacity distribution only shifts during the course of time through changes in C and β^o. These changes are Sato's (1975, p. 27-29) cases of 'scaling-up' and 'stretching-out' of the capacity distribution, respectively.

3. Estimation of the capacity distribution

It is obvious that the normalised capacity distribution ω is a density function. The integral

$$\int_L^H \omega(\beta;\beta^o,\pi)d\beta$$

gives the fraction of aggregate output being produced by production units whose productivities lie between L and H. When one interprets this as the probability of a unit of output being produced by a production unit whose productivity lies between L and H, ω can be interpreted as a probability density function. The observed values of β are sample values of a random variable with probability density function ω. And the observed output corresponding to an observed value of β represents the frequency of observations on that particular value of β.[3)]

Let data be available for an industry on x_i and β_i for each production unit i (i=1,...,n). Interpreting the normalised capacity distribution as a probability density function, its parameters π and β^o can be estimated by means of the maximum likelihood method[4)]. That is, for an assumed form of ω

$$(5) \qquad \ln L(\beta^o,\pi) = \sum_{i=1}^{n} \ln\left[\frac{1}{\beta^o} \cdot f(\frac{\beta_i}{\beta^o};\pi)\right]$$

is maximised with respect to π and β^o. From equation (5) one sees that the maximum likelihood estimation does not require data on x_i. The reason is that the frequency of observations on β_i, measured by x_i in this interpretation, is already contained in the form of ω.

When data on more years are available, it is also possible to test whether the normalised capacity distribution is invariant over time. Assuming that the observations are stochastically independent over time, this can be done by means of the generalised likelihood ratio test: When the distribution is invariant over T years, we have $\pi_1 = \ldots = \pi_T = \pi$. The generalised likelihood ratio is given by:

(6)
$$\Lambda = \frac{\displaystyle \max_{\pi, \beta_1^o, \ldots, \beta_T^o} \prod_{t=1}^{T} L(\beta_t^o, \pi)}{\displaystyle \prod_{t=1}^{T} \max_{\pi_t, \beta_t^o} L(\beta_t^o, \pi_t)}.$$

Under the null-hypothesis $-2 \ln \Lambda$ has the $\chi^2(\eta)$ distribution as its limiting distribution.[5]

It will frequently occur that for an industry, data are only available in grouped form. For instance, data on the fraction of total output produced by production units whose labour productivities (or wage shares) lie within a certain interval. Let Y_j stand for the fraction of output produced by all production units (assuming they operate at full capacity) whose productivities lie between L_j and H_j. This fraction is measured by

(7)
$$Y_j = \sum_{i \in J_j} x_i / C$$

where $J_j = \{i \,|\, L_j < \beta_i \leq H_j\}$ for $j = 1, \ldots, m$. The m intervals (L_j, H_j) are such that they partition the interval $(0, \beta^o)$.

When only data on Y_j, L_j, and H_j are available, it will often be difficult to estimate the parameters of the capacity distribution by means of the maximum likelihood method. A more tractable method then is to estimate these parameters from the moments of the distribution, which in their turn can be estimated from the grouped data.[6] We elaborate this below for the case of a beta capacity distribution.

4. The beta-capacity distribution

In Muysken (1983) it is demonstrated that the beta distribution:

$$(8) \qquad \omega(\beta) = \frac{1}{\beta^o} \cdot \frac{1}{B(\lambda,\mu)} \cdot (\frac{\beta}{\beta^o})^{\lambda-1} \cdot (1 - \frac{\beta}{\beta^o})^{\mu-1}, \qquad 0 < \beta < \beta^o$$

with parameters β^o, λ and μ, is a very general form of the normalised
capacity distribution. To each different pair of λ and μ of the distribution
corresponds a different aggregate production function. For instance, to
a $B(\alpha,1)$-distribution corresponds the Cobb-Douglas function, to a
$B(1,\sigma/1-\sigma)$-distribution the CES function, and to a $B(2,\gamma)$-distribution a
VES function. Moreover, the flexibility of its form makes it plausible that
a specific set of data will fit the beta distribution. Therefore we discuss
the estimation of its parameter values below.

When data on individual production units are available, the parameter
values of the capacity distribution (8) can be estimated according to the
maximum likelihood method. Hence, according to equation (5), the maximum
likelihood estimators of these parameters are found by maximising

$$(9) \qquad -n \cdot \ln \beta^o - n \cdot \ln B(\lambda,\mu) + (\lambda-1) \sum_{i=1}^{n} \ln(\beta_i/\beta^o) + (\mu-1) \sum_{i=1}^{n} \ln(1-\beta_i/\beta^o)$$

with respect to λ, μ, and β^o. Moreover, the invariance of the distribution
over time can be tested by means of the generalised likelihood ratio test,
presented in equation (6). The above is elaborated in Appendix 1.

On the other hand, when data are available only in grouped form,
the parameters can be estimated from the moments of the beta distribution
(8). The mean and variance of this distribution, α and σ^2, respectively,
are related to its parameters as follows:

$$(10) \qquad \alpha = \frac{\lambda}{\lambda+\mu} \cdot \beta^o$$

$$\sigma^2 = \frac{\lambda \cdot \mu}{(\lambda+\mu)^2(\lambda+\mu+1)} \cdot \beta^{o^2}.$$

Furthermore, when the capacity distribution is expressed in labour input
coefficients instead of labour productivities, its mean is equal to the
industry's labour input coefficient when operating at full capacity.[7] As
a consequence, in the case of the beta distribution:

$$(11) \qquad \frac{\bar{V}}{C} = \frac{1}{\beta^o} \cdot \frac{\lambda + \mu - 1}{\lambda - 1}$$

holds. Here $\bar{V}$ stands for the amount of labour employed when the industry is operating at full capacity.

The values of α and σ^2 can be estimated in a straightforward manner from the grouped data. Moreover, if the values of $\bar{V}$ and C are also known, then equations (10) and (11) consist of three equations which provide estimators for the three parameters, λ, μ, and β^o. This is elaborated in Appendix 2.

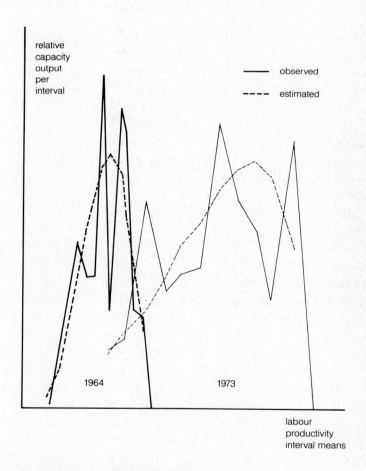

Fig. 1. The capacity distribution in 1964 and 1973

5.   The case of the Swedish dairy industry

In this section we shall illustrate the above for the Swedish dairy industry. For each of the years 1964-1973 data on x_i and β_i for individual dairies are available. Capacity output, x_i, is measured in tons of milk and the labour productivity, β_i, is measured in tons of milk per hour worked. The number of dairies varies from 75 in 1964 to 41 in 1973. A precise description of the data is given in Førsund and Hjalmarsson (1984, ch. 9). In this description Førsund and Hjalmarsson argue that the dairy process is of a putty-clay nature, with labour as the only variable input. Hence, the above analysis can be applied to their data.

For each year we aggregate over the individual data to $C = \Sigma_i x_i$ and $\bar{V} = \Sigma_i x_i / \beta_i$. Moreover, grouped data are calculated from the individual data according to equation (7). They are presented for 12 intervals in Appendix 3. From these grouped data the capacity distribution can be constructed. In Figure 1 it is presented for the years 1964 and 1974 in twelve intervals. Both distributions exhibit a bell-shaped form, although there are several peaks.[8] Such a bell-shaped form is consistent with a beta distribution. Moreover, the distribution obviously is stretched-out in the course of time, which seems consistent with Sato's invariance condition of equation (4).

We estimate for each year the parameters of the beta distribution. As was discussed above, we use the maximum likelihood method on individual data and the method of moments on grouped data for 12 intervals.[9] The estimation results for both methods are presented in Table 1, together with the observed values on $\bar{V}/C$ (cf. col. (2)), and β^o (cf. col (3)). This last value is the highest value of β observed in any one year.[10]

The results of the maximum likelihood estimation method are presented in Table 1, columns (4) - (6). The estimated values of β^o, presented in column (4), generally differ highly significantly from zero. They are remarkably close to the directly observed values (cf. column (3)), except for the years 1968 and 1969. The estimated values of λ, column (5), also differ significantly from zero for all years. Except for the years 1968 and 1969, they vary between 2.1 and 3.6. Finally, the estimated values of μ have larger variances (cf. column (6)). They only differ significantly from zero for five years: 1964, 1965, 1967, 1971 and 1972. For those years μ varies between 1.37 and 3.28.

Since the observed values of $\bar{V}/C$, presented in column (2), are reliable observations, it is worthwhile to compare these values to those calculated according to equation (11) from the maximum likelihood estimates of λ, μ, and β^o. These calculated values are presented in column (7). They consistently lie somewhat above the directly observed values. Hence, the estimated values of μ are somewhat too high or those of λ are somewhat too low, or both.

The results of the method of moments estimation are presented in Table 1, columns (8) - (10).[11] Again the estimated values of β^o, column (8), are remarkably close to the observed ones, except for the year 1968. Hence they also are close to the maximum likelihood estimates in column (4). The estimated values of λ, column (9), consistently lie above their maximum likelihood counterparts in column (5). They show a decreasing tendency over time from 6.3 in 1964 to 3.3 in 1973. The values of μ on the

Table 1. The estimation results for the Swedish dairy industry

year (1)	$\bar{V}/C$ (2)	β^o (3)	maximum likelihood estimation				method of moments				ML
			β^o (4)*	λ (5)*	μ (6)*	$\bar{V}/C$ (7)	β^o (8)	λ (9)	μ (10)	R^2 (11)	R^2 (12)
1964	0.612	2.69	2.94 (9.26)	3.57 (3.66)	3.28 (2.08)	0.774	3.58	6.34	6.34	0.84	0.76
1965	0.562	2.78	2.83 (26.98)	2.23 (3.24)	1.51 (2.40)	0.787	3.71	5.56	4.99	0.81	0.83
1966	0.540	3.12	3.62 (5.73)	3.35 (2.90)	3.52 (1.48)	0.690	3.65	4.89	3.77	0.68	0.64
1967	0.514	3.39	3.27 (14.58)	2.75 (3.67)	2.33 (2.46)	0.713	3.46	4.61	2.87	0.89	0.79
1968	0.457	4.05	6.05 (2.48)	3.94 (3.09)	7.62 (1.10)	0.594	6.94	6.22	11.39	0.91	0.82
1969	0.395	4.94	8.24 (1.62)	4.07 (2.74)	9.84 (0.83)	0.507	4.93	3.65	2.51	0.69	0.70
1970	0.380	5.25	4.90 (8.86)	2.95 (3.16)	2.79 (1.87)	0.488	4.95	4.28	2.96	0.92	0.86
1971	0.319	5.68	4.90 (32.42)	2.40 (2.76)	1.42 (2.19)	0.411	5.14	4.28	2.15	0.59	0.58
1972	0.285	6.27	5.59 (33.16)	2.19 (2.72)	1.37 (2.16)	0.385	5.29	3.48	1.27	0.81	0.86
1973	0.269	6.08	5.89 (25.45)	2.05 (1.99)	1.29 (1.51)	0.378	6.06	3.26	1.48	0.85	0.79

* the values between brackets are t-values.

other hand, column (10), lie much closer to the corresponding estimates
presented in column (6), except for the years 1968 and 1969. They also
show a decreasing tendency from 6.3 in 1964 to 1.2 in 1973.

The average value of λ over the whole period, except for 1968/69, is
2.7 in the case of maximum likelihood estimation and 4.6 when estimated
by the method of moments. The average values of μ are 2.2 and 3.3,
respectively.[12] This suggests, in line with our conclusion above, that
in order to find better estimates of $\bar{V}/C$ in column (7), the maximum likelihood estimates of λ should be higher.

From these results one might wonder to what extent the capacity
distribution does fit a beta distribution. To get an impression of the
goodness of fit, we calculate the coefficient of determination, R^2. However, in order to be able to do so, we have to calculate, $\hat{Y}_j$, the estimated capacity output produced by production units in the interval
$L_j < \beta \leq H_j$. It is defined by:

$$(12) \qquad \hat{Y}_j = \int_{L_j}^{H_j} \omega(\beta;\hat{\beta}^o,\hat{\pi})\,d\beta$$

where $\hat{\beta}^o$ and $\hat{\pi}$ stand for the estimated values of β^o and π, respectively.
However, since the integral of a beta-function cannot be solved in general,
we use the approximation:[13]

$$(13) \qquad \int_{L_j}^{H_j} \omega(\beta;\hat{\beta}^o,\hat{\pi}) \simeq (H_j - L_j) \cdot \omega(\frac{L_j + H_j}{2}; \hat{\beta}^o,\hat{\pi}).$$

This enables us to calculate $\hat{Y}_j$ and hence R^2 straightforwardly.[14]

The goodness of fit to the data on 12 intervals is calculated both for
the method of moments (cf. column (11)), and for the maximum likelihood
method (cf. column (12). On the whole the method-of-moments estimates
show a good fit; for the years 1966, 1969, and 1971 the fit is reasonable.
Hence a beta distribution with parameters estimated by the method of
moments gives a reasonable approximation of the capacity distribution of
the Swedish dairy industry. The estimated distributions for the years
1964 and 1973 are presented in Figure 1.

The fit of the maximum likelihood estimates is also good, although
somewhat worse than the fit of the method-of-moments estimates. Therefore, we conclude that both estimates are sufficiently close to each other.

However, we cannot help but notice that, for instance, in 1965 the method-of-moment estimates of λ and μ are about three times the maximum likelihood ones, whereas the coefficients of determination are 0.81 and 0.83, respectively.

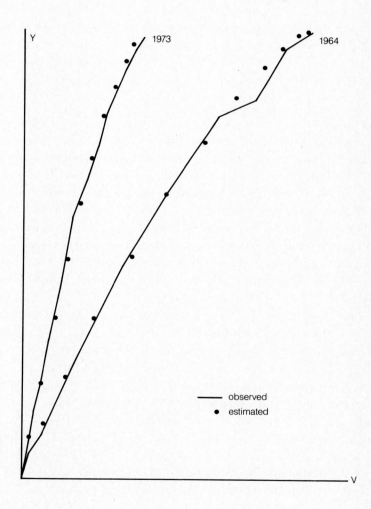

Fig. 2. The aggregate short-run production function in 1964 and 1973

The fit of the capacity distribution to the beta distribution may also be demonstrated by comparing the aggregate production function which can be constructed from the estimated capacity distribution with the aggregate production function that can be constructed directly from the grouped data. Apart from data on Y_j and $\hat{Y}_j$ we then need data on V_j and $\hat{V}_j$. V_j stands for the amount of labour employed by production units in the interval $L_j < \beta \leq H_j$ and $\hat{V}_j$ stands for its counterpart estimated from the capacity distribution. Using the approximation from equation (13) we find

$$(14) \qquad V_j \simeq Y_j \frac{2}{L_j + H_j} \quad \text{and} \quad \hat{V}_j \simeq \hat{Y}_j \frac{2}{L_j + H_j}.$$

Assuming efficient behaviour in the industry, the aggregate production function is constructed from the data by cumulating simultaneously Y_j on one axis and V_j on the other one, where j is ranked in decreasing productivity. In the same way a function is constructed from the estimated capacity distribution by cumulating $\hat{Y}_j$ and $\hat{V}_j$ simultaneously. Both functions are presented in Figure 2 for the years 1964 and 1973. It is obvious that the fit is very good, although the capacity output of the least efficient units is overestimated. Hence, for the purpose of constructing the aggregate short-run production function, the beta distribution represents the capacity distribution of the Swedish dairy industry very well.[15]

It also is interesting to know whether the estimated distributions satisfy the invariance conditions. As elaborated above, we apply the generalised likelihood ratio test to test the invariance of λ and μ over time (see also Appendix 1). The values of λ and μ that maximise the likelihood function over the whole period, given the values of β_t^o presented in column (4) of Table 1, are 2.04 and 1.98, respectively. The corresponding value of $-2 \ln \Lambda$ is 201.7 which amply exceeds the critical value of 1.49 at a 5%-level. Hence the capacity distribution cannot be said to be invariant over time. Although it can be represented for each year by a beta distribution, the parameters of the distribution can differ from year to year.

The results for the Swedish dairy industry, presented in Figures 1 and 2, could be extensively extended. First, one might try to explain the shifts in the capacity distribution over the course of time. Such an explanation would include an analysis of both the ex-ante production function for milk-processing and of entrepreneurial behaviour with respect to buying, utilising and scrapping of milk-processing units. The empirical investigation of the Swedish dairy industry presented in Førsund and Hjalmarsson (1984) seems a good starting point for such an analysis. Next, one might try to infer some characteristics of the short-run aggregate production function from the estimation results for the beta distribution, along the lines of Sato (1975, Ch. 17). Finally, one might try to look for a form of the aggregate production function that shows these characteristics. Such a form should be both analytically manageable and approximately consistent with a beta-capacity distribution. However, an analysis along these lines exceeds the scope and purpose of the present paper.

6. Concluding remarks

In this paper we discussed the estimation of the industry capacity distribution for a given functional form. We discussed this for the case of a beta distribution. This form of the capacity distribution has been chosen on a priori grounds, namely it allows for a bell-shaped form and it is consistent with well-known forms of the aggregate production function. Moreover, the flexibility of its form makes it plausible that a specific set of data will fit the beta distribution.

In order to corroborate this last statement we estimated the capacity distribution for the Swedish dairy industry for each of the years 1964-1973. This led to the conclusion that the capacity distribution of this industry fits a beta distribution with parameter values of λ in the range 2-6 and of μ in the range 1-6.[16] However, the invariance conditions are not satisfied.

An obvious method for estimating the parameters of the capacity distribution is the maximum likelihood method. However, this method can only be applied to a beta distribution when individual data are available. When the data are presented in grouped form, as is usually the case, estimation by means of the method of moments is a useful alternative. We demonstrated that the estimated results from the method of moments employing grouped data lie close to the maximum likelihood estimation results employing individual data. This suggests that plausible estimates of the coefficients of the capacity distribution can be obtained from grouped data by means of the method of moments.

One should realise that the choice of a beta distribution was made on a priori grounds: The capacity distribution of the Swedish dairy industry might also fit other distributions. Nonetheless, the good fit of the beta distribution contradicts Hildenbrand's statement, cited above, that "there is no justifiable reason for the hope that the distribution... has a simple parametric representation." Moreover, the empirical results of Sato (1975) and Muysken (1983a) also indicate that "the Beta distribution gives a passable approximation in some instances."[17]

Utilising as much scarce data as available, it seems worthwhile to verify whether the beta distribution shows a good fit for many other industries. If this is the case, an algorithm should be constructed to derive the aggregate production function corresponding to a $B(\lambda,\mu)$-distribution, for any value of λ and μ. The properties of the production function should then be investigated both analytically and numerically.[18] Moreover, as is continuously stressed in Johansen's seminal book Produc-tion Functions, the analysis should be extended to the case of more vari-able inputs. Such a fruitful mixture of both theoretical and empirical analysis seems to us very much in the spirit of Leif Johansen.

Appendix 1

Maximum likelihood estimation of the beta distribution

According to the maximum likelihood method, the parameters of the beta distribution are found by maximising

$$(A1.1) \quad \ell = -n \cdot \ln\beta^o - n \cdot \ln B(\lambda,\mu) + (\lambda-1) \sum_{i=1}^{n} \ln(\beta_i /\beta^o)$$

$$+ (\mu-1) \sum_{i=1}^{n} \ln(1-\beta_i /\beta^o)$$

with respect to λ, μ and β^o. This yields:[19]

(A1.2) $\quad \frac{\lambda}{\mu-1} = \frac{1}{n} \cdot \sum\limits_{i=1}^{n} \frac{\beta_i}{\beta^o - \beta_i}$

(A1.3) $\quad \ln\left\{\frac{\lambda}{\lambda+\mu}\right\} - \frac{\mu}{2\lambda(\lambda+\mu)} = \frac{1}{n} \cdot \sum\limits_{i=1}^{n} \ln\left\{\beta_i / \beta^o\right\}$

(A1.4) $\quad \ln\left\{\frac{\mu}{\lambda+\mu}\right\} - \frac{\lambda}{2\mu(\lambda+\mu)} = \frac{1}{n} \cdot \sum\limits_{i=1}^{n} \ln\left\{1 - \beta_i / \beta^o\right\}.$

The estimators of β^o, λ and μ then can be found iteratively from equations (2)-(4).[20]

The asymptotic covariance matrix, S, of these estimators is:

(A1.5) $\quad S = \begin{bmatrix} -\dfrac{\partial^2 \ell}{\partial \beta^{o2}} & & \\[2em] -\dfrac{\partial^2 \ell}{\partial \beta^o \partial \lambda} & -\dfrac{\partial^2 \ell}{\partial \lambda^2} & \\[2em] -\dfrac{\partial^2 \ell}{\partial \beta^o \partial \mu} & -\dfrac{\partial^2 \ell}{\partial \lambda \partial \mu} & -\dfrac{\partial^2 \ell}{\partial \mu^2} \end{bmatrix}^{-1}$

In order to compute the generalised maximum likelihood ratio, we also have to maximise

(A1.6) $\quad -\sum\limits_{t=1}^{T} n_t \cdot \ln\beta_t^o - \ln B(\lambda,\mu) \cdot \sum\limits_{t=1}^{T} n_t + (\lambda-1)\sum\limits_{t=1}^{T}\sum\limits_{i=1}^{n_t} \ln(\beta_{it}/\beta_t^o)$

$\quad +(\mu-1)\sum\limits_{t=1}^{T}\sum\limits_{i=1}^{n_t} \ln(1-\beta_{it}/\beta_t^o)$

with respect to λ, μ and $\beta_1^o, \ldots, \beta_T^o$. The resulting equations are similar to equations (A1.2)-(A1.4). The right-hand sides of equations (A1.3) and (A1.4) are summed over time, and equation (2) holds for each β_t^o. Hence we have T+2 equations and T+2 unknown variables.

We were not able to solve the system simultaneously for the Swedish dairy industry. Therefore we took the values of β_t^o as given, and used the values estimated for the individual years. The values of λ and μ could then be found along the lines described in note 20.

Using Stirling's approximation to approximate $B(\lambda,\mu)$, the generalised likelihood ratio then can be straightforwardly calculated according to equation (6) in the text. The values of λ, μ and β^o found from equations (A1.2)-(A1.4) should be substituted in the numerator, and those found from maximising equation (A1.6) should be substituted in the denominator.

Appendix 2

Estimation of the parameters of the beta distribution from its moments

Let only data on Y_j, L_j and H_j be available. Moreover, let $v = \bar{V}/C$ be known. Then estimators of α and σ^2 are given by:

(A2.1)
$$a = \sum_{j=1}^{m} Y_j \cdot i_j$$

$$s^2 = \frac{n}{n-1} \cdot \sum_{j=1}^{m} Y_j (i_j - a)^2$$

respectively, where $i_j = \frac{1}{2}(L_j + H_j)$. From equation (10) in the text we find:

(A2.2) $\lambda = \dfrac{a}{\beta^o - a} \cdot \mu = \dfrac{a}{\beta^o} \cdot (a \cdot \dfrac{\beta^o - a}{s^2} - 1)$

(A2.3) $\mu = s^2 \cdot \dfrac{\beta^o + (a/\lambda)}{a \cdot (a/\lambda)^2}.$

Now the estimation procedure runs as follows. First calculate a and s^2 from the data, according to equation (A2.1). Next calculate values of λ and μ from equations (A2.2) and (A2.3), respectively, assuming a value for β^o. Then since v is known, β^o can be calculated according to equation (11) from

(A2.4) $\beta^o = \dfrac{1}{v} \cdot \dfrac{\lambda + \mu - 1}{\lambda - 1}.$

When this calculated value of β^o exceeds the assumed value, the initially assumed value should be increased, and vice versa. Then a new iteration is begun, resulting in new values for λ and μ and a new value for β^o. The procedure continues until the assumed value and the new value of β^o differ by less than 1 per cent.

Appendix 3

Data on the Swedish dairy industry, 1964-1973

For each year the intervals of the labour input coefficient (by their interval mean, Int. mean) and the corresponding relative fraction of capacity output (Rel. fr.) are presented.

Year 1964 Int.mean	Rel.fr.	Year 1965 Int.mean	Rel.fr.	Year 1966 Int.mean	Rel.fr.	Year 1967 Int.mean	Rel.fr.	Year 1968 Int.mean	Rel.fr.
2.5965	0.0499	2.6871	0.1001	3.0140	0.1136	3.2810	0.0315	3.9173	0.0939
2.4174	0.0552	2.5018	0.1921	2.8062	0.0177	3.0547	0.0537	3.6472	0.0339
2.2384	0.1547	2.3165	0.0594	2.5983	0.0293	2.8284	0.0481	3.3770	0.0109
2.0593	0.1651	2.1311	0.0852	2.3904	0.2641	2.6021	0.1052	3.1069	0.0833
1.8802	0.0549	1.9458	0.1399	2.1826	0.0728	2.3759	0.2181	2.8367	0.0931
1.7012	0.1833	1.7605	0.0742	1.9747	0.1138	2.1496	0.1034	2.5665	0.1449
1.5221	0.0721	1.5752	0.1115	1.7669	0.0653	1.9233	0.1273	2.2964	0.1258
1.3430	0.0738	1.3899	0.0709	1.5590	0.1239	1.6970	0.0825	2.0262	0.1617
1.1640	0.0883	1.2046	0.0702	1.3511	0.0703	1.4708	0.1118	1.7560	0.1135
0.9849	0.0613	1.0192	0.0496	1.1433	0.0950	1.2445	0.0787	1.4859	0.0727
0.8058	0.0373	0.8339	0.0330	0.9354	0.0190	1.0182	0.0112	1.2157	0.0486
0.6267	0.0031					0.7920	0.0178	0.9456	0.0142
								0.6754	0.0019

Year 1969 Int.mean	Rel.fr.	Year 1970 Int.mean	Rel.fr.	Year 1971 Int.mean	Rel.fr.	Year 1972 Int.mean	Rel.fr.	Year 1973 Int.mean	Rel.fr.
4.7727	0.0759	5.0776	0.0130	5.4935	0.0389	6.0601	0.0142	5.8778	0.1503
4.4435	0.0478	4.7274	0.0273	5.1146	0.0328	5.6421	0.0649	5.4725	0.0592
4.1144	0.0311	4.3773	0.0357	4.7357	0.0245	5.2242	0.0577	5.0671	0.0978
3.7852	0.0358	4.0271	0.0378	4.3569	0.0871	4.8063	0.1063	4.6617	0.1134
3.4561	0.0881	3.6769	0.1571	3.9780	0.0959	4.3883	0.1138	4.2564	0.1637
3.1269	0.0671	3.3267	0.1513	3.5992	0.3369	3.9704	0.1912	3.8510	0.0809
2.7978	0.2584	2.9765	0.1626	3.2203	0.0528	3.5525	0.1263	3.4456	0.0755
2.4686	0.1327	2.6264	0.1471	2.8414	0.0281	3.1345	0.1503	3.0403	0.0638
2.1395	0.0650	2.2762	0.0563	2.4626	0.2035	2.7166	0.0637	2.6349	0.1141
1.8103	0.0903	1.9260	0.1204	2.0837	0.0367	2.2986	0.0259	2.2295	0.0380
1.4812	0.0646	1.5758	0.0650	1.7049	0.0344	1.8807	0.0474	1.8242	0.0328
1.1520	0.0415	1.2256	0.0249						

Notes

1) Hildenbrand (1981), pp. 116-117. For a non-parametric approach see also Forsund and Hjalmarsson (1984).

2) When time-series data on the industry are also available over a sufficiently long period, the properties of the aggregate short-run production function estimated from these data can be compared to the properties implied by the distribution approach, given the estimation of the capacity distribution. Cf. Muysken (1983a).

3) One might argue that the frequency of observations on a particular value of β is given by the number of observed production units whose labour productivity is equal to that value. However, usually all production units will not be of an equal size. Then the capacity distribution, ω, which refers to output produced, no longer gives the frequency of observations on a particular value of β. As a consequence, in order to be able to interpret ω as a probability density function all production units in the analysis are assumed to be of equal size. For example, an observed dairy producing 100 tons of milk is assumed to consist of 100 production units producing 1 ton of milk. Cf. Levhari (1968, p. 151) who states, "we normalize the cells such that each of them is capable of producing one unit of output" and then interpret the capacity distribution as "a density function of the various cells". See also Sato (1975, p. 16).

4) An alternative is to estimate the parameters by means of least squares (Sato, (1975, Ch. 14), Muysken (1983a)). However, one should realise that the assumption of independent random error terms is not justified, in particular when the approximation of equation (13) below is made. Hence the statistical properties of the estimates are hard to find.

5) The number of degrees of freedom is $\eta = (a+1)\cdot(T-1)$, where a is the number of parameters in π.

6) Aitchison and Brown (1957, Ch. 5) suggest this procedure when estimating the parameters of the log-normal distribution. Obviously the method of moments is less efficient than the maximum likelihood method.

7) Define $\xi = 1/\beta$. Then the capacity distribution, corresponding to equation (4), is $\phi(\xi)$, which is defined for $\xi > \xi^0 = 1/\beta^0$. The aggregate amount of labour employed at full capacity is by definition $\bar{V} = \int_{\xi^0}^{\sim} \xi\cdot\phi(\xi)d\xi$, which also is the mean of the distribution $\phi(\xi)$.

8) At first sight the observed distributions do not appear to have the characteristic smooth, bell-shaped forms of a beta-distribution. However, one should realise that this partly depends on the choice of the interval lengths of labour productivity.

9) Actually we did not use the data on the last interval since its mean is undetermined.

10) For each year, except 1973, we omitted from the data the dairy with the highest value of β, and for 1965 and 1967 also the one with the

next highest value. Considering the other observations on dairies, these values seemed very implausible on a-priori grounds. We omitted: '64 3.73, '65 3.51 4.37, '66 3.51, '67 3.95 5.10, '68 9.62, '69 8.00, '70 5.95, '71 6.02, '72 8.62. Compare also Table 1, column (3).

11) We omitted the last intervals from the years 1964 and 1969, since both intervals contain only one dairy producing less than 0.17% of total output.

12) When we use the least-squares method (note 4 above) we find average values for λ and μ of 3.8 and 2.1, respectively.

13) See also Sato (1975), p. 200.

14) The coefficient of determination is calculated from

$$R^2 = 1 - \frac{\sum_i (\hat{Y} - Y)^2}{\sum Y^2}.$$ See also Theil (1971), p. 176.

15) For an excellent survey of the properties of the production structure for the Swedish dairy industry, we refer to Førsund and Hjalmarsson (1984, Ch. 9).

16) Sato (1975, Ch. 14) found for the Japanese cotton spinning industry and several US-manufacturing industries a satisfactory fit with λ in the range 2-4 and μ in the range 9-15. Muysken (1983a) found for the Japanese cotton spinning industry a satisfactory fit for $\lambda=2$ and $\mu=2$.

17) Sato (1975), p. 205. See also note 16.

18) See Sato (1975), Ch. 17.

19) Using Stirling's approximation, $\Gamma(h) \approx \sqrt{2\pi} \cdot e^{1-h} \cdot (h-1)^{h-1/2}$, it can easily be seen that

$$\frac{1}{B(\lambda,\mu)} \cdot \frac{dB(\lambda,\mu)}{d\lambda} = \frac{\Gamma'(\lambda)}{\Gamma(\lambda)} - \frac{\Gamma'(\lambda+\mu)}{\Gamma(\lambda+\mu)}.$$

20) Define $a = \lambda/\mu$ and $b = \mu/[2\lambda(\lambda+\mu)]$. Then equations (A1.3) and (A1.4) can be rewritten as follows:

(A1.3') $\quad b = a^2 \cdot [\ln\{a/a+1\} - S1]$

(A1.4') $\quad b = -\ln\{a+1\} - S2.$

where $S1 = (1/n) \cdot \sum_{i=1}^{n} \ln\{\beta_i/\beta^o\}$ and $S2 = (1/n) \cdot \sum_{i=1}^{n} \ln\{1-\beta_i/\beta^o\}$. Since $b > 0$ should hold, we find a lower limit a_0 for a:

$$a > a_0 = 1/(e^{-S1} - 1).$$

Then, for each value of $a > a_0$, b can be calculated both from equations (A1.3') and (A1.4'), given β^o. By increasing the value of a gradually, starting from a_0, one finds a unique point where both calculated values of b coincide. This point is found, however, for a given value of β^0. An obvious initial value is the maximum value of the observed β_i's.

The values of λ and μ can be calculated from the values found for a and b. Then the left-hand side of equation (A1.2) can be calculated and compared to its right-hand side, which is calculated for the given value of β^0. Since $(1 - \beta_i/\beta^0)$ is an increasing function of β^0, β^0 should be increased when the calculated left-hand side exceeds the right-hand side, and decreased otherwise.

With a new value of β a new iteration can be made, from which newer values of a and b are calculated. This procedure is continued until all parameter values change less than 0.1% after an additional iteration.

References

Aitchison, J. and J.A.C. Brown (1957), The Lognormal Distribution, Cambridge University Press, Cambridge.

Førsund, F.R. and L. Hjalmarsson (1984), Analysis of Industrial Structure: A Production Function Approach, Working paper No. 135, the Industrial Institute for Economic and Social Research, Stockholm.

Hildenbrand, W. (1981), "Short run production functions based on micro-data", Econometrica 49, 1095-1126.

Johansen, L. (1972), Production Functions. An integration of micro and macro, short run and long run aspects, North-Holland Publ. Co., Amsterdam.

Levhari, D. (1968), "A note on Houthakker's aggregate production function in a multi-firm industry", Econometrica 36, 151-154.

Muysken, J. (1983), "Transformed beta-capacity distributions of production units", Economics Letters 11, 217-221.

Muysken, J. (1983a), "Aggregation of putty-clay production functions", European Economic Review 22, 351-362.

Sato, K. (1975), Production Functions and Aggregation, North-Holland Publ. Co., Amsterdam.

Seierstad, A. (1981), "The macro production function uniquely determines the capacity distribution of micro units", Economics Letters 7, 211-214.

Theil, H. (1971), Principles of Econometrics, J. Wiley and Sons, New York.

Production, Multi-Sectoral Growth and Planning
F.R. Førsund, M. Hoel, and S. Longva (Editors)
© Elsevier Science Publishers B.V. (North-Holland), 1985

PROPERTIES OF PRODUCTION AND PROFIT FUNCTIONS ARISING FROM THE AGGREGATION OF A CAPACITY DISTRIBUTION OF MICRO UNITS

by Atle Seierstad
University of Oslo

This article reviews some properties of production and profit functions for a sector containing possibly a large number of firms producing one and the same kind of output. The approach has its origin in a paper by H.S. Houthakker (1955). L. Johansen worked out its many implications in his 1972 book Production functions. More recently W. Hildenbrand (1981) has given a treatment of the topic, relating it to the mathematical theory of zonoids.

The present article is divided into two parts. Part I gives a survey of results related to properties of the capacity distribution of firms and to the macro production and profit functions. The second part, Part II, gives a more detailed mathematical exposition, including brief proofs of the more elementary results.

Part I. Survey of results

Two methods for representing the situation at the micro level have been presented in the literature:

i)   In the approach of W. Hildenbrand (1981) each micro unit is characterized by its production capacity and input requirements at full capacity. Hildenbrand takes as a point of departure the - so to speak

I have benefited from comments on an earlier draft made by Kalle Moene. Comments on the last draft made by Bruce Wolman and Knut Sydsæter were also very useful. In my work on the themes of this article I have had stimulating discussions with Eivind Bjøntegård and Leif Johansen.

- empirically given distribution of micro units, denoted by ν in this article. If each micro unit is described by a vector $z = (v,x)$, where $v = (v_1,\ldots,v_n)$ is the input requirement at full capacity and x is the production capacity, then ν gives the number of micro units of type z.

ii) In the approach of Houthakker and Johansen, the empirically given data are re-edited in the following way: The capacities of all micro units with the same input coefficients are added together. If input coefficients are denoted by the vector $\xi = (\xi_1,\ldots,\xi_n)$, i.e., $\xi_i = v_i/x$, we can say that this procedure leads to a distribution μ that gives the total capacity of all the micro units for any given vector of input coefficients ξ.

In the present article the discussion will be carried out mainly in terms of the latter approach.

Each firm can be run at any fraction ϕ of full capacity. Then, by assumption, both the output and the inputs are equal to ϕ times their full capacity levels. Assume now that each micro unit is run at some individually fixed fraction of full capacity, and suppose we sum the total output and total inputs of all the firms, denoted x and $v = (v_1,\ldots,v_n)$, respectively. The set of points (v,x), obtained by going through all possible combinations of individually chosen capacity utilizations of the micro units, is the macro technology set Y. This set is convex. The macro production function, F, is then found by searching for each fixed v through the technology set for the pair (v,x) with the highest production x. This function becomes concave and its domain of definition D will be some convex subset of $R_+^n = \{v \in R^n, v \geq 0\}$, where $v \geq 0$ means $v_i \geq 0$ for all i.

A standard approach in economics is to map out the technological constraints, and in particular the most efficient technologies, by observing the reactions of firm owners to varying input prices. In theory this is carried out by mental experiments. For example, profit-maximising input vectors and the corresponding outputs (or simply the profit itself) are recorded for all possible input prices. In duality theory, such information makes it possible to construct the production function. In smooth cases, any input vector v is profit maximising for some choice of input prices, and if the corresponding output is known, we then know any point on the graph of the production function.

The same ideas are used in the approach originating with Houthakker: When given an output price p and input prices q_i, all micro units with positive profits, or quasi-rents, will produce at full capacity and all micro units with negative quasi-rents will produce at zero capacity. (The quasi-rent per unit of output is given by the expression $p - \Sigma_i q_i \xi_i$.)

Summing the inputs and outputs of all the firms, we obtain the profit-maximising input and corresponding output of the whole sector. In smooth cases, the production function can be obtained by varying the input prices as above.

If the (cumulative) distribution μ has a density f, the sector's inputs v_i and output x at prices p, q_i can be written

$$(\text{'}) \qquad v_i(-q,p) = \int \cdots \int_{G(-q,p)} \xi_i \, f(\xi_1,\ldots,\xi_n) d\xi_1 \ldots d\xi_n$$

$$(*) \qquad x(-q,p) = \int \cdots \int_{G(-q,p)} f(\xi_1,\ldots,\xi_n) d\xi_1 \ldots d\xi_n$$

where $G(-q,p)$ is the set of firms (or of input coefficients) with positive or zero quasi-rent: $G(-q,p) = \{\xi : p - \Sigma q_i \xi_i \geq 0\}$, $(q = (q_1,\ldots,q_n))$. When calculating v and x we included above all firms with zero quasi-rent. All other profit-maximising points (v,x) are obtained by allowing firms with zero quasi-rent to run at arbitrarily fixed fractions of full capacity (see II.3 below).

An interesting feature of the present set-up is that knowing the macro profit function $\pi(-q,p) = px(-q,p) - qv(-q,p)$ not only makes it possible to reconstruct the macro production function, but also the underlying capacity distribution of micro units (see II.12). However, it is not possible to reconstruct the Hildenbrand empirical distribution of micro units. The reason is the following: When prices change, all micro units with a given vector of input coefficients will switch at the same time from having positive to having negative quasi-rents (or vice versa), so prices cannot differentiate between them.

In its general version, the present approach allows the distribution of micro units to be of any type – discrete, continuous, or a mixture. It is assumed that the region of micro units with nonzero capacity is a bounded set, i.e. the distribution has a bounded support.

Define the region of substitution D* of the macro production function F to be the set consisting of inputs v with the property that smaller

inputs produce less, i.e. $F(v') < F(v)$ for all $v' \leq v$, $v' \neq v$. If the
distribution is given by a continuous density f, the set of firms with zero
quasi-rent will always be negligible, and the profit-maximising input is
unique, continuous in (q,p) and given by the expression (') above.
Furthermore, if the set $E = \{\xi : f(\xi) > 0\}$ lies truly inside R^n_+ (i.e. for
some $\delta > 0$, $\xi_i \geq \delta$, $i=1,\ldots,n$, for all $\xi \epsilon E$), then each point v in the
region of substitution D* of the macro production function equals $v(-q,1)$
for some price vector $q \geq 0$ (see II.10).

When the profit-maximising input is unique (as in the continuous density case), both profit-maximising inputs and profit-maximising output are
functions nonincreasing in q and nondecreasing in p. (If some or all of
the q_i's increase, then the set $G(-q,p)$ shrinks.) In particular, expansion lines are nondecreasing.

When the distribution is given by a continuous density f, and the set
$E = \{\xi : f(\xi) > 0\}$ is connected (any two points in it can be connected by
an unbroken curve lying in E), then different price vectors q in the set
$Q = \{q\epsilon R^n_+ : 0 < v(-q,1) < v(0,1)\}$ give rise to different input vectors
$v(-q,1)$; here e.g. $0 < v$ means $0 \leq v$, $0 \neq v$ (see II.10). In this case, the
function $v(-q,1)$ is continuous on Q and has a continuous inverse defined
on $D' = D*\backslash\{0,v(0,1)\}$ if E lies truly inside R^n_+. (Note that $q_i \leq 1/\delta$ if $0
< v(-q,1)$.) Furthermore, the macro production function is differentiable
at any point $v \epsilon D'$ in the interior of D. In a sense, it is also differentiable at all boundary points v of D, $v \epsilon D'$. Finally, the free disposal hull
of the macro production function is differentiable at all points v, $0 < v <
v(0,1)$. The free disposal hull is the production function obtained by
assuming that any output which can be produced by some input vector v
can also be produced by any larger input vector $v' \geq v$. On D* it coin-
cides with the original production function F (see II.10 again).

The technology set Y is convex and contains the origin. The point $\bar{z}
= (\bar{v},\bar{x})$, $\bar{v} = v(0,1)$, $\bar{x} = x(0,1)$, is the largest point in Y, ($z \leq \bar{z}$ for all
$z\epsilon Y$). Furthermore, the point $z' = \frac{1}{2}\bar{z}$ is a center of symmetry of the set
Y, i.e. $z'+z\epsilon Y$ implies $z'-z\epsilon Y$. This property is reflected in the following
property of the macro production function F, namely that $F(v) + F(v'') \geq
F(\bar{v})$ if $v+v'' = \bar{v}$ and $v,v''\epsilon D$ (see II.4).

Above we mentioned that the distribution can be reconstructed from its
macro profit function. In fact, different capacity distributions give rise to
different macro profit functions and different macro production functions.
This means that, in principle, it is possible to reconstruct the capacity

distribution either from the knowledge of the profit function $\pi(-q,1)$, defined on R_+^n, or from the macro production function or its free disposal hull. Mathematical techniques exist that can be applied to this reconstruction problem (see II.12).

Writing q instead of $-q$, the (macro) profit function $\pi(q,p)$ for $q \leq 0$ and $p \geq 0$ is continuous, nondecreasing, convex, and linearly homogeneous. Furthermore, for any given q, $\pi(q,p) = p\bar{x}-q\bar{v}$ for large enough p, (i.e. for p so large that $G(q,p)$ contains the region of micro units with nonzero capacity).

Note that D, the domain of definition of the production function F, is bounded, so we can define the profit function $\pi(q,p)$ for both positive and negative input prices, i.e. for $q \epsilon R^n$. Moreover be aware of our convention of writing the profit as $px + \Sigma_i q_i v_i$, where both the output and the inputs v_i are nonnegative.

Define $\pi^+(q,p) = \pi(q,p) - \frac{1}{2}(q\bar{v}+p\bar{x})$. The symmetry of Y is equivalent to the fact that the function $\pi^+(q,p)$ defined on $R^n \times [0,\infty)$, has a convex symmetric extension to all R^{n+1}. The latter property can be expressed solely in terms directly obtained from π, since $\bar{v} = \left[\partial\pi(q,p)/\partial q\right]_{\substack{q=0 \\ p=1}}$ and $\bar{x} = \pi(0,1)$; and hence

(**) $\pi^+(q,p) = \pi(q,p) - \frac{1}{2}(q\left[\dfrac{\partial\pi(q,p)}{\partial q}\right]_{\substack{q=0 \\ p=1}} + p\pi(0,1))$.

The convex symmetric extension property of π^+ is equivalent to F having the property $F(v)+F(v') \geq F(\bar{v})$ when $v,v'\epsilon D$, $v+v' = \bar{v}$ even if F does not arise from a distribution of micro units (see II.14).

The macro profit function arising from a distribution of micro units exhibits even further special and crucial properties. One such property is that the function $\exp(-\pi^+(q,p))$ is <u>positive definite</u> (see (13) in Part II for a definition of this term). This property together with linear homogeneity of π^+ and symmetry of $q \to \pi^+(q,0)$ is not only necessary but also sufficient for $\pi(q,p)$ to originate from a capacity distribution of micro units.

Another crucial property that the macro profit function $\pi(q,p)$ satisfies is the following:

Define

$$(***) \qquad C(q) = \int_0^\infty e^{-P} \pi(q,p)dp$$

$q \ll 0$ (i.e. $q_i < 0$ for all i). Then all partial derivatives of $C(q)$ of any order are nonnegative for all $q \ll 0$. (This property is often called absolute monotonicity).

Assume that $\pi(q,p)$, defined for $q \le 0$ and $p \ge 0$ is any continuous, convex, nondecreasing, and linearly homogeneous function. Assume in addition that $\pi(q,p)$ is linear in p when p is large, i.e. for some constants K, K_q and Q_q, $K \ge 0$, $\pi(q,p) = Kp+Q_q$ for all $p \ge K_q$. If $\pi(q,p)$ is also absolutely monotonous in the above sense, then $\pi(q,p)$ is the macro profit function of some capacity distribution of micro units (see II.12).

Part II. Precise definitions and results

In this paper both the Hildenbrand "empirical" distribution ν and the Houthakker-Johansen capacity distribution μ will be bounded Borel measures with bounded support if nothing explicitly is said to the contrary.

It is natural to assume that ν has its support in $R_+^{n+1} = \{z \varepsilon R^{n+1}, z \ge 0\}$. We shall below even assume that ν has its support in $R^+ = \{z \varepsilon R_+^{n+1}, z_{n+1} > 0\}$. This means simply that we disregard production units with zero production capacity.

1.   Note that μ is formally related to ν as follows:

$$\mu = \tilde{\nu} \circ f^{-1} \text{ where } f: z \to (z_1/z_{n+1}, \ldots, z_n/z_{n+1}) \text{ and } \tilde{\nu}: E \to \int_E z_{n+1} d\nu.$$

The Hildenbrand approach can be framed in the setting of the theory of so-called zonoid of moments (Bolker 1969). Each bounded Borel measure ν with bounded support gives rise to a zonoid of moments Y_ν defined by

$$(1) \qquad Y_\nu = \{\int_{R^{n+1}} \phi(z)z d\nu(z): \phi \text{ a Borel function on } R^{n+1} \text{ with values in } [0,1]\}.$$

The Houthakker-Johansen approach can also be framed in the setting of the theory of zonoid of moments. Instead of the measure μ defined on R_+^n, we can imagine that we have a measure ν_1 defined in R^{n+1}, with support in the set $R_1 = \{z \varepsilon R_+^{n+1}, z^{n+1} = 1\}$. Indeed, another way of expressing that the total capacity of all micro units with input coefficients ξ is μ, is to say that we have a number ν_1, $\nu_1 = \mu$, of micro units of type $(\xi, 1)$, each unit having, as we see, unit production capacity. Formally, if $\alpha(\cdot)$ is the one-to-one map $(v, 1) \to v$, $R_1 \to R_+^n$, then $\nu_1 = \mu \circ \alpha$.

2. Y_ν was defined above. When $\nu = \nu_1$, the set Y_{ν_1} can equivalently be defined as:

(2)

$\qquad Y_\mu$ is the set of vectors $z = (v, x) \varepsilon R_+^{n+1}$, where

$$z = (v, x) = (\int_{R_+^n} \xi \phi(\xi) d\mu(\xi), \int_{R_+^n} \phi(\xi) d\mu(\xi)),$$

ϕ any Borel function on R_+^n with values in $[0,1]$. Next, define the domain of the macro production function by

(3) $\qquad D_\mu = \{v: \text{There exists a number } x \text{ such that } (v, x) \varepsilon Y_\mu\}.$

The production function corresponding to μ is defined by

(4) $\qquad F_\mu(v) = \sup \{x: (v, x) \varepsilon Y_\mu\}, \quad \text{for } v \varepsilon D_\mu.$

Furthermore, for each $q' \varepsilon R^n \times [0, \infty)$, define the (macro) profit function:

(5) $\qquad \pi_\mu(q') = \sup q'Y_\mu = \sup_{v \varepsilon D_\mu} (pF_\mu(v) - qv), \quad q' = (-q, p).$

Define, for $q' \varepsilon R^n \times [0, \infty)$, the set of profit-maximising vectors by

(6) $\qquad A(q') = \{z: q'z = \pi_\mu(q'), z \varepsilon Y_\mu\}.$

Define, finally, for $q' = (-q,p)$:

(7) $z(q')=(\int\limits_{G(q')} \xi d\mu, \int\limits_{G(q')} d\mu)$, $G(q')=\{\xi:p-q\xi \geq 0, \xi\epsilon R^{n}_{+}\}$.

Write $z(q') = (v(q'),x(q'))$. Then, $x(q') = F_{\mu}(v(q'))$ if $p > 0$. This follows from the fact that, for any $q' \epsilon R^{n} \times [0,\infty)$, $z(q')$ maximises profits, as we shall now show.

3.   Note that $z(q')$ belongs to $A(q')$: For any z of the type (2), we have for $q'= (-q,p)$,

$$q'z = \int\limits_{R^{n}_{+}} (p-q\xi)\phi(\xi)d\mu(\xi) \leq \int\limits_{G(q')} (p-q\xi)\phi(\xi)d\mu(\xi)$$

(8)

$$\leq \int\limits_{G(q')} (p-q\xi)d\mu(\xi) = q'z(q')$$

(the first inequality since $p-q\xi < 0$ in $\complement G(q')$, the second one since $\phi \leq 1$). This proves that $z(q')\epsilon A(q')$.

When z is given by (2), it is natural to write $z = z_{\phi}$. The first inequality in (8) is strict if, μ-essentially, $\phi(\cdot) > 0$ in $\complement G(q')$. Thus if $z_{\phi}\epsilon A(q')$, $\phi(\cdot) = 0$ μ-a.e. on $\complement G(q')$ and $z_{\phi} \leq z(q')$. If, μ-essentially, $\phi(\cdot) < 1$ on $G^{0}(q') = \{\xi\epsilon R^{n}_{+}:p-q\xi > 0\}$, then the second inequality in (8) is strict. Hence,

(9) $z_{\phi}\epsilon A(q') \Rightarrow \phi(\cdot) = 1$ μ-a.e. in $G^{0}(q')$.

And if $\mu(H(q')) = 0$, $H(q') = \{\xi\epsilon R^{n}_{+}:p-q\xi = 0\}$, then, evidently, $A(q')$ contains a single point.

4.   Define

(10) $\bar{v} = \int\limits_{R^{n}_{+}} \xi d\mu(\xi)$, $\bar{x} = \int\limits_{R^{n}_{+}} d\mu(\xi)$

Note that F_{μ} satisfies the following property:

(11) $v, v'' \epsilon D_\mu$, $v + v'' = \bar{v} \Rightarrow F(v) + F(v'') \geq F(\bar{v}) = \bar{x}$.

The property in (11) easily follows from the following observation: Let $(v, x) = z_\phi$ for some ϕ. Then $(v', x') = z_{1-\phi}$ evidently has the property that $z_\phi + z_{1-\phi} = \bar{z} = (\bar{v}, \bar{x})$, i.e. $v' = v''$ and $x + x' = \bar{x}$. Finally, $F(v) \geq x$ and $F(v'') \geq x'$.

5.   Let $q' = (-q, 1)$. Observe that (5) and $z(q') \epsilon A(q')$ imply that q is a supergradient to F_μ at $v(-q, 1)$. If F_μ is differentiable at $v = v(-q, 1)$, $dF_\mu/dv = q$ at this point by convexity theory.

Next, consider the equality $z(\hat{q}') = z(q')$. For this equality to hold, $\phi = \chi_{G(q')}$ has to equal 1 μ-a.e. on $G^0(\hat{q}')$ (see (9)), and $\chi_{G(\hat{q}')}$ has to equal 1 μ-a.e. on $G^0(q')$.

Thus

(12) $\mu[G^0(\hat{q}') \setminus G(q')] = 0$ and $\mu[G^0(q') \setminus G(\hat{q}')] = 0$.

6.   Define the free disposal hull Y_μ^h of Y_μ by $Y_\mu^h = Y_\mu + (R_+^n \times (-\infty, 0])$ and define the free disposal hull of F_μ by $F_\mu^h(v) = \sup\{x : (v, x) \epsilon Y_\mu^h\}$, $v \epsilon R_+^n$. Define the region of monotonicity $D_\mu'' = \{v \epsilon D_\mu : F_\mu(v) = F_\mu^h(v)\}$. Both F_μ and F_μ^h are concave, and thus exhibit nonincreasing returns to scale. Furthermore, $\mu\{0\} = 0 \Leftrightarrow F_\mu(0) = F_\mu^h(0) = 0$, (see Appendix, a).

7.   Next, note that Y_μ is a compact set, (use weak* compactness of the set of functions ϕ considered as elements of the dual of $L_1(R_+^n, \mu)$). Furthermore, if μ has no atoms, Y_μ can be generated by restricting the functions ϕ in (2) to be indicator functions of Borel sets (see Liapunov's Theorem, Rudin (1974), Theorem 5.5). The closedness of Y_μ immediately implies that F_μ and F_μ^h are upper semicontinuous. A theorem in convexity theory [Rockafellar (1970), Theorem 10.2] gives that F_μ^h is continuous, and thus also F_μ becomes continuous on the closed set D_μ''.

8.   Observe that F_μ has a unique maximum point $\bar{v} \epsilon D_\mu$. Let $q' = (0, 1)$,

then $G^0(q') = R^n_+$. Since Y_μ is closed, $(v,F(v)) \epsilon Y_\mu$ for any $v \epsilon D_\mu$. If
$F(v) = F(\bar{v})$, then $(v,F(v)) = z_\phi$ for some ϕ. By (9), $\phi = 1$ μ-a.e in R^n_+,
which gives $v = \bar{v}$.

By definition, $\pi(\hat{q}') \geq \hat{q}'z(q')$, $\pi(q') = q'z(q')$, which means that
$\pi(\hat{q}') - \pi(q') \geq (\hat{q}'-q')z(q')$, i.e. $z(q')$ is a subgradient at q' to the
convex function $\pi(\cdot)$. Any $z \epsilon A(q')$ has this property. On the other
hand, $\pi(\hat{q}') - \pi(q') \geq (\hat{q}' - q')z$ for all $\hat{q}'$ implies $z \epsilon A(q')$, (put
$\hat{q}' = 0$). For $q' = (0,1)$ the subgradient is unique, as seen above, i.e.
π is differentiable at $(0,1)$.

9. By convexity theory, F^h_μ has a supergradient at any point $v \gg 0$.
Since F^h_μ is nondecreasing, this supergradient must be ≥ 0. Any super-
gradient to F^h_μ at a point $v \epsilon R^n_+$ is also a supergradient to F_μ if $v \epsilon D''_\mu$,
hence F_μ has a nonnegative supergradient at each point v in $D''_\mu \cap R^n_{++}$,
$R^n_{++} = \{q \epsilon R^n: q \gg 0\}$. If there exists a vector $v' \gg 0$, such that the
support of μ is contained in the set $R_{v'} = \{v \epsilon R^n: v \geq v'\}$, then $D_\mu \setminus \{0\} \subset$
R^n_{++}. Moreover, in this case, F^h_μ even has supergradients at all points in
$R^n_+ \setminus R^n_{++}$ (see Appendix, b).

10. Hence, we can conclude that if $\mu(H(-q,1)) = 0$ for all $q \geq 0$ and
$\mu(R^n_+ \setminus R_{v'}) = 0$, there exists a supergradient $q \geq 0$ to F_μ at any $v \epsilon D''_\mu$,
(i.e. a support functional $q' = (-q,1)$ to Y_μ at $(v,F_\mu(v))$, and
$(v,F_\mu(v)) = z(q')$ where $z(q')$ is given by (7). Thus, the map
$q \rightarrow v(-q,1)$, $q \epsilon R^n_+$ defined by $q' \rightarrow z(-q,1)$, is onto D''_μ. It is one-to-one
on $Q = \{q \epsilon R^n_+: 0 < v(-q,1) < \bar{v}\}$ if one of the equalities in (12) fails to
hold for any pair $q' = (-q,1)$, $\hat{q}' = (-\hat{q},1)$, $q \neq \hat{q}$, $q, \hat{q} \epsilon Q$, and in this case
F_μ is differentiable at any point $v \epsilon D''_\mu \setminus \{0,v(0,1)\}$ and, F^h_μ is differentiable at any point $v' \epsilon \{v:0 < v < v(0,1)\}$. (If q is a supergradient at v' to
F^h_μ, then for some $v \leq v'$ and $v > 0$, $v \epsilon D''_\mu$, $0 < F^h_\mu(v') = F_\mu(v)$, thus q is a
supergradient to F_μ at v.) The last argument also implies that if also
$v' \epsilon D''_\mu$, then $v' < v$ is impossible, since both equal $v(-q,1)$. Thus $D''_\mu =$
$D^* = \{v:F(v')<F(v)$ for all v', $0 \leq v' < v\}$ if the properties in the first
sentence of this paragraph hold.

11.   Note that Y_μ^h is closed and that the epigraphs of F_μ and F_μ^h are closed. Furthermore, by convexity theory, the support function $\pi_\mu(q')$, which is defined (finite) for all $q' \varepsilon R^{n+1}$, is dual to the set Y_μ, while $\pi(-q,p)$ with domain $\{(q,p):q \geq 0,\ p \geq 0\}$ is dual to F_μ^h.

The remarks above summarize essentially well-known results that can be found in one form or another in one or more of the references: Houthakker (1955), Johansen (1972), Hildenbrand (1981), Bolker (1969), and, for convexity theory, Rockafellar (1970).

All the remarks above also hold if μ is bounded and has finite first-order moments, an assumption placed upon ν in Hildenbrand (1981)). The results can even be generalized to the case where μ is simply assumed to be bounded, provided Y_μ is taken to be the closure of the set of vectors z of the type (2) for all ϕ giving finite integrals. In this case, however, Y_μ may fail to be compact and $\pi_\mu(q')$ is not necessarily finite for all q'. (The points 7, 8, 10, and property (11) thus do not hold. In (10), note that $\bar{v}$ in this case perhaps has infinite components.   We can only be sure that $z(-q,p)$ is defined when $q \gg 0$.)

Note that the "transform" $x(q')$ of μ has very much in common with the so-called Radon transform (Helgason (1980)).

12.   Consider for a moment a function F^h defined on R_+^n that is bounded, nondecreasing, upper semi-continuous, concave, and nonnegative. Define $\pi^F(q') = \sup_{v \varepsilon R_+^n} pF(v)+qv,\ q'=(q,p),\ q \ll 0,\ p > 0$, and define $C^{F^h}(q) = \int_0^\infty e^{-p}\pi^{F^h}(q,p)dp$. Then we have the following result:

F^h stems from a unique bounded Borel measure μ with support in R_+^n, if and only if, $C^{F^h}(q)$ is absolutely monotonous. If the former (or latter) condition is satisfied, then $C^{F^h}(q)$ is the Laplace transform of μ.

By the theory of inverse Laplace transforms, μ can thus be reconstructed from F_μ^h (see Seierstad (1982b) or the more detailed Seierstad (1982a)).   In this connection, note that $F_\mu^h = F_{\mu'}^h \Rightarrow \mu=\mu'$ (these results hold in the general case of μ being a bounded Borel measure). An elementary proof of the very last result was given in Seierstad (1981), for μ's with bounded support. Compare also the classical result of Cramer and

Wold (1936).

Note, finally, that μ has a bounded support, if and only if, $F_\mu(v(-q,p))$ is a constant for $p \geq a$ for some number $a > 0$ and for some fixed $q \gg 0$, say $q=(1,\ldots,1)$. Use the formula $F_\mu(v(-q,p)) = x(-q,p) = \int_{G(-q,p)} d\mu$.

13. We shall now present some other results concerning the duality between μ and π_μ. The results are mere translations of certain results in the theory of zonoids (Bolker (1969)) that exploit results in probability theory for the representation of infinitely divisible characteristic functions of a special stable type.

The next theorem states that if a macro profit function is of a certain type, it can be considered to arise from an aggregation of the profits of a distribution of micro-units.

Theorem 1. Let π be a real function with domain of definition $D' = R^n \times [0,\infty)$. Then $\pi = \pi_\mu$ for some bounded Borel measure μ with support in R^n_+ and with finite first-order moments, if and only if:

i) π is linearly homogeneous, continuous, and nonnegative.

ii) $\pi(q,0) = 0$ for $q \leq 0$.

iii) $\pi(q,0) \leq \pi(q,p)$ for all $p \geq 0$, all q.

iv) $q \to \pi(q,1)$ is differentiable at $q = 0$.

Furthermore, defining $\pi^+(q,p) = \pi(q,p) - \frac{1}{2}(q\bar{v} + \pi(0,p))$, where $\bar{v} = [d\pi(q,1)/dq]_{q=0}$, we have

v) $\pi^+(q,0)$ is symmetric.

Finally, defining $\pi^+(q,p)$ for all $(q,p) \epsilon R^{n+1}$ by letting $\pi^+(q,p) = \pi^+(-q,-p)$ if $p < 0$, we have:

vi) The function $q' \to e^{-\pi^+(q')}$ on R^{n+1} is positive definite.

A real-valued function $d(q')$ is called positive definite if

$\sum\limits_{i,j=1}^{r} c_i \bar{c}_j d(q'_i - q'_j) \geq 0$ for every choice of $q'_1,\ldots,q'_r$ in R^{n+1} and for

every choice of complex numbers $c_1,\ldots,c_r$, r arbitrary (it is linearly

homogeneous if $d(\lambda q') = \lambda d(q')$ for all q', $\lambda > 0$).

Since π^+ is symmetric, it would be sufficient for positive definiteness

of π^+ to require the following property:

Let q_i, $i=1,\ldots,r$ be any vectors in R^n, let a_i be any real numbers and

let p_i be any nonincreasing sequence of numbers. Then

(13) $\sum\limits_{\substack{i,j \\ i<j}} 2a_i a_j d(q_i - q_j, p_i - p_j) + \sum\limits_{i} a_i^2 \geq 0$

where $d(q,p) = \exp(-\pi^+(q,p))$. The property (13) uses the definition of

π^+ only in $R^n \times [0,\infty)$.

Proof. We first prove that i) – vi) imply the existence of μ. The symme-

try and linear homogenity of π^+ together with property vi) imply the

following result from probability theory (see [Bolker (1969), Theorem

2.7] or Appendix c): There exists a bounded Borel measure α on $S_1 = $

$\{z \in R^{n+1}, \|z\| = 1\}$ such that $\pi^+ = \frac{1}{2} \int\limits_{S_1} |q'z| d\alpha(z)$. Let y' be the center of

the zonoid of moments Y_α. Then $Y'_\alpha = Y_\alpha - y'$ is a zonoid (the words "of

moments" deliberately omitted). Moreover, $\pi^+(q') = \max q'Y'_\alpha$, cf.

[Bolker 1969, (9)], and, defining $Y^+ = \{z : q'z \leq \pi^+(q')$ for all $q'\}$, we

have $Y'_\alpha = Y^+$ by duality.

The last expression for π^+ gives that π^+ is convex. Now, at $q=0$, $p=1$,

$\partial\pi^+/\partial q = \frac{1}{2}\bar{v}$ and $\partial\pi^+/\partial p = \frac{1}{2}\pi(0,1)$, since $\pi^+(0,p) = \frac{1}{2}p\pi(0,1)$. Thus, by

convexity, $\pi^+(q,p) - \pi^+(0,1) \geq \frac{1}{2}\bar{v}q + (p-1)\frac{1}{2}\pi(0,1)$. Since $\pi^+(0,1) = $

$\frac{1}{2}\pi(0,1)$, we get $\pi^+(q,p) \geq (q,p)y''$, for all (q,p), where $y'' = $

$\frac{1}{2}(\bar{v},\pi(0,1))$, hence $y'' \in Y^+$. By symmetry, $-y'' \in Y^+$.

Now $Y'_\alpha = Y^+$ is a zonoid and also $Y = Y^+ + y''$ is a zonoid since

$0 \in Y$. Furthermore, $\pi^+(q') = \max q'Y^+ \Rightarrow \pi(q') = \max q'Y$, and ii) of

Theorem 1 then implies that $Y \subset R^n_+$. As Y is a zonoid, it can always be

written as a zonoid of moments [Bolker (1969), Theorem 2.5] by means of

a bounded measure with support in S_1 (the measure is here denoted ν),

and from the construction of the measure in that theorem we even have that v has support in $S^+ = \{z \varepsilon S_1, z \geq 0\}$, i.e. $Y = Y_v$ (see (1)), and $\pi = \pi_v$ $= \max q'Y_v$. Now, any maximum point v' of $F_v(v) = \sup\{x:(v,x)\varepsilon Y\}$ provides a subgradient $(v', F_v(v'))$ to $\pi_v(q')$ at $q' = (0,1)$, (cf. Sec. 8 above). Since $q \rightarrow \pi_v(q,1)$ is differentiable at $q = 0$, it has a unique subgradient. However, if $v(C) \neq 0$ where $C = \{z \varepsilon R_+^n: z_{n+1} = 0\}$, then (1) furnishes two different maximum points for $\phi = \chi_{R_+^n}$ and $\phi = \chi_{R_+^n \setminus C}$.

Hence, $v(C) = 0$, the support of v is contained in R^+, and there exists by Sec. 1, a bounded Borel measure μ with finite first-order moments such that $Y_v = Y_\mu$, i.e. $\pi_\mu = \pi_v = \pi$.

The proof of the fact that π_μ satisfies i) - vi) is essentially rather trivial: i) - iii) are obvious, iv) follows from Sec. 8, and from that section we also know that $\partial\pi(0,1)/\partial q = \bar{v}$, the maximum point of F_μ. The point $\frac{1}{2}(\bar{v}, F_\mu(\bar{v})) = y''$ is a point of symmetry of Y_μ ($2y'' = z_\phi$ for $\phi \equiv 1$, while, generally $z_\phi + z_{1-\phi} = 2y''$ or $z_\phi - y'' + z_{1-\phi} - y'' = 0$). Since $\pi_\mu^+(q') = \max q'(Y_\mu - y'')$ and $Y_\mu - y''$ has the origin as a point of symmetry, then π_μ^+ is symmetric and $\pi_\mu^+(q,p) = \pi_\mu^+(-q,-p)$, which is consistent with the extension of π^+ in the Theorem. In particular, v) holds. Finally, $\pi_\mu^+ = \frac{1}{2}\int|q'z|d\mu(z)$ (see [Bolker (1969), (7)]). Probability theory (see e.g. [Feller (1966) Ch.XVII] or [Levy (1937) Ch. VII]) gives that $-\pi_\mu^+$ is the logarithm of a (special stable) characteristic function, which implies that $e^{-\pi_\mu^+}$ is positive definite.

14. Actually, we have not yet justified the conditions placed upon π in the preceding theorem. Though most of them perhaps are evident to the reader, let us formally justify the conditions by relating them to properties of macro production functions by means of a duality theorem. Unfortunately, we have no convenient geometric property of the production function that reflects the positive definiteness assumption on $e^{-\pi^+}$. In the course of the proof, we mentioned that convexity of the extended π^+ was a consequence of this property. Thus, we have explored that property of the production function which corresponds to this convexity of π^+.

Before we state the next theorem, let us list the properties of the macro profit function π and of the macro production function F that enters the theorem (D is the domain of F, and D' the domain of π):

a) D is convex and compact and F is upper semi-continuous, concave
   and bounded from above.
b) D is a subset of R_+^n and contains the origin. F is nonnegative.
c) F has a unique maximum at a point $\bar{v} \in D$.
d) $\frac{1}{2}\bar{v}$ is a center of symmetry of D.
e) $F(v) + F(v') \geq F(\bar{v})$ for all v, $v' \in D$ such that $v + v' = \bar{v}$.

a') $D' = R^n \times [0,\infty)$, π is linearly homogeneous, convex, and continuous.
b') $\pi \geq 0$, $\pi(q,0) = 0$ for $q \leq 0$, $\pi(q,p) \geq \pi(q,0)$ for all $p \geq 0$.
c') $q \to \pi(q,1)$ is differentiable at $q = 0$.
d') $\pi^+(q,0)$ is symmetric (where, generally, $\pi^+(q,p) = \pi(q,p)$
   $-\frac{1}{2}(q,p)(\bar{v},\bar{x})$, $\bar{v} = \partial\pi(0,1)/\partial q$ and $\bar{x} = \pi(0,1)$).
e') Defining $\pi^+(q,p) = \pi^+(-q,-p)$ if $p < 0$, the function $\pi^+(q,p)$ becomes
   a convex function on all R^{n+1}.

A necessary condition for a compact, convex set Y to be a zonoid is
that it has a center of symmetry. It turns out that properties a) – e)
imply the existence of a technology set Y that has a largest point $\bar{z} =$
$(\bar{v},\bar{x})$ and has $\frac{1}{2}\bar{z}$ as a center of symmetry.

Another observation is also useful. For a function π^+ defined
on $R^n \times [0,\infty)$, linear homogenity, convexity, symmetry of $q \to \pi^+(q,0)$ and
property e') is equivalent to the following property:
$|\alpha|\pi^+(q,p)+|\beta|\pi^+(q',p') \geq \pi^+(\alpha q+\beta q', \alpha p+\beta p')$ for all q, $q' \in R^n$, all $p \geq 0$,
$p' \geq 0$ and all real numbers α, β for which $\alpha p + \beta p' \geq 0$.

There is a one-to-one correspondence between a function F defined
on a set D and its epigraph $Y = \{(v,\gamma): v \in D, \gamma \leq F(v)\}$, $(F(v) =$
$\sup\{\gamma:(v,\gamma)\in Y\})$. For any set Y, define $\pi_Y(q,p) = \sup\{qv+px:(v,x)\in Y\}$,
the domain of π_Y being those pairs $(q,p)\in R^{n+1}$ for which this supremum
is finite. For any function π with domain D', define $Y_\pi = \{(v,x):qv+px$
$\leq \pi(q,p)$ for all $(q,p)\in D'\}$. When Y is the epigraph of F we write
$\pi_F = \pi_Y$, and we write the function F having Y_π as epigraph as F_π. A
pair of functions (F,π) is called a dual pair if either $F = F_\pi$ or $\pi = \pi_F$.

Then we have the following theorem:

Theorem 2. Let (F,π) be a dual pair. Then a) $\Leftrightarrow$ a') and under either of
these equivalent assumptions $F = F_{\pi_F}$ and $\pi_{F_\pi} = \pi$. Furthermore, a),b) $\Leftrightarrow$

a'),b'); a),b),c) $\Leftrightarrow$ a'),b'),c'); a),b),c),d) $\Leftrightarrow$ a'),b'),c'),d'); and
a),b),c),d)e) $\Leftrightarrow$ a'),b'),c'),d'),e').

Sketch of proof

When F is given, a) holds and π is defined by $\pi = \pi_F$, the relation F
$= F_{\pi_F}$ follows from the relation $Y = Y_{\pi_Y}$, Y being the epigraph of F (see
[Rockafellar (1970), Theorem 13.1]). Furthermore, by compactness of D
and boundedness of F, it is evident that sup $\{qv+px:(v,x)\varepsilon Y\}$ is finite
iff $p \geq 0$, i.e. $D' = R^n \times [0,\infty)$. These properties also imply that π becomes
continuous on D'. Hence, a) $\Rightarrow$ a').

When π is given, a') holds and F is defined by $F = F_\pi$, the relation π
$= \pi_{F_\pi}$ follows from the relation $\pi = \pi_{Y_\pi}$ (see [Rockafellar (1970), Theorem
13.2.]). Furthermore, a' $\Rightarrow$ a):

Note that $(v,x)\varepsilon Y_\pi \Rightarrow (v,x)\cdot(0,1) \leq \pi(0,1)$, which entails that F is
bounded. Defining $D'' = \{v:qv \leq \pi(q,0)$ for all $q\varepsilon R^n\}$, we have
$D'' \supseteq D_\pi = \{v:(v,\gamma)\varepsilon Y_\pi$ for some $\gamma\varepsilon R\}$. The continuity of π implies that
$\pi(q,0) \leq K$ for some constant K when $\|q\| \leq 1$. And $v\varepsilon D'' \Rightarrow v\tilde{v} \leq$
$\pi(\tilde{v},0) \leq K$, $\tilde{v} = v/\|v\|$, hence D'' and D_π are bounded.

The implication b) $\Rightarrow$ b') is trivial. To show b' $\Rightarrow$ b), π given, note that
$\pi \geq 0 \Rightarrow 0\varepsilon D_\pi$. By a separation argument, $\pi(q,0) = 0$ for $q \leq 0 \Rightarrow D'' \subset R^n_+$.
Next, the property $\pi(q,p) \geq \pi(q,0)$ for all $p \geq 0$ entails $(v,0)\varepsilon Y_\pi$ for
all $v\varepsilon D''$. Thus $D_\pi \times \{0\} \subset D'' \times \{0\} \subset Y_\pi$, hence F_π is nonnegative.

Next, assume that a'),b'),c') hold (π given, $F = F_\pi$). We then have
that $\bar{v}q + \pi(0,1) \leq \pi(q,1)$ for all q ($\bar{v}$ is a subgradient of $\pi(\cdot,1)$ at q =0).
By homogenity, $(\hat{q},p)(\bar{v},\bar{x}) \leq \pi(\hat{q},p)$ for all $\hat{q}$, all $p > 0$. By continuity,
this inequality even holds for $\hat{p} = 0$. Thus $(\bar{v},\bar{x})\varepsilon Y_\pi$. On the other
hand, any point $(v,\gamma)\varepsilon Y_\pi$ has the property that $\gamma = (v,\gamma)(0,1)$
$\leq \pi(0,1) = \bar{x}$. Thus $F_\pi(\bar{v}) = \bar{x}$. A unique subgradient of π_F at q=0 is, as
well known, equivalent to a unique profit maximum for F at q=0. This
maximum is the same as a maximum of F since q = 0. Finally, using the
fact that $\pi = \pi_F$, c) follows (any maximum point $\bar{\bar{v}}$ of F satisfies $F(\bar{\bar{v}}) =$
$\pi_F(0,1)$ by definition of π_F and $\bar{\bar{v}}q + \bar{x} \leq \pi_F(q,1)$, $\bar{x} = \pi_F(0,1)$. The last
inequality is equivalent to the fact that $\bar{\bar{v}}$ is a subgradient to the convex
function $\pi_F(\cdot,1)$ at q = 0).

When a), b), c) hold with F given, $\pi = \pi_F$, the arguments in the last paragraph implies that $\pi(q,1)$ has a unique subgradient at $q = 0$, i.e. is differentiable at $q = 0$. (If $\overline{\overline{v}}$ is any subgradient to $\pi(\cdot,1)$ at $q = 0$, then an argument above gave that $(\overline{\overline{v}},\overline{x}) \varepsilon Y$, Y is the epigraph of F, and $\overline{x} = \pi_F(0,1)$. Now, $\overline{x} = \pi_F(0,1) \Rightarrow \overline{x} = \max F = F(\overline{v})$ and $(\overline{\overline{v}},\overline{x}) \varepsilon Y \Rightarrow F(\overline{\overline{v}}) \geq \overline{x}$, i.e. $F(\overline{\overline{v}}) = \overline{x}$.)

When d) holds, the symmetry of d') is trivial. On the other hand, to show that d) is implied by a') - d'), it suffices to show that the origin is a point of symmetry of $D-\{\tfrac{1}{2}\overline{v}\}$. Arguments showing the latter property are contained in the proof of the ofllowing Lemma. (Note that $0 \varepsilon Y_\pi$, $\overline{z} = (\overline{v},\overline{x}) \varepsilon Y_\pi$ [see above], so $\tfrac{1}{2}\overline{z} \varepsilon Y_\pi$ and $0 \varepsilon Y_\pi^+$.)

Lemma Assume that a') - e') hold for a given π. Then $\pi^+(q') = \pi^+(-q')$ for all q' implies that the origin is a center of symmetry of $Y^+ = \{z: q'z \leq \pi^+(q')$ for all $q' \varepsilon R^{n+1}\}$.

To prove this lemma, it suffices to test if $-y \varepsilon Y^+$ when y belongs to the boundary of Y^+. If the latter property is the case, then for some q', $q'y \geq \sup q'Y^+ = \pi^+(q')$. If $-y \notin Y^+$, then for some q'', $q''(-y) > \sup q''Y^+ = \pi^+(q'') = \pi^+(-q'')$ (the strict inequality since Y^+ is closed. Then $\tfrac{1}{2}(q'-q'')y = \tfrac{1}{2}q'y + \tfrac{1}{2}q''(-y) > \tfrac{1}{2}\pi^+(q') + \tfrac{1}{2}\pi^+(-q'')) \geq \pi^+(\tfrac{1}{2}(q'-q''))$. Thus $y \varepsilon Y^+$, and a contradiction is obtained.

Finally, we turn to the equivalence a) - e) $\Leftrightarrow$ a') - e'). We first prove the implication $\Rightarrow$ in the case F is given. Let Y be the epigraph of F. Define $F^+(v-\tfrac{1}{2}\overline{v}) = F(v) - \tfrac{1}{2}\overline{x}$, $\overline{x} = F(\overline{v})$, $D^+ = D - \tfrac{1}{2}\overline{v}$. Let v, $v' \varepsilon D$, $v + v' = \overline{v}$ and define $v^+ = v - \tfrac{1}{2}\overline{v}$, $v'^+ = v'- \tfrac{1}{2}\overline{v}$. Note the equivalences $F(v) + F(v') \geq F(\overline{v}) \Leftrightarrow F^+(v^+) + F^+(v'^+) \geq 0 \Leftrightarrow (v^+, F^+(v^+))=(-v'^+, -\gamma)$ for some $\gamma \leq F^+(v'^+) \Leftrightarrow (v^+, F^+(v^+)) \varepsilon Y^+ \cap(-Y^+)$, where Y^+ is the epigraph of F^+. Define $Z = Y^+ \cap (-Y^+)$, $\phi(q') = \sup q'Z$, $q' \varepsilon R^{n+1}$. Evidently, $Z \subset Y^+ \Rightarrow \phi(q') \leq \sup q'Y^+ = \pi^+(q')$, when $q' = (q,p)$, $p \geq 0$. On the other hand, for such q', $\pi^+(q') = \sup \{qv^+ + pF^+(v^+): v^+ \varepsilon D^+\} \leq \phi(q')$, since $(v^+, F^+(v^+)) \varepsilon Z$ for any $v^+ \varepsilon D^+$. Hence $\phi(q,p) = \pi^+(q,p)$ for $p \geq 0$. If π^+ is extended as described in e'), then π^+ becomes symmetric ($q \to \pi^+(q,0)$ is symmetric due to d)). Since ϕ is symmetric due to the symmetry of Z, $\phi(q,p) = \pi^+(q,p)$ for all (q,p). Since ϕ is convex, so is π^+.

Next, consider the implication $\Leftarrow$. To show e), it evidently suffices to show that $(v^+, F^+(v^+)) \varepsilon Z$, where now $F = F_\pi$, $F^+(v^+) = F_\pi(v) - \tfrac{1}{2}\overline{x}$, $v^+ = v - \tfrac{1}{2}\overline{v}$ with $\overline{v}$, $\overline{x}$ given in d'), and $Z = Y^+ \cap(-Y^+)$ with Y^+ the epigraph of F^+ i.e. $Y^+ = \{(v,x): qv + px \leq \pi^+(q,p)$ for all (q,p), $p \geq 0\}$. Note that $Z = \{z: q'z \leq \pi^+(q') \text{ for all } q'\}$. We shall first show that

(14) $(v^+, F^+(v^+)) \in \{z: q'z \leq \pi^+(q') \text{ for all } q'\}$

for v^+ in the relative interior $D*$ of D^+. By duality,

$$\pi^+(q,p) = \sup_{v^+ \in D^+} \{qv^+ + pF^+(v^+)\}, \ (q,p) \in R^n \times [0,\infty).$$

   If (14) fails for some $v^+ \in D*$, it must be the case that $(-q,-p)(v^+, F(v^+)) > \pi(-q,-p)$ for some $p > 0$, $q \in R^n$.

   Let $D'' = \text{lin span } D^+$. Since $(v^+, F^+(v^+))$ is a boundary point in $Y^+ \subset D'' \times R$, there exists a linear functional q'' on D'' and a $p' \geq 0$ such that $q''(v^+) + p'F^+(v^+) \geq q''(\tilde{v}^+) + p'F^+(\tilde{v}^+)$ for all $\tilde{v}^+ \in D^+$. Since $v^+ \in D*$, $p' > 0$. Representing q'' by a vector q' in R^n, by (15) we get $q'v^+ + p'F^+(v^+) = \pi^+(q',p')$. We can assume that $p' \geq p$. Then $\frac{1}{2}(q'-q)v^+ + \frac{1}{2}(p'-p)F^+(v^+) = \frac{1}{2}(q',p')(v^+, F^+(v^+)) + \frac{1}{2}(-q,-p)(v^+, F^+(v^+)) > \frac{1}{2}\pi^+(q',p') + \frac{1}{2}\pi^+(-q,-p) \geq \pi^+(\frac{1}{2}q' - \frac{1}{2}q, \frac{1}{2}p' - \frac{1}{2}p)$ by e'), a contradiction of (15) since $\frac{1}{2}p' - \frac{1}{2}p \geq 0$. Thus, (14) holds for all v^+ in $D*$.

   Next, note that if (v^+, γ) belongs to the relative interior Y^i of Y^+, then $v^+ \in D*$. For any point $(v^+, F^+(v^+))$ there exists a sequence $(v_n^+, \gamma_n) \to (v^+, F(v^+))$, $(v_n^+, \gamma_n) \in Y^i$. Then also $(v_n^+, F^+(v_n^+)) \to (v^+, F^+(v^+))$, (otherwise Y^+ was not closed). Thus, (14) holds for all $v^+ \in D^+$.

Appendix

__a.__   Proof of the fact that $F_\mu(0) = 0 \Rightarrow \mu\{0\} = 0$: Assume $F_\mu(0) = 0$. Define $q_n = n(1,\ldots,1)$. Since F_μ is bounded, $v(-q_{n,1}) \to 0$ when $n \to \infty$ (otherwise $\pi(-q_n,1)$ becomes negative). Thus also $F_\mu^h(v(-q_n,1)) \to F_\mu(0) = 0$. Now $0 \in G(-q_n,1))$ and $F_\mu^h(v(-q_n,1)) \geq x(-q_n,1) \geq \mu\{0\}$.

__b.__   Let $0 < \delta < v'_i$ for all components i. Note that the integrals in (2) do not change when R_+^n is replaced by $R_{v'}$. For any i, z in (2) has the property that $v_i \geq \int_{R_{v'}} \delta\phi d\mu$, i.e. $x \leq \bar{\delta}^Y v_i$. Thus $v_i \to F_\mu^h(v_1,\ldots,v_n)$ has a right derivative $\leq 1/\delta$ at $v_i = 0$. Being nondecreasing and concave, $v_i \to F_\mu^h$ has $1/\delta$ as Lipschitz constant for all $v_i \geq 0$.

Finally, F_μ^h is then simultaneously Lipschitzian continuous in $v \geq 0$ with constant $K = n/\delta$ in the norm $\max |v_i|$. A standard separation argument now gives that F_μ^h has a supergradient at each point $\tilde{v} \geq 0$. (Define $B = (\tilde{v}, F_\mu^h(\tilde{v})) + C$, $C = \{(v,x): x > 2K \|v\|\}$. The set B is disjoint from the epigraph E of F_μ^h. A linear functional $\underline{a}$ separates these two sets, i.e. $\sup a E \leq \inf a B$. By necessity, $a_{n+1} > 0$: Since C is open, $0 < ac$ for all $c \epsilon C$, in particular for $c = (0,1)$).

Finally, note that any point $(v, F_\mu(v))$, $v \epsilon D''_\mu$ is also a point on the graph of $(v, F_\mu^h(v))$.

<u>c.</u>   This result can be found e.g. in [Levy (1937) Ch. VII]. Since, however, most standard texts only discuss the one-dimensional case, a few remarks may be pertinent:

Since, for all $n = 1,2 \ldots, e^{-\pi^+(q/n)}$ is positive definite, then $e^{-\pi^+}$ is an infinitely-divisible characteristic function.

A characteristic function $\omega(\zeta)$, $\zeta \epsilon R^n$ is infinitely divisible if and only if ω is of the form $\omega = e^\rho$, $\rho(\zeta) = \psi(\zeta) + ib\zeta$, b some fixed n-vector and

$$(*) \qquad \psi(\zeta) = \iint_S \frac{e^{i\zeta\theta r} - 1 - i\zeta\theta\sin r}{r^2} d\widehat{M}(\theta,r), \quad S = S_1 \times [0,\infty)$$

for some Borel measure $\widehat{M}$. Here $S_1 = \{y \epsilon R^n : \|y\| = 1\}$. When $r \to 0$, the integrand has a limit. $\widehat{M}$ is bounded on bounded sets and has the property that $1/r^2$ is integrable with respect to it for $r > \delta > 0$. The proof of this formula is essentially the same in one and several dimensions, (see [Feller (1966), XVII 2, Theorem 1, and XVII.11]). $\widehat{M}$ is uniquely determined by $\psi(\zeta)$ in the formula $(*)$; the proof is the same in one and several dimensions (see [Feller 1966, XVII. 2, Lemma 4]). If $\rho(-\zeta) = \rho(\zeta)$, a property we shall assume from now on, then from $(*)$ we get $\rho(\zeta) = \frac{1}{2}(\rho(-\zeta) + \rho(\zeta)) = \iint_S \frac{\cos(\zeta\theta r) - 1}{r^2} d\widehat{M}$, and this relation also determines $\widehat{M}$ uniquely (by a similar proof).

From the property $\rho(\zeta) = \frac{1}{\lambda}\rho(\lambda\zeta)$, $\lambda > 0$, which we also assume, we obtain

84   A. Seierstad

$$\int\int_S \frac{\cos(\zeta\theta r) - 1}{r^2} d\widetilde{M}(\theta,r) = \lambda^{-1} \int\int_S \frac{\cos(\lambda\zeta\theta r) - 1}{r^2} d\widetilde{M}(\theta,r)$$

$$= \int\int_S \frac{\cos(\zeta\theta y) - 1}{y^2} \lambda d\widetilde{M}(\theta,\frac{y}{\lambda})$$

(the last equality by the change of variable $\lambda r = y$). By uniqueness,
$\lambda\widetilde{M}(\theta, \frac{y}{\lambda}) = \widetilde{M}(\theta,y)$, which means that $r\widetilde{M}(C_1) = \widetilde{M}(C_r)$ for any set $C_r = \{(\theta,r'): \|\theta-\bar\theta\| \le \delta, 0 < r' \le r\}$, $\bar\theta$, $\delta > 0$, arbitrarily given. Then
$\widetilde{M}(C_{r'} \setminus C_r) = (r'-r)\widetilde{M}(C_1)$ if $r' > r$. Defining $W(D) = \widetilde{M}(C_1)$, $D = \{\theta: \|\theta-\bar\theta\| \le \delta\}$, we see that $\widetilde{M}(C_{r'} \setminus C_r) = W(D) \cdot (r' - r)$, i.e. $\widetilde{M}$ is the product of
the measure W (W extended to Borel sets) and the Lebesque measure.
Hence, $\rho(\zeta) = \int_{S_1} (\int_0^\infty \frac{\cos(\zeta\theta r) - 1}{r^2} dr) dW(\theta)$. By complex integration, the
inner integral equals $-\pi|\zeta\theta|/2$, so $\rho(\zeta) = \int_{S_1} -\frac{1}{2}\pi|\zeta\theta|dW(\theta)$.

References

Bolker, E. (1969), "A class of convex bodies". Trans. Amer. Math.
     Society 149, Nov., 323-345.

Cramer, H. and Wold, H. (1936), "Some theorems on distribution func-
     tions", J. of London Math. Society 11, 290-294.

Feller, W. (1966), An introduction to Probability Theory and its Applica-
     tions, John Wiley & Sons, New York.

Helgason, S. (1980), The Radon transform, Birkhäuser, Boston.

Hildenbrand, W. (1981), "Short Run Production Functions Based on
     Microdata", Econometrica 49. No. 5, 1095-1125.

Houthakker, H.S. (1955),"The Pareto distribution and the Cobb-Douglas
     function in activity analysis", Review of Economic Studies 23, 27-31.

Johansen, L. (1972), Production Functions, North-Holland Publ.
     Company, Amsterdam.

Levy, P. (1937), <u>Theorie de l'additions des variables aléatoires</u>,
    Gauthiers-Villars, Paris.

Rockafellar, R.T. (1970), <u>Convex Analysis</u>, Princeton University Press,
    Princeton, New Jersey.

Rudin, W. (1974), <u>Functional analysis</u>, Mc. Graw-Hill, New York.

Seierstad, A. (1981), "The macro production function uniquely determines
    the capacity distribution of the micro units", <u>Economics Letters</u> 7,
    211-214.

Seierstad, A. (1982a), "Capacity distributions derived from macro
    production functions", <u>Memorandum</u> from Institute of Economics,
    University of Oslo.

Seierstad, A. (1982b), "Capacity distributions derived from macro
    production functions", <u>Economics Letters</u> 10, 23-27.

Production, Multi-Sectoral Growth and Planning
F.R. Førsund, M. Hoel, and S. Longva (Editors)
© Elsevier Science Publishers B.V. (North-Holland), 1985

FLUCTUATIONS AND FACTOR PROPORTIONS:
PUTTY-CLAY INVESTMENTS UNDER UNCERTAINTY

Karl Ove Moene

University of Oslo

1. Introduction

Central to the approach Leif Johansen developed within production
and investment theory[1] is i) an emphasis on the embodiment of production techniques in durable capital equipment, ii) a distinction between
substitution possibilities ex ante and ex post, and iii) a focus on indivi-
sible and irreversible projects. Hence, in Johansen's view investment
decisions are fundamental for determining the structure of the supply side
of the economy. The "putty-clay" nature of capital equipment (i.e. malleable ex ante and hard ex post) implies that investment decisions have
lasting consequences many periods into the future. Once the production
technique has been chosen, only that technique is available until new
equipment can replace the old.

When decision makers make investment decisions, they need some
information about future prices and demands. This information can be
very difficult to obtain in a decentralized market economy. In his article
"Some problems of pricing and optimal choice of factor proportions in a
dynamic setting" Leif Johansen discussed these and related issues. He
concluded that his analysis "raises serious questions as to the ability of
an unguided competitive system to reach optimal decisions about factor
proportions" (Johansen (1967) p. 151). The present paper pursues this
line of thought, emphasizing the impact of fluctuations and uncertainties
on the profit-maximizing choice of factor proportions. For this purpose we
shall consider an environment where prices and demands fluctuate about a
trend. It is likely that plants in such an environment will have idle capacity in some future periods due to short-run unprofitableness or sales

---

I wish to thank Finn R. Førsund and Sverre Munck for helpful
comments.

constraints. When calculating optimal investment decisions these possibilities must be taken into account. However, future cycles in prices and sales are impossible to foresee with certainty. From experience firms usually know that the future will not evolve as smoothly as projected trends indicate. Moreover, the past cycles have not been sufficiently regular to enable one to predict with confidence when future recessions will occur and of what type they will be. Therefore it is reasonable to assume that investors explicitly incorporate uncertain expectations into their investment calculations.

We shall compare in this paper the case of an economy subject to uncertainty and fluctuations, and visualized as the outcome of an unguided market development with a hypothetical bench-mark certainty case. In this bench-mark case prices and demands will be assumed to evolve smoothly, a development which could for instance be the result of successful macroeconomic planning.

Our main intention is to draw some economic implications from the comparison between the two cases outlined above. For example, we ask the question "does the anticipation of fluctuations induce employers to choose plant designs that when operated optimally have utilization rates that are more sensitive or adaptable to fluctuations?" A further intention is to touch upon some aspects of vertical integration that concern the division of production between main producers and subcontractors, modelling the division as part of the investment decision. A third aim is to discuss the impact of different types of economic stabilization policies and to identify possible long-run productivity gains. The need for coordination of investment decisions is also briefly discussed. Finally, we focus attention on possible differences between the private and social optimum with respect to the choice of factor proportions in a system with public unemployment compensation.

In Section 2 we outline the technological assumptions and characterize the optimal strategy for utilization of the plant. In Section 3 the optimality conditions for plant design is derived under both uncertainty and certainty. In Section 4 the comparison between the bench mark and the uncertainty case is presented, and in Section 5 the economic interpretations mentioned above are finally discussed.

2. Plant design and capacity utilization

A typical problem of plant design facing the entrepreneur is the choice of the optimal combination of factors of production, in particular the optimal combination of factors that <u>can</u> be varied during the utilization of the plant with factors that <u>cannot</u> be varied ex post. The fixed factors (e.g. buildings, machinery, equipment) are determined only during the investment decision. The flexible factors can be varied ex post, but the relationship between these inputs and the amount of output is determined by the choice of technique that is embodied in the fixed factors.

One aspect of this problem is to what degree the entrepreneur should mechanize. Ex ante he has a choice between labor-intensive and capital-intensive techniques. Once the machinery is in place, however, its costs are sunk, while labor costs vary with utilization rates as long as workers are hired on spot market terms. The productivity of the workers is then completely determined by the manning requirements of the equipment.

Another aspect of this problem, also related to the mixture of variable and fixed costs, can be found in the context of vertical integration: A part of the investment problem is to decide which tasks should be assigned to subcontractors and which should be performed at the plant. Subcontracted inputs are variable ex post while self-reliance entails fixed-cost commitments.

A simple formulation which incorporates the technological aspects sketched out above is the following: Let a plant be defined by X, K and L. X is the capacity of the plant, K is a production factor whose quantity is fixed ex post, and L indicates the quantity of the ex post variable factor needed if the capacity of the plant is to be fully utilized. We can, for simplicity, think of K as capital equipment and L as the labor requirements at full capacity. The set of possibilities from which the investor makes his choice can be represented by the "choice-of-technique-function"

(1) $X = F(K,L)$,

which summarizes the relevant technological knowledge available to the investor.

Ex post the plant design is assumed to be "frozen" in the following sense. The production capacity is fixed and there is no substitution possibility between L and K. It is assumed that the factor proportion

(2) $a = L/X$

is fixed so that the ex post production function of the plant is

(3) $X(t) = \min \left[\frac{1}{a} N(t), X \right].$

In this expression $X(t)$ represents production and $N(t)$ the use of labor in period t.

Equivalently, the ex post technology can be expressed as

$$(4) \quad \begin{cases} X(t) = h(t)X \\ \\ N(t) = h(t)L \end{cases}$$

where h indicates the degree of capacity utilization,

$0 \le h \le 1;$

$h(t)$ is then a decision parameter of management in period t.

The ex post production function in (3) (and (4)), with fixed coefficients and a given capacity, is a realistic representation for many manufactoring process industries and some of the transport sectors. It is also analytically tractable. Nevertheless, no general empirical validity for this formulation can be claimed.[2] However, compared to the neo-classical approximation which has full substitution possibilities at every moment of time, the putty-clay approach constitutes a more empirically realistic alternative.

During the short-run operating of the plant, we assume the firm to behave as if it was a price taker facing possible sales constraints. The existence of sales constraints could simply mean that trade takes place outside of Walrasian equilibrium. For example, the output market may be characterized by oligopolistic traits such as price leadership or other types of implicit price contracts among firms.

In the following we will also employ the Hicksian terms "fixprice" and "flexprice" markets. Firms in fixprice markets simply assume, for whatever reason, that prices will be slow to adjust to demand variations and that quantity adjustments clear the markets in the short run. Firms in flex-price markets assume that prices adjust instantaneously in order to balance supplies and demands on the markets so that there are no prevailing sales constraints perceived in the short run.

When capacity utilization decisions are made in the respective future periods, we assume that possible sales Y, the output price p, and the wage rate w for that period will be known to the firm. Assuming inventories are neglected, the optimal utilization rule is as follows: produce as much as can be sold within capacity constraints as long as the quasi-rent per unit,

(5) $s = p - aw$

is positive; let the plant stand idle when s is negative. Formally, this optimal strategy can be expressed by

(6) $h = \begin{cases} \frac{1}{X} \min\left[Y, X \right] & \text{when } s \geq 0 \\ 0 & \text{when } s < 0. \end{cases}$

When the degree of plant utilization is being decided (i.e. when, according to (4), the decision with respect to the production level at the plant in the relevant period is made) both X and $a = L/X$ (in (5) and (6)) have already been determined by the investment decision. The value of aw indicates the short-run break-even price of the plant in the sense that p=aw implies zero quasi-rent.

3. Optimal plant designs

Let us start with the uncertainty case. It is assumed that the investor is risk neutral. The optimal plant design is then represented by the values of L and K which maximize expected present value of the project subject to the choice of technique function in (1) and the optimal strategy of capacity utilization in (6).[3]

For the problems focused upon in this paper, nothing of interest is lost if we assume a stationary market trend, i.e. by assuming no long-run

growth of markets. The expected present value of the project is then
defined by

$$(7) \qquad E\Pi = E\left[\sum_{t=1}^{T} hs\,X(1+r)^{-t} \right] - qK = \beta(T)\,E(hs)\,X - qK$$

where the shorthand $\beta(T) = \sum_{t=1}^{T} (1+r)^{-t}$ is used. Defining s by (5), r is
the discount rate, T is the technical lifetime of the equipment, and q is
the price per unit of K. Taking (6) into account, expectations in (7) are
with respect to Y, p, and w. Note that the economic lifetime of the project
is determined endogenously from (6).

Let us define:

R as the event that $s \geq 0$ and $Y \geq X$; and
Q as the event that $s \geq 0$ and $Y < X$.

Here both R and Q denote periods in which the plant is profitable to
operate. Q indicates that production is demand constrained, while R indicates that production is capacity constrained.

The optimality conditions[4] can then be written as

$$(8) \qquad BF_K = q$$

$$(9) \qquad BF_L = C$$

where

$$(10) \qquad B = \left[Pr(R)\,E(p\,|\,R) + Pr(Q)\,a\,E(hw\,|\,Q) \right]\beta(T)$$

$$(11) \qquad C = \left[Pr(R)\,E(w\,|\,R) + Pr(Q)\,E(hw\,|\,Q) \right]\beta(T).$$

B is the expected present value of the revenues associated with a marginal
increase in capacity. C is the expected present value of the ex post costs
associated with a unit increase in L. Hence, (8) and (9) simply imply that
the optimal plant design is determined such that the expected present
value of marginal gains should equal expected present value of marginal
costs for increasing K and L, respectively.

Let us go into a little more detail. Consider first C, the expected ex post costs per unit of L, and recall from (6) that workers will be hired only when quasi-rents are positive. If no sales constraints prevail, the probability of this event being $Pr(R)$, capacity will be fully utilized. Hence, a marginal increase in L is expected to cost $E(w|R)$. If sales constraints do prevail, the probability of this event being $Pr(Q)$, there will be cutbacks in employment. Hence, only a fraction h of the full-capacity total of workers are paid, and the expected wage-bill per unit of L becomes $E(hw|Q)$. From this we see that the expression within brackets in (11) is expected ex post costs of a unit increase in L. Observe that by applying the optimal utilization rule in (6), the expected wage payments per unit of L are

$$E(hw) = Pr(R)\ E(w|R) + Pr(Q)\ E(hw|Q)$$

such that (11) becomes

(11)' $C = E(hw)\beta(T).$

Next, consider B, the expected revenues of a marginal capacity expansion, and recall that the firm wants to produce only when quasi-rents are positive. Hence, when $s < 0$ no (gross) revenue is obtained from a higher capacity. If $s \geq 0$ and no sales constraints prevail, the marginal revenue from a higher capacity is p with the expected value $E(p|R)$. When sales constraints do prevail, the situation becomes a little more complicated. All else equal, there is a variable cost reduction effect of a higher capacity: production of Y involves variable costs waY, which is equivalent to hwL. Increasing X by one marginal unit (all else equal) reduces capacity utilization by $\partial h/\partial X = -h/X$. Hence, total variable costs are reduced by $(h/X)wL = hwa$. In a demand constrained period this "cost reduction" constitutes a positive gross revenue with the expected value $aE(hw|Q)$. Therefore the expression within the brackets in (10) is the expected gain from a capacity expansion, i.e. the sum of expected revenues for the capacity constrained and the demand constrained cases, weighted by their respective probabilities.

We now turn to the hypothetical bench mark where deterministic prices and demands are assumed to induce full capacity utilization in all future periods, and where the bench-mark prices are assumed to be equal to the mean value of the uncertain prices. We can obtain the optimality conditions by setting the probabilities of negative quasi-rents and sales constraints equal to zero in (8) and (9), i.e.

(12) $\bar{B}F_K = q$

(13) $\bar{B}F_L = \bar{C}$

where

(14) $\bar{B} = \sum\limits_{t=1}^{T} E(p)(1+r)^{-t} = E(p)\beta(T)$

(15) $\bar{C} = \sum\limits_{t=1}^{T} E(w)(1+r)^{-t} = E(w)\beta(T).$

These conditions determine the bench-mark plant design with which the optimal plant design for the case with market fluctuations will be compared.

4. The impact of fluctuations

Since no revenue is obtained in periods of unprofitable recession and since revenues are reduced in periods with constrained sales, the expected revenue per capacity unit is lower in the case with fluctuations than in the bench-mark case. Further, no wages are paid in unprofitable recession periods and only part of the labor pool is paid during sales constrained recessions. Therefore, the expected wage cost per full capacity labor force is the lowest in the case with fluctuations.

Accordingly,

(16) $B \leq \bar{B}$

(17) $C \leq \bar{C}$

with strict inequalities holding whenever the probability of negative quasi-rents is positive and/or the probability of sales constraints (Y < X) is positive. This is demonstrated formally in the appendix at the end of the paper.

The implications of these inequalities can be seen from (8), (9), (12), and (13): the effect of uncertainty compared to certainty is to reduce both the "price" $\bar{B}$ and the "wage level" $\bar{C}$. Hence, uncertainty has both a substitution effect and a scale effect. The substitution effect (i.e. the effect for a given capacity) is unambiguous: L increases and K decreases. The scale effect is ambiguous, however, since both B and C are reduced. If the substitution effect dominates, uncertainty about demands, prices and wage levels leads to the choice of a more labor-intensive technique. This results in cost flexibility when short-run unprofitableness or sales constraints are experienced. To hedge against future imbalances it is optimal to construct a plant with a rather labor-intensive technique, i.e. to have less fixed and more variable production factors. As a consequence the chosen plant design may be different from the cost-minimizing one, the latter being defined as the design that can produce the chosen full capacity output at the lowest total costs. Consider, for example, the case of a predetermined capacity X and a deterministic wage rate $\bar{w}$. The cost minimizing design is then given by

$$(18) \qquad F_L/F_K = \bar{w}\beta(T)/q.$$

This yields a more capital-intensive production technique than in the corresponding profit-maximizing case, since the latter also takes possible fluctuations into account:

$$(19) \qquad F_L/F_K = \bar{w}E(h)\beta(T)/q.$$

The capital-labor ratio K/L determined by (18) is higher than the ratio determined by (19) since Eh < 1.

With a predetermined capacity, the labor productivity of the plant X/L = 1/a is obviously lower in the profit-maximizing case with fluctuations and uncertainty than in the certainty case. The same also holds in the general case (without a predetermined X) when the substitution effect of uncertainty dominates the capacity effect. Hence, in these cases uncertainty and fluctuations induce a higher break-even price aw.

The impact of uncertainty and fluctuations on the present value of the plant depends on the nature of the fluctuations, i.e. whether the markets can be considered to be of the fixprice type or the flexprice type.

Increased dispersion of prices and wages for given mean values in flexprice markets increases the probabilities of both high and low (negative) quasi-rents. However, since management can take the plant out of operation when quasi-rents are negative, the value of these negative rents are irrelevant. Hence, by utilizing the capacity in an optimal way the firm is able to reap the potential higher profits while avoiding the potential heavier losses caused by increased price and wage dispersion. Therefore, there is an expected gain due to increasing price and wage risks in flexprice markets. This can be demonstrated more formally by applying the familier results from Rothschild and Stiglitz (1970): since hsX is convex in p and w according to (5) and (6), mean-preserving spreads in p and w increases the value of $E(hs)X$ and therefore also of $E\Pi$ defined by (7).

The result is just the opposite with respect to the degree of risk attached to future sales. The firm cannot avoid the realized quasi-rents which correspond to low sales quantities; and due to capacity limitations will be unable to capture all the large profits that would be forthcoming if all potentially high sales could be fulfilled. Therefore, increased dispersion in possible sales reduces the expected quasi-rent. Formally, since hsX is concave in Y according to (5) and (6), a mean-preserving spread in the probability distribution of Y reduces the value of $E(hs)X$ and therefore also of $E\Pi$ defined by (7).

5.   **Economic interpretations**

Above I have made a case for the proposition that in response to price and sales fluctuations, a risk-neutral entrepreneur will choose a plant design which entails relatively less fixed costs and more variable costs . Further, the entrepreneur dislikes sales risks but benefits from price risks. Let us now turn to some economic interpretations of these results.

5.1 The sensitivity of utilization rates to price fluctuations

Consider the case with a deterministic wage, and a stochastic price fluctuating around $\bar{p}$ = Ep. Two firms are about to construct new plants with the same capacity. The first firm only takes the market trend into account in its investment calculations and chooses a relatively more capital-intensive technique, i.e. a plant design with a relatively lower labor-output ratio $\bar{a}$. The other firm taking possible fluctuations into account chooses a more labor-intensive plant design with a relatively higher labor output-ratio a*. The situation is illustrated in Figure 1 where the variable unit costs for the plant chosen by the first firm is $\bar{a}$w, an amount which is lower than the variable unit costs a*w implied by the investment decision of the second firm. In the figure, a possible development of the output price is also drawn. When the price falls below the variable unit costs of a plant, the plant is temporarily closed down. As seen from the figure, due to periods of unprofitableness, the plant with the a*-technique will lay off its labor force more often and for longer periods than the plant with the $\bar{a}$-technique. Hence, when the investor takes possible fluctuations into account he chooses a plant design with utilization rates that are more sensitive to future price fluctuations than otherwise would be the case. Further, since lay-offs and unemployment normally shift the demand of the workers more than the corresponding reduction in income should imply, sensitive utilization rates result in price shocks being more easily propagated through the economy.

Next, consider an employer who has the option of selling his product either in accordance with long-term price contracts or in a spot market with fluctuating prices. If the value of the expected price in the spot market is the same as the one offered on long-term contracts, a risk-neutral employer prefers the former. This will be reflected in his choice of technique, since he will prefer labor-intensive methods. Hence, we suggest the following outcome: Choosing among different selling strategies or types of contracts, the firm chooses the one in which prices fluctuate the most. Anticipating such fluctuations, the optimal plant design will be relatively more labor intensive with a higher break-even price. A higher break-even price implies that the utilization rates will be more sensitive to price fluctuations. The probability of temporary shutdowns increase both because the spot market is preferred to long-term contracts and because the chosen technique is relatively more labor intensive.

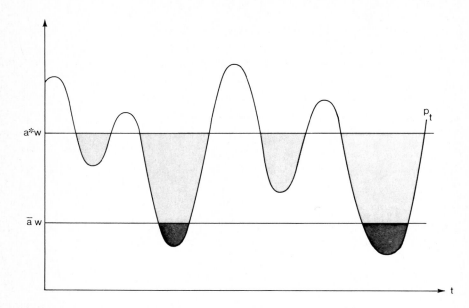

Figure 1. Fluctuating output price and choice of technique

5.2 The optimal degree of subcontracting

We now consider the case where the fundamental choice with respect to technique is the degree of subcontracting. Semi-finished inputs are assumed to be offered in competitive markets at constant reservation prices. The variable costs (ex post) which serve as payments for subcontracted services and semi-finished inputs should be thought of as follows:

The production process is separated into many tasks and operations which are ordered for given shadow prices according to the efficiency with which the firm can undertake them. If some of these tasks can be performed by subcontractors, the firm first contracts out those operations at which it is least efficient. We can then define the degree of subcontracting per unit of capacity by an index a such that the higher the value of a, the greater the number of tasks and operations that are subcontracted. Further, L = aX can be defined as the total amount of a composite semifinished input needed to operate at full capacity with a unit price w. This composite input will increase if either the degree of subcontracting is increased or capacity is increased. [5)] After an investment is made the firm is committed to the chosen technique which requires a prescribed amount of the semi-finished inputs per unit of output. Before the investment is made, however, the firm can choose among different arrangements according to the function X = F(K,L), which indicates that subcontracted inputs can be substituted for fixed capital commitments (for more details see footnote 5).

We can now define the cost-minimizing arrangement for each capacity level, i.e. the choice of K and L which minimizes the present value of the cost of the arrangement (cf. (18)). This describes the division of work between producers and subcontractors which takes advantage of all possible cost reductions. At first glance one might expect that a market economy would implement just that degree of vertical integration. Producers would plan to buy inputs from subcontractors if they are offered at prices lower than the production costs within their own plants, while no semi-finished inputs would be bought which could be produced more cheaply by the producers themselves. However, the preceding discussion provides some evidence that this is not always the case. The combination of fixed capital commitments and market uncertainty can result in other solutions even when firms are risk neutral.

When the demand for the finished output is fluctuating and/or uncertain, the typical firm will not choose the cost-minimizing arrangement. An even higher degree of subcontracting is optimal from the firm's point of view. This means that it will be profitable to parcel out tasks and operations to subcontractors even when the prices that have to be paid for these inputs are higher than the full costs of their production within feasible plant designs. To be able to undertake these tasks within the plant, fixed capital investment is required. Subcontracting saves on these fixed costs. These savings are profitable when capacity utilization varies. Subcontracting provides cost flexibility to firms faced with demand fluctuations and uncertainty. Moreover, this flexibility also results in higher break-even prices for each capacity level. As a consequence, utilization rates will be more sensitive to price fluctuations; the resulting variations in capacity utilization will spread more easily throughout the economy due to the high degree of subcontracting. Using Frisch's (1933) terminology, the strength of both the "impulse" mechanisms and the "propagation" mechanisms of fluctuations are thereby affected. When firms take into account possible demand shocks, they choose production techniques and plant designs which inadvertently increase their exposure to price shock impulses. In addition these impulses propagate more easily into the rest of the economy through the chains of vertical interdependencies. Thus the propagation mechanism of demand shock impulses also is strengthened when firms take possible fluctuations into account since backward linkages increase in importance due to the extensive use of subcontractors.

5.3 Stabilization policies

Within the context of our model, stabilization policies have effects which have not been fully recognized in the debate on the desirablity of such policies. Let us consider economic policies which are successful in stabilizing demand along the trend path. When firms anticipate this stable path, they no longer have a reason to hedge against fluctuating capacity utilization rates. Accordingly, a forecast predicting a stable path induces the choice of more capital-intensive techniques in new production units as compared to a forecast expecting fluctuations around the same trend. Plant designs and arrangements with subcontractors will tend towards the ones which minimize costs for any chosen capacity. Therefore a stabilization policy not only results in short-run gains (in the form of a more efficient utilization of the existing production units), but it also results in long-term gains as well, since the production techniques and the industrial organization induced by this stabilized development will be more cost efficient. That is, the full capacity output is produced at lower costs and the division of work between firms is more in accordance with real cost advantages. These long-term effects should be considered when assessing the desirability of stabilization policies.

However, not every stabilization policy leads to this result. For example, one failure in this respect would be a selective economic policy of government subsidies to industries during unprofitable recession periods. Roughly speaking this policy means that no workers would be laid off even in periods when short-run revenues do not exceed variable costs. The government would pay the difference during these periods in the form of short-run subsidies, conditional on no workers being laid off. [6]

Let us examine the implications of this type of policy in its simplest

form. Consider a flexprice market. The subsidy "rule" followed by the
government can then be described as

$$(20) \quad \theta = \begin{cases} 0 & \text{when } s \geq 0 \\ -sX & \text{when } s < 0 \end{cases}$$

where θ is the amount of subsidy paid to the firm. This "rule" implies that
the government pays short-run losses if they occur, and pays nothing
otherwise. Given this policy, the firm has no incentive to lay off workers.
It is optimal to produce at full capacity utilization even in periods where
$s < 0$. The realized quasi-rent will be the sum of ordinary quasi-rents and
government subsidies, $sX + \theta$. The rate of capacity utilization will now be
one in each period. Nevertheless, we can define a parameter h: h = 1
when $s \geq 0$, and h = 0 when $s < 0$. Using this definition of h in (20), we
can write $sX + \theta = sX + (1-h)(-sX)$.

The expected realized quasi-rent then becomes

$$(21) \quad E(sX) + E\theta = E(sX) + E((1-h)(-sX)) = E(hs)X.$$

Hence, we obtain the equivalent expression to the one included in (7) for
the expected present value of the plant without sales constraints, thereby
implying that the values of K and L that maximize EΠ must be identical to
the optimal values for the case with possible lay-offs during recession
periods.

The exercise above shows that our conclusion that price fluctuations
lead to labor-intensive techniques also has relevance in cases where
short-run variations in employment at the plant level is not "accepted".
Suppose the investor knows that it will not be possible to lay off workers
during future unprofitable recessions periods. At the same time, suppose
he anticipates the type of selective subsidy policy described above. If
this is the case, the outcome of his investment decision will be identical to
the case where labor power is in fact a flexible factor ex post. Furthermore,
the government policy also implies that fluctuations in prices are preferred
to stable prices with identical expected values, since the subsidy "rule",
just as in the case with lay-offs, protects the firm against negative quasi-
rents while allowing it to hold onto the higher quasi-rents earned at the
peaks.

It should also be noted that the anticipation of such subsidy "rules" induces investment policies which will increase both the probability of subsidies being paid and the amount of subsidy actually paid. Firstly, given the subsidy rule, uncertain prices are preferred to stable prices (with the same mean value). Consequently the firm may choose to invest in sectors with wide fluctuations, thereby inducing the government to pay larger subsidies and to pay them more often. Secondly, uncertain prices, combined with the subsidy rule, make labor-intensive techniques profitable; hence the plants will have higher variable unit costs. As a consequence even small price declines may require some subsidies from the goverment to cover short-run costs. Figure 1, also illustrates this case: when the chosen technique is the capital-intensive one, $\bar{a}$, total subsidies paid out are indicated by the darkly-shaded areas; when the chosen technique is the labor-intensive one, a*, total subsidies are indicated by the sum of the lightly-shaded and darkly-shaded areas. As seen from the figure, total subsidies are higher and are paid out more frequently in the case with the labor-intensive technique as compared to the capital-intensive technique.

5.4 Coordination of investments

If it is impossible to reduce fluctuations and/or market uncertainty, one may ask whether there are gains to be made by the coordination of firm investment behavior. Would the government make different investment decisions than the ones resulting from a noncoordinated, decentralized structure? We assume that the market conditions (prices and sales constraints) are determined independently of the activity level in the sector under consideration. Hence, the central decision maker faces exactly the same market situation as the decentralized agents. However, he is allowed to coordinate the production and investment activities among firms.

In the case of flexible prices, there is no need for coordination of the capacity utilization decisions within the sector. Those units with positive quasi-rents at the going prices will be operated at full capacity while those with negative quasi-rents will be taken out of use. This is also optimal for the sector as a whole when the sector is considered to be a price-taker. If the central decision maker were deciding upon all new investment projects, he would hedge against price fluctuations and uncertainties for each project in exactly the same way as analyzed above. The central decision maker would choose L-intensive plant designs due to market uncertainty and fluctuations. Nothing could be gained by coordination.

In the case of possible sales constraints this is no longer true. In an economy with slowly adjusting prices there is no mechanism which will direct a sales-constrained production level to the most efficient production units. Central coordination, however, can implement such short-run efficiency. Furthermore, if the central decision maker were deciding upon all investments, additional efficiency improvements could be obtained since it will be nonoptimal to hedge against sales uncertainty in every new production unit. Instead, the optimal policy is to aim at cost flexibility only at the sector level. Production in future periods should be coordinated among the production units. Hence, given the sales expectations for the sector as a whole, the central decision maker can implement the construction of some capital-intensive plants which will produce at full capacity utilization in every period, and some L-intensive plants which will absorb all the variations in total sales. This is more profitable compared to having cost flexibility in every micro unit since the same total sector production can be undertaken at lower costs.

5.5 The effect of public unemployment compensation

Uncertainty and fluctuation, in addition to what has already been mentioned, may also lead to other types of misallocation of the productive resources. Irrespective of whether prices in output markets are fixed or flexible, private firms may not face the full cost of their ex post flexible inputs. In particular, this is the case with idle labor when the government pays unemployment benefits. Let us focus upon this possible difference between private and public interests in the simplest manner possible.

Consider an economy with short-run immobility between sectors. Suppose there are only two sectors, one operating in a market with fluctuating demand and one in a stable market. If our assumptions about irreversible choices of techniques hold, the medium-run allocation of both capital and labor between these sectors is determined by the investment decision. Let the shadow price of labor, $\bar{w}$, be equal to the remuneration of workers in the stable sector. Furthermore, let w_u be the unemployment compensation. Finally, let w be the wage of those working in the fluctuating sector. Due to temporary cutbacks caused by short-run unprofitableness or sales constraints, the expected (or average) payment to a representative worker in the fluctuating sector is

$$(22) \qquad E\left[hq + (1-h)w_u \right]$$

where h as before indicates the capacity utilization. Each worker in the fluctuating sector will on average be unemployed a fraction $E(1-h)$ of any sufficiently long period of time. Long-run equilibrium in the labor market requires that expected payment in the fluctuating sector just balances the wage level in the stable sector. If this condition does not hold migration will, after a while, take place to the sector with the highest expected payment. Accordingly, in equilibrium

$$(23) \qquad \bar{w} = E(hw) + E((1-h)w_u)$$

which implies that

$$(24) \qquad \bar{w} > E(hw).$$

From (11') we know that $E(hw)$ is the relevant marginal costs per period if a more L-intensive production technique has been chosen, while $\bar{w}$ is the corresponding cost to society as a whole.

This simple exercise suggests the following conclusion: A private firm in the fluctuating sector will choose a production technique that is too labor intensive in comparison to the social optimum. The reason is that the firm faces too low a price for the variable input labor. Lay-offs are cheaper for the firm than they are for society. When considering different production techniques the firm should be made to take into account that each unit of L is worth $\bar{w}$ in an alternative application. However, the firm only has to pay $E(hw) < \bar{w}$ on average. One could say that in the long run public unemployment benefits function as a subsidy to employers in fluctuating sectors of the economy. If other "insurance schemes" were available, e.g. one where the workers had the opportunity to borrow money to cover their living expenses while unemployed, firms in fluctuating sectors would have to pay higher wages to attract workers.

There are reasons to believe that unguided private investments lead to a situation where more workers are in the labor pools of fluctuating sectors than socially optimal. First, too much capacity is invested in these sectors because the "low" wage-cost makes it too profitable not to enter. Secondly, for any given capacity the firms choose too labor-intensive production techniques, since they face too low wage costs. This conjecture has some bearing on the allocation of resources between exporting and sheltered sectors (of small open economies). The former produces for an uncertain world market while the latter is protected from the same kind of uncertainties. The analysis above asserts that the export sector easily can grow too large with too many workers.

6. Concluding remarks

Given the putty-clay nature of capital equipment, uncertainty as such does play an important role for the optimal investment decisions even when the decision makers are risk neutral. Further, unguided investment decisions may lead to factor proportions different from the socially optimal ones. In this respect our analysis reminds us of a typical feature characterizing Leif Johansen's thinking: despite his widespread interests and specialties he was always careful to make his various analyses mutually consistent, a typical example being the connection between his arguments in favor of economic planning[7] and his approach to production and investment theory.

Appendix

We want to demonstrate that

$$B = \left[\Pr(R) E(p|R) + \Pr(Q) a E(whQ) \right] \beta(T) \leq E(p)\beta(T) = \bar{B}$$

$$C = \left[\Pr(R) E(w|R) + \Pr(Q) E(whQ) \right] \beta(T) \leq E(w)\beta(T) = \bar{C}.$$

Observe first that

$$Ew = E(hw) + E((1-h)w) \geq E(hw).$$

This shows that $C \leq \bar{C}$ and that a strict inequality holds when there is a positive probability of h being less than 1 (i.e. at least one of the probabilities $Pr(Q)$ and $Pr(s < 0)$ are positive.

Next, we know that

$$Ep = Pr(R)E(p|R) + Pr(Q)E(p|Q) + Pr(s < 0)E(p|s < 0)$$

$$\geq Pr(R)E(p|R) + Pr(Q)E(p|Q)$$

$$\geq Pr(R)E(p|R) + Pr(Q)aE(wh|Q).$$

The latter inequality is true since $E(sX|Q) = E(p|Q)X - E(w|Q)L \geq 0$, by definition of Q implying that

$$E(p|Q) \geq aE(w|Q) \geq aE(wh|Q).$$

This shows that $B \leq \bar{B}$ and that a strict inequality hold if $Pr(Q)$ and/or $Pr(s < 0)$ are positive.

Notes

1) Leif Johansen's production and investment theory goes back to his (1959) article and is more fully developed in his (1972) book <u>Production Functions</u>. See also the contribution of Salter (1960).

2) Another analytically simple alternative is the following: Ex ante K is determined given the relationship X = F(K,N). Ex post, after the values of some uncertain variables have been revealed, N is determined given the relationship X = F(K, Ñ). This approach is used by Hartman (1972), Smith (1970); Nickell (1978 ch. 5) and others. In my opinion it is more restrictive than the simple putty-clay approach described above, even though it has a non-linear ex post relationship between X and N. No choice of technique is modelled. The investment decision is only with respect to the dimension of the plant.

3) In the light of the importance of uncertainty over future market conditions for optimal putty-clay investments, it is surprising to discover that these aspects are so little discussed in the literature. While working with my own study of putty-clay investments (Moene (1984)) my attention has been drawn to two papers with an approach similar to mine: Kon (1983) discusses the impact of price uncertainty within a putty-clay framework, while Albrecht and Hart (1983) discuss implications of sales uncertainties. A recent paper by Abel (1983) concern-

ing energy price uncertainty and optimal factor intensity is also relevant. In addition, a paper by Fuss and McFadden (1978, Ch. II.4) is
related to our topic.

4)   For a more thorough derivation of the optimality condition, see Moene
     (1984) Ch. 4 and Appendix I.

5)   Let there be a total of M different tasks and operations that can be
     subcontracted with the inputs f_1, f_2, ... f_M per unit of X. If sub-
     contracting takes place operation no. 1 will be set out first, operation
     no. 2 second, and so on. The unit prices of these inputs are denoted
     by w_1, w_2, ...w_M. Let $w = \sum_{i=1}^{M} w_i f_i$. The degree of subcontracting
     when m operations are put out can be defined by $a(m) = \sum_{i=1}^{m} w_i f_i / w$
     and the maximum degree of subcontracting a(M) is one.   Ex ante
     there are substitution possibilities between K and m according to the
     funtion X = G(K,m) (with positive partial derivatives of both argu-
     ments). Now, L = a(m)X defines m as a function of L and X. Substi-
     tuting this into the G-function we can write X = F(K,L) where L has
     the unit price w defined above.

6)   This kind of policy was to some extent followed in Norway during the
     1970's.

7)   See for example his Lectures on Macroeconomic Planning, Vol. I and II,
     especially ch. 7.

References

Abel, A. (1983), "Energy Price Uncertainty and Optimal Factor Intensity:
     A Mean-Variance Analysis", Econometrica 51, No 6, 1839-45.

Albrecht, J. and Hart, A. (1983), "A Putty Clay Model of Demand Uncer-
     tainty and Investment", The Scandinavian Journal of Economics 85,
     393-402.

Frisch R. (1933), "Propagation Problems and Impulse Problems in Dynamic
     Economics" in Economic Essays in Honor of Gustav Cassel, G. Allen
     and Unwin, Ltd.

Fuss, M. and D. McFadden (1978), "Flexibility versus Efficiency in Ex
     Ante Plant Design", in M. Fuss and D. McFadden (eds.), Production
     Economics: A Dual Approach to Theory and Applications, Vol. I, 311-
     364, North-Holland Publ. Co., Amsterdam.

Hartman, R. (1972), "The Effect of Price and Cost Uncertainty on Invest-
      ment", Journal of Economic Theory 5, 258-66.

Johansen, L. (1959), "Substitution versus Fixed Production Coefficients
      in the Theory of Economic Growth: A Synthesis", Econometrica 27,
      157-76.

Johansen, L. (1967), "Some Problems in Pricing and Optimal Choice of
      Factor Proportions in a Dynamic Setting", Economica 34, 131-52.

Johansen, L. (1972), Production Functions, North-Holland Publ. Co.,
      Amsterdam.

Johansen, L. (1977), Lectures on Macroeconomic Planning, Vol. I (1977)
      and II (1978), North-Holland Publ. Co., Amsterdam .

Kon, Y. (1983), "Capital Input Choice under Uncertainty - A Putty Clay
      Technology Case", International Economic Review 24, pp. 183-97.

Moene, K. (1984), "Investment and Fluctuations. Optimal 'Putty-Clay'
      Investments under Uncertain Business Prospects", Memorandum from
      the Department of Economics, University of Oslo, No 9, February
      1984.

Nickell, S. (1978), The Investment Decisions of Firms, James Nisbet &
      Co. Ltd., Welwyn.

Rothschild, M. and J. Stiglitz (1970), "Increasing risk: I. A Definition",
      Journal of Economic Theory 2, 66-84.

Salter, W. (1960), Productivity and Technical Change, Cambridge Univer-
      sity Press, Cambridge.

Smith, K. (1970), "Risk and the Optimal Utilization of Capital", Review of
      Economic Studies 37, 253-59.

Production, Multi-Sectoral Growth and Planning
F.R. Førsund, M. Hoel, and S. Longva (Editors)
© Elsevier Science Publishers B.V. (North-Holland), 1985

THE INTERPLAY BETWEEN SECTORAL MODELS BASED ON MICRO DATA AND MODELS FOR THE NATIONAL ECONOMY

Finn R. Førsund

University of Oslo

Eilev S. Jansen

Norges Bank

1. Introduction

In a paper on large scale econometric models for national planning presented at the symposium commemorating the twenty-fifth anniversary of the Econometric Institute at Erasmus University, Rotterdam, Leif Johansen (1982, p. 112) pointed out

"...that much of the modelling of the supply side will fail to come to grips with important problems because it relies too much on smooth, neo-classical formulations of production functions and derived concepts."

To increase the realism and explanatory power of econometric planning models, Johansen urged the adoption of the putty-clay approach. Concerning the data requirement for implementing such an approach he stated:

"It seems that much more of data from the micro level of the economy would be necessary for more reliable econometric implementations of the ideas of putty-clay technology" (Johansen (1982, p. 112)).

In Norway the annual Industrial Statistics from the Central Bureau of Statistics is the most important source of micro information on industrial

The authors wish to thank Olav Bjerkholt, Ådne Cappelen, Arne Jon Isachsen, and Svein Longva for helpful comments.

economic activity. All firms in Norwegian industry with more than five
employees are obliged to render each year very detailed information concerning their production and employment, and their use of energy and
other inputs. Several production studies have been based on this vast
body of data. Griliches and Ringstad (1971) used data from the 1963
Census of Manufacturing Establishments to estimate CES production functions for broad industry sectors, and Ringstad (1971) gave a similar analysis based on time-series of cross-section data for the years 1959-1967.
Recent developments include attempts to estimate frontier (micro) production functions via cost functions for the mechanical pulp industry (see
Førsund and Jansen (1974), (1977)), and the construction of industry
production functions of the Johansen type, e.g. for the Norwegian
aluminium industry (Førsund and Jansen (1982)).

The purpose of this paper is to outline how sectoral models based on
putty-clay production functions can interact with models for the national
economy. The questions posed can be stated as two distinct problems:

Problem 1: How can past and present micro information, viz. as
           summarised in a sectoral model, be utilised within a dynam-
           ic macro model of the total economy?

Problem 2: How can the results of a macro model, expressed in terms
           of time paths for production aggregates, be translated into
           information about industrial structure for use within the
           framework of a sectoral production model based on micro
           units?

In the next section, the concepts of the industry production function and
the frontier production function are presented. The interplay between
these concepts, which are tools for sectoral analysis, and a multisectoral
but otherwise unspecified macro model is discussed in Section 3. We consider first the short-run case where no new capacity is generated through
investments, and then extend the analysis to include new capacity within
a vintage-capital approach. The concluding section points to a number of
problems which are likely to emerge if these procedures are implemented
in the planning process.

2. Micro-based models for one sector

2.1 The industry production function

The concept of a short-run industry production function derived from micro observations was first put forward by Leif Johansen in his book Production Functions (see Johansen (1972)).[1] He considered the case of an industrial sector consisting of production units (firms) which produce a reasonably homogeneous output. Johansen's key assumption – which makes industrial structure an interesting concept – was that substitution possibilities for each firm are more restricted ex post than ex ante.

The ex ante production function at the micro level can be thought of as a neo-classical production function with continous substitution possibilities. It is assumed to summarise the relevant technological knowledge available at the moment of investment, and the choices of technique related to this function. Once the choice is made, fixed factors – such as capital – determine the capacity of that particular production unit, which is now characterised by fixed unit requirements for current inputs. Ex post, the production possibilities embodied in each unit are therefore assumed to follow a limitational law, i.e.

(1) $0 \leq x \leq \bar{x}$

(2) $v_j = (\bar{v}_j / \bar{x}) x = \xi_j x, \quad j=1,\ldots,n.$

(1) states that current production, x, cannot exceed capacity, $\bar{x}$, and (2) expresses that current inputs are required in the same proportion to output as they would be at full capacity utilisation, $\bar{v}_j / \bar{x}$. In practice, the input coefficients ξ_j are estimated from the observed coefficients.

The short-run industry production function

(3) $X = F(V_1,\ldots,V_n)$

can thus be defined as the solution to the classical problem of maximising output for given levels of inputs:

(4) $\text{Max } X = \sum\limits_{i=1}^{N} x^i$

subject to

(5) $\sum\limits_{i=1}^{N} \xi^i_j \, x^i \leq V_j, \quad j = 1, \ldots, n,$

(6) $x^i \leq \bar{x}^{-i}, \quad i = 1, \ldots, N,$

(7) $x^i \geq 0, \quad i = 1, \ldots, N,$

where X denotes output, $V_1, \ldots, V_n$ denote current inputs for the industry as a whole, and where $i=1, \ldots, N$ refers to plants with a capacity of $\bar{x}^{-i}$.

The industry production function (3) is a technical relationship which is not dependent upon prices or economic behaviour. We may obtain a deeper insight into the nature of this function by formulating the dual problem of (4)-(7). Let the dual variables $q_1, \ldots, q_n$ correspond to the restrictions on current inputs in (5) and $r^1, \ldots, r^N$ correspond to the capacity limitations in (6). The full dual problem is then:

(8) $\text{Minimise } \sum\limits_{j=1}^{n} q_j V_j + \sum\limits_{i=1}^{N} r^i \bar{x}^{-i}$

subject to

(9) $\sum\limits_{j=1}^{n} q_j \xi^i_j + r^i \geq 1, \quad i = 1, \ldots, N.$

With respect to the capacity utilisation of each unit the correspondence between the solutions of the primal and the dual problem yields

$$\sum\limits_{j=1}^{n} q_j \xi^i_j > 1 \;\Rightarrow\; x^i = 0,$$

(10) $\sum\limits_{j=1}^{n} q_j \xi^i_j = 1 \;\Rightarrow\; 0 \leq x^i \leq \bar{x}^{-i},$

$$\sum\limits_{j=1}^{n} q_j \xi^i_j < 1 \Rightarrow x^i = \bar{x}^{-i}.$$

The variables $q_1, \ldots, q_n$ are shadow prices of the current inputs and express the marginal productivities in the industry production function.

Whether a production unit is operated or not is decided according to (10), i.e. by whether operation "costs" calculated at these shadow prices are less than unity. The units which are utilised are those with non-negative quasi-rents (r^i). This is illustrated in Figure 1 for the case of two current inputs where only the units on or below the zero quasi-rent line are in operation.

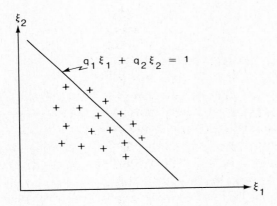

Fig. 1.   The zero quasi-rent line in an input coefficient diagram. Observations are indicated by crosses

This procedure enables us to derive supply and input-demand functions which correspond to the short-run industry production function. This production function can be interpreted as prescribing the optimal allocation of production within the industry (i.e. the degree of capacity utilisation assigned to each unit) when factor prices and current output vary, and given that all units face the same prices. Conditional upon this interpretation, we can determine the supply of output by substituting actual real prices[2] for the shadow prices in (10) and then summing the outputs of the production units which yield a non-negative quasi-rent. The corresponding demand for inputs can be obtained from (2). These analytical functions of the real prices may not be unique.

If the input coefficients ($\xi_1, \ldots, \xi_n$) have a discrete distribution, the implicit supply and demand functions in this approach will not be "well-behaved". Johansen (1972) showed that well-behaved functions follow if we can assume a continuous capacity distribution, $f(\xi_1,\ldots,\xi_n)$, over an n-dimensional region in the $(\xi_1,\ldots,\xi_n)$ space. If G denotes the set of points in this region where the quasi-rent is non-negative, we can write the supply and demand functions in the following way:

(11) $X = \int\ldots\int_G f(\xi_1,\ldots,\xi_n) \, d\xi_1\ldots d\xi_n,$

(12) $V_j = \int\ldots\int_G \xi_j f(\xi_1,\ldots,\xi_n) \, d\xi_1\ldots d\xi_n, \quad j = 1,\ldots,n.$

2.2 The frontier production function

One theoretical requirement for the frontier production function of an industry is that it should represent the most efficient transformation of inputs into outputs given the available technology. The empirical estimations from this concept may be considered as a pessimistic estimate of the choice of technique function, i.e. the ex ante production function as described in the previous section.

Let us again consider an industrial sector with production units producing a homogeneous output. It is assumed that the industry frontier function is composed of the production units' functions – either observed or hypothetical production possibilities – that yield maximum output for a

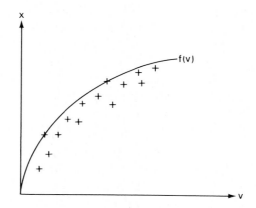

Fig. 2.   The frontier production function f(v). The case of one input. Observations are indicated by crosses

given set of inputs (see Førsund and Hjalmarsson (1974)). During the last
decade such functions have been estimated from observed performances,
normally assuming perfect substitutability between all inputs ex post as
well as ex ante.[3] The standard approach is to fit an envelope function
to all observations available in the space defined by inputs and output.
This procedure is illustrated in Figure 2 for the case of one input.

If we revert to our assumption of fixed input coefficients ex post, each
unit provides only one observation for the estimation, and this sample
point is a realisation of the ex ante production function at the time of
investment. Under certain assumptions with respect to technical change in
the ex ante function for the industry, it is still possible to estimate the
function. Note that this function contains capital as a variable factor.

3. The interaction between sectoral models and models for the national economy.

The macroeconomic model considered in this paper is a multisectoral
model at a moderate level of disaggregation intended for medium-term
projections of, say, four to ten years.[4]

Let us, for sake of simplicity, first look at the short-run interaction
between a macroeconomic model of this kind and a sectoral model. This
means that we can disregard investment flows and their effect on productive capacity. Let us further assume that this sector produces a relatively
homogeneous output (the volume of which is X) by means of two current
inputs, labour (N) and raw materials, e.g. energy (E), and that we have
reliable data for these entities. In this situation, the interplay between
the sectoral information (S), represented by the data underlying the
industry production function, and the macro model (M) is quite straightforward, as shown in Figure 3.

Suppose that the sector price p and the factor prices of energy and
labour, q^E and w, are determined in the macro model M. As explained in
Section 2, these prices define the zero quasi-rent line in the unit input
diagram. With a given capacity distribution for the micro units in the
sector – in Figure 3 symbolised by a continuous capacity distribution
function $f(\xi_N, \xi_E)$ defined over a region of positive capacity – we can
derive the supply of output of X^S and the demand by the sector for the

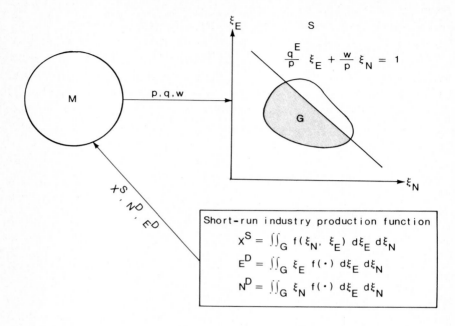

Fig. 3.   The interaction between the macroeconomic model M and the
               sectoral model based on the micro information S

current inputs E^D and N^D.

We have therefore one answer to Problem 2 set out in the introduction. If <u>at least one</u> of the price variables are endogenous in the macro
model M, and the price solution of M is dependent on the sectoral quantum
variables (X, E and N), which are considered as predetermined variables
in the macro model, then both models can be solved iteratively until convergence with respect to the prices is obtained. In this case we have also
provided a simplistic answer to Problem 1 for the short run.

In order to go beyond the short run and make medium-term projections, we shall extend the analysis to include a model of investment
demand for the sector. The investment demand can be captured by
applying a vintage-capital model to the sector as a whole. After the last
observed period, we lose track of the individual establishments in the
future periods, so that vintage capital at the aggregated level is the only
operational unit available for analysis.[5]

The vintage-capital approach is consistent with the assumptions underlying the construction of an industry production function made in
Section 2.[6] These assert that the industry production can be described
by a putty-clay technology, and that a frontier (ex ante) production
function for the industry exists and is known to the investors in the sector. Again simplifying, we shall assume that the investors behave as if
they have certain expectations about future output prices as well as about
future prices in the factor markets, including the price of capital, q_K.
The discounted profit function π for the sector can then be established,
in which the discount rate can be interpreted as a required rate of return
on capital, z. Assuming that the investors maximise π, it can be shown
that, under certain regularity conditions, this maximum is obtained when
the present value of the marginal productivity of capital (MPK) - derived
from the ex ante function - equals the price of capital. It is conceivable
that investment demand calculated in this way, ΔK^D_{calc}, may take on
unrealistically high values. In practice, however, it is likely that investment demand will be constrained by an upper limit ΔK, determined by
institutional conditions such as credit availability. Alternatively, adjustment costs may be introduced. The sector demand for capital can then be
written

(13) $\quad \Delta K^D = \begin{cases} 0 \text{ when } MPK \leq q_K \text{ at } \Delta K=0 \\ \\ Min (\Delta K, \Delta K^D_{calc}) \text{ when } MPK \geq q_K \text{ at } \Delta K=0. \end{cases}$

We shall assume that ΔK_t (realised investments in period t) manifests
itself as new production capacity at time t+1 and we let $f^+(\xi_N, \xi_E)$ represent the corresponding capacity distribution function. The links
between the investment model for the sector, the macro model M, and the
sectoral information contained in S are illustrated in Figure 4.

The sector investment model is connected to the sectoral information S
through the frontier production function, which also figures in the investors' profit function. Moreover, it is plausible to assume that the investors' price expectations are determined by changes in the current prices,
p, q^E, and was well as by past changes in these prices.[7]

We assume that the price of capital q_K and the required rate of return z are determined in the macro model M. If z and q_K are endogenous

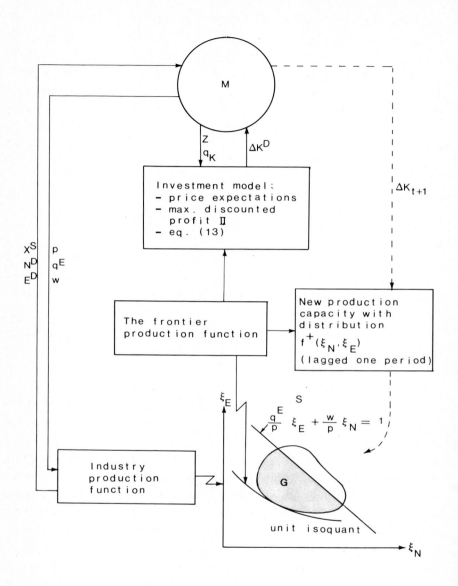

Fig. 4.   The interaction between the macroeconomic model M and the
               sectoral models based on the micro information S: the case
               with new capacity added through investments

variables in M and their solutions are dependent on ΔK^D, we shall have
to solve the investment model for the sector and the macro model iteratively.

It is, however, conceivable that investment demand from the sector
does not influence the solutions of the price variables in M to any significant extent. In that case, the investment model enters the model system,
outlined in Figure 4, as a recursive block, which for each period can be
solved after we have found the iterative market solutions (prices and
quantities) for the sector's output and current inputs.

Under these conditions, the short-run answers stated above to problems 1 and 2 of the introduction are not dramatically changed by the
presence of a model of investment which generates new capacity in the
sector.

4. Some further considerations

In this concluding section we shall comment briefly on some problems
which are likely to emerge if the procedures described in Section 3 are
to be implemented. We shall not dig deeper into the various ways in which
the macro model M can be formulated, but shall take a closer look at some
of the building blocks used in modelling at the sectoral level.

The first problem is one of aggregation: the industry production
approach requires that the sector produce a reasonably homogeneous
output which is measureable in technical units. One obvious limitation to
the applicability of our analysis is that only a few branches of industry
satisfy these assumptions. The next best we can hope for is that for some
industries, the sector specified in the macro model consists of several
branches, each one of which fulfills the requirements. For example, the
pulp and paper industry may be divided into three relatively homogeneous
branches: mechanical pulp, sulphate & sulphite pulp, and paper.

If the following assumptions hold, the interactive scheme of the previous section may still apply:

- The changes in prices are proportional within the aggregated sector
  (pulp and paper, say).
- The initial price levels are known for all branches.

We can then use the macro model to determine the common rate of change
in the prices, while the sectoral analysis is carried out at the
disaggregated branch level. The quantum variables to be used in the
macro model are then determined by simple aggregation to the appropriate
sector level.

A quite different problem is posed by the question of whether to
choose a continuous or a discrete representation of the capacity distribution for the sector production. For industries with a small number of firms
- like the aluminium industry in Norway - the best alternative is probably
to utilise the primary input coefficient observations in a discrete form. If
the number of firms in the sector is large, it may be a considerable advantage to condense the data by using a continuous capacity distribution
function to represent the observations. Even with only two current inputs, however, it is extremely difficult to find functional forms for this
distribution function which are both simple enough to be estimated empirically and sophisticated enough to yield a realistic description of the underlying observations.[8] Moreover, we also require that the capacity
distribution function should be integrable in order to obtain the sector's
supply of output and input-demands via eqs. (11) and (12).[9]

The change over time of a sector's production capacity is composed of
two factors: creation of new capacity and scrapping of existing capacity.
The scrapping criterion may be the quasi-rent criterion, i.e. capacity
with negative quasi-rent according to the prices generated by the macro
model is scrapped within each time period. With a view towards reality,
this strict criterion may be relaxed to allow for a certain share of unprofitable operations, but if full employment is obtained at the macro level, it
is logical to maintain the strict quasi-rent criterion.

In regard to creation of new capacity, we encounter a problem due to
the fact that the notion of individual production units disappear from the
model at future points of time, whereas individual units, of course, do
exist in the real world. If the formation of uniform price expectations
based on the prices generated in the macro model is applied to the sectoral investment calculations, we end up realising just one point on the ex
ante function. In the case of a discrete distribution this means one artificial unit is created each time the sector increases its capacity, and for a
continuous distribution the incremental capacity mass is concentrated at
just one input coefficient point.

The more realistic situation where investors may have different price expectations and new investments take place within existing plants could be simulated by "stretching out" the investment point on the ex ante function.   The degree of "stretching out" may be imposed directly or may be based on observed variation. The two alternatives are illustrated in Figure 5 in the case of rapid technical change.

Technical change takes place through the movement of the ex ante function. Such changes may be predicted parametrically from estimations based on observed data and/or engineering information. Our analysis of the

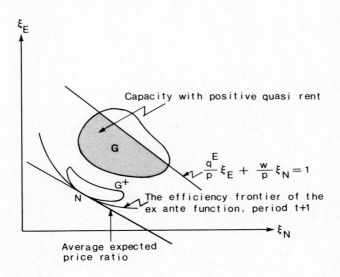

$$\frac{q}{p}\xi_E + \frac{w}{p}\xi_N = 1$$

Capacity with positive quasi rent

The efficiency frontier of the ex ante function, period t+1

Average expected price ratio

+ G = New capacity created when "stretching" the optimal choice of input coefficients.

N   = Optimal point on the ex ante function for new investment with uniform price expectations and full information

Fig. 5.   Creation of new capacity in the sectoral model

Norwegian aluminium industry (Førsund and Jansen (1982)), for example,
showed a typical movement towards a steady-state structure of almost
equal units in the sector. Further estimates of technical progress, especially as regards unit electricity consumption, could have only be inferred
from the use of engineering information.

Disembodied technical change may also be introduced in accordance
with "the complete growth equation" found in Johansen (1972). This
means that the region G in Figure 5 of existing utilised capacity also
moves over time.

Finally, in view of the problems and loose ends confronting the model-
builder of putty-clay production structures, it seems pertinent to again
quote Johansen (1982, p. 112):

".....this case is of course much easier to argue from a theoretical than
from an econometric point of view, since the econometrics of putty-clay
production is much more complicated than the econometrics of pure
neo-classical production."

Notes

1) For a further discussion of the concept of the short-run industry
    production function, see Førsund and Hjalmarsson (1983), (1984).

2) I.e. prices of inputs relative to the output price.

3) For a survey, see Førsund, Lovell and Schmidt (1980).

4) The model we have in mind is the Norwegian planning model MODAG (see
    Cappelen et al. (1981)) with 30 production sectors which are identical
    to the sectors specified in the MSG model, see Bjerkholt et al. (1982)
    and the original text by Johansen (1974).

5) The use of the Industrial Statistics as a data source implies that the
    situation is quite different for each period of observation: all direct
    information refers to the actual establishments, while information on
    capital vintages is available only indirectly as annual investments.

6) See Førsund and Hjalmarsson (1984) for a further discussion of the
    capital-vintage approach in this context.

7) This assumption is discussed further in Section 4 below.

8)   Mathematical examples of capacity distribution functions are analysed
     in Johansen (1972, ch. 5) and Muysken (1981). Refer also to Levhari
     (1968) and Hildenbrand (1981).

9)   See Seierstad (1981), (1982).

References

Bjerkholt, O., S. Longva, Ø. Olsen and S. Strøm (eds.) (1983),
Analysis of Supply and Demand of Electricity in the Norwegian
Economy, Samfunnsøkonomiske Studier 53, Central Bureau of
Statistics, Oslo.

Cappelen, Å., E. Garaas and S. Longva (1981), "MODAG. En modell for
makroøkonomiske analyser", (MODAG. A model for macroeconomic
analysis), Reports 81/30, Central Bureau of Statistics, Oslo.

Førsund, F.R., C.A. Knox Lovell and P. Schmidt (1980), "A Survey of
Frontier Production Functions and of Their Relationship to Efficiency
Measurement", Journal of Econometrics 13, 5-25.

Førsund, F.R. and L. Hjalmarsson (1974)," On the Measurement of Productive Efficiency", Swedish Journal of Economics 76, 141-154.

Førsund, F.R. and L. Hjalmarsson (1983), "Technical Change and Structural Change in the Swedish Cement Industry 1955-1979", Econometrica 51, 1449-1467.

Førsund, F.R. and L. Hjalmarsson (1984), Analysis of Industrial Structure: A Production Function Approach, Working Paper No. 135, The
Industrial Institute for Economic and Social Research, Stockholm.

Førsund, F.R. and E.S. Jansen (1974), "Average Practice and Best Practice Production Functions with Variable Scale Elasticity. An Empirical
Analysis of the Structure of the Norwegian Mechanical Pulp
Industry", Memorandum, 2 January, Department of Economics, University of Oslo.

Førsund, F.R. and E.S. Jansen (1977), "On Estimating Average and Best Practice Homothetic Production Functions via Cost Functions", International Economic Review 18, 463-476.

Førsund, F.R. and E.S. Jansen (1982), "Analysis of Energy-Intensive Industries - The Case of Norwegian Aluminium Production 1966-1978", in O. Bjerkholt et al. (eds.), Analysis of Supply and Demand of Electricity in the Norwegian Economy, 221-259, Samfunnsøkonomiske Studier 53, Central Bureau of Statistics, Oslo.

Griliches, S. and V. Ringstad (1971), Economies of Scale and the Form of the Production Function, North-Holland, Amsterdam-London.

Hildenbrand, W. (1981), "Short-Run Production Functions Based on Microdata", Econometrica 49, 1095-1125.

Johansen, L. (1972), Production Functions, North-Holland, Amsterdam-Oxford.

Johansen, L. (1974), A Multi-Sectoral Study of Economic Growth. (Second Enlarged Edition), North-Holland, Amsterdam-Oxford.

Johansen, L. (1982), "Econometric Models and Economic Planning and Policy: Some Trends and Problems", in M. Hazewinkel and A.H.G. Rinnooy Kan (eds.), Current Developments in the Interface: Economics, Econometrics, Mathematics, 91-122, D. Reidel Publishing Co., Dordrecht.

Levhari, D. (1968), "A Note on Houthakker's Aggregate Production Function in a Multifirm Industry", Econometrica 36, 151-154.

Muysken, J. (1981), "Transformed Beta-Capacity Distributions of Production Units in an Industry", Memorandum, 6 July, Department of Economics, University of Oslo.

Ringstad, V. (1971), Estimating Production Functions and Technical Change from Micro Data, Samfunnsøkonomiske Studier 21, Central Bureau of Statistics, Oslo.

Seierstad, A. (1981), "The Macro Production Function Uniquely Determines the Capacity Distributions of the Micro Units", Economics Letters 7, 211-214.

Seierstad, A. (1982), "Capacity Distributions Derived from Macro Production Functions", Economics Letters 10, 23-27.

Production, Multi-Sectoral Growth and Planning
F.R. Førsund, M. Hoel, and S. Longva (Editors)
© Elsevier Science Publishers B.V. (North-Holland), 1985

EXTENSIONS AND APPLICATIONS OF THE MSG-MODEL:
A BRIEF SURVEY

Lars Bergman

Stockholm School of Economics

1. Introduction

The model presented in Johansen's A Multi-Sectoral Study of Economic Growth, the so-called MSG-model, was a remarkable achievement. Not only has it been used as a tool for long-term planning and forecasting purposes in Norway for more than two decades, thereby avoiding the fate of early death and oblivion experienced by most economic models, but it has also been a source of continuing inspiration for later students of resource allocation problems in national economies. As a result a good deal of the multisectoral models presented in recent years can be regarded as extensions and applications of the MSG approach.

The MSG-model has no doubt been a main source of inspiration because of the way it incorporates basic notions of Walrasian general equilibrium theory into the context of macroeconomic planning and forecasting. Thus, in the MSG-model the sectoral allocation of resources and sectoral output rates are determined by the interplay of profit-maximizing producers and utility-maximizing consumers in competitive markets. A solution to the model is defined as a state of the economy where all product and factor markets simultaneously clear, and product prices are equal to the unit costs of production, including a "normal" rate of return on capital.

In other words the (relative) prices and quantities are _simultaneously_ determined in the MSG-model, whereas input-output and linear programming type of resource allocation models typically determine equilibrium quantities at given (relative) prices or vice versa. Seen in this perspective,

I am grateful to Jaime de Melo, Svein Longva, Stefan Lundgren, and Øystein Olsen for comments on an earlier version of this paper. I have also benefitted from discussions with Sherman Robinson and John Whalley. Of course I am solely responsible for remaining errors and mistakes.

the MSG-model can be regarded as the first example of what nowadays is called computable general equilibrium, or simply CGE-models.

The challenge provided by the MSG-model to later model builders stems to a large extent from its incompleteness. That is, a good deal of the factors influencing the resource allocation pattern in the MSG-model are exogenously given. Thus, while the MSG-model allows price-induced substitution between inputs, the substitutability is restricted to capital and labor. Consequently intermediate inputs such as energy and materials are used in fixed proportions in 'the usual input–output fashion. Moreover, in spite of the openness of the Norwegian economy, foreign trade is essentially exogenously determined. This means that the domestic price system determined within the model is largely independent of world market prices.

It should also be mentioned that although the MSG-model endogenously determines factor prices, it only distinguishes one type of labor and one aggregated household sector. As a result the income distribution aspects of endogenously determined resource allocation patterns are essentially neglected. Moreover, although the MSG-model is a model of economic growth it has no explicit time dimension; a solution to the original MSG-model only gives the development tendencies at a particular point in time.

The purpose of this article is two-fold. The first is to briefly survey the links between Johansen's MSG-model and the resource allocation models usually referred to as "computable general equilibrium" (CGE) models.[1] The second purpose is to present and discuss some of the approaches CGE-model builders have adopted when trying to extend MSG-type of models into more complete models of resource allocation in an open economy.

2. A Stylized Version of the MSG-model

In order to give a brief account of the MSG-model, and to get a point of departure for the ensuing discussion, a "stylized" MSG-model will be presented in this section. In the course of describing that model, I will briefly discuss some of the particular features of Johansen's original MSG-model. However, I shall disregard throughout the empirical problems raised in the practical implementation of a model such as the MSG-model. I begin with the representation of technological constraints and producer behaviour.

The basic behavioural assumption is that producers maximize profits. Each sector produces a single output, and there is a one-to-one mapping between production sectors and types of output. Each one of the n outputs is produced by means of capital, labor and intermediate inputs, and the technological constraints can be represented by a well-behaved neoclassical production function. Under these conditions the technological constraints and the behaviour of producers can be neatly summarized by a unit cost function. Letting κ_j denote the unit cost of output in sector j, we get

$$(1) \qquad \kappa_j = \kappa_j(P_1,\ldots,P_n,W_j,\ R_j,\ \bar{P}_o,\ X_j),\ j=1,2,\ldots,n.$$

where $P_1,\ldots,P_n$ denote prices of outputs and thus intermediate inputs, W_j the wage rate in sector j, R_j the user cost of capital in sector j, $\bar{P}_o$ the price of "complementary" imports, and X_j the gross output level in sector j.

Except for Agriculture and Fishing, Johansen assumed profit maximization behaviour on the part of the producers. With the exception of these two sectors and Mining and Electricity Generation, the sectoral production functions were assumed by Johansen to exhibit constant returns to scale, i.e. that κ_j was independent of X_j. To simplify the exposition, I will assume constant returns to scale and profit-maximizing behaviour in all sectors.

In the original MSG-model there is very limited substitution possibilities between inputs. Thus, while the elasticity of substitution between capital and labor is assumed to be unity, it is set equal to zero between all pairs of intermediate inputs including complementary imports. This means that the unit cost functions, assuming constant returns to scale in all sectors, can be written

$$(1^*) \qquad \kappa_j = \kappa_j^*(W_j,R_j) + \sum_{i=1}^{n} P_i a_{ij} + \bar{P}_o b_{oj},\ j=1,2,\ldots,n$$

where $\kappa_j^*(\cdot)$, the "net" unit cost function, represents the minimum labor and capital cost per unit of output in sector j, while a_{ij} and b_j are Leontief input-output coefficients for domestically produced intermediate inputs and complementary imports, respectively. Moreover, producer equilibrium implies equality between P_j and κ_j for all j. That is

$$(2) \qquad P_j = \kappa_j^*(W_j, R_j) + \sum_{i=1}^{n} P_i a_{ij} + \bar{P}_o b_{oj}, \quad j=1,2,\ldots,n.$$

Given the unit cost function (1'), the input demand functions are directly given by Shephard's lemma. That is, the demand by sector j for labor (L_j), capital (K_j), domestically produced intermediate inputs (X_{ij}), and complementary imports $(\bar{M}_{oj})$ can be written

$$(3) \qquad L_j = \frac{\partial \kappa_j^*(\cdot)}{\partial W_j} X_j , \quad j = 1,2,\ldots,n$$

$$(4) \qquad K_j = \frac{\partial \kappa_j^*(\cdot)}{\partial R_j} X_j , \quad j = 1,2,\ldots,n$$

$$(5) \qquad X_{ij} = a_{ij} X_j , \qquad j = 1,2,\ldots,n$$

$$(6) \qquad \bar{M}_{oj} = b_{oj} X_j , \qquad j = 1,2,\ldots,n.$$

Before turning to the representation of final demand, a few words should be said about the sectoral wage and rental rates, i.e. W_j and R_j. Beginning with the wage rate, it should be noted that only one type of labor is distinguished in the MSG-model. Moreover, the formulation of the model implies that labor could costlessly move between sectors. This means that, in equilibrium, there should be no wage differentials across sectors. Yet the wage rates do differ across sectors in the MSG-model.

More precisely sectoral wage rates are defined by

$$(7) \qquad W_j = \omega_j W , \quad j = 1,2,\ldots,n$$

where ω_j is a parameter which differs across sectors, and W is an index of the overall wage level in the economy. In much the same way, the model contains a set of intersectoral profit differentials. Thus, even though capital is homogeneous and mobile, the net real rates of return on capital differ across sectors in the MSG-model.

Strictly speaking intersectoral wage and profit differentials are not consistent with the general specification of the MSG-model. This is, however, only true in a narrow sense. Johansen apparently did not believe that a model entirely based on Walrasian general equilibrium theory could explain the resource allocation pattern at a certain point in time in a real-world economy. In other words, his vision of the "true and complete" model was something much more elaborate than the MSG-model.

A more complete model would account for such phenomena as inter-sectoral differences in working conditions, uncertainty about future pros-pects, and degree of monopolization, i.e. phenomena which would produce intersectoral wage and profit differentials. Thus the MSG-model is just an approximation of a largely unknown "model", and the exogenous wage and profitability structures should be regarded as shorthand representations of phenomena which cannot be explained within the model.

This modelling strategy also reveals the purpose and emphasis of the MSG-model. Johansen was not particularly concerned with the estimation of possible welfare losses due to various distortions in the functioning of the economic system. Instead, he wanted the model to elucidate and pro-ject the sectoral reallocation of resources during a process of economic growth. Consequently, he emphasized the model's forecasting ability rather than its consistency with Walrasian general equilibrium theory. As I will point out in Section 3, this is in quite sharp contrast to the model-ling strategy adopted by some later CGE-modellers.

Turning now to our stylized MSG-model, and working in the spirit of Johansen's original formulation, the user cost of capital variables can be written

$$(8) \qquad R_j = P_{n+1}(\delta_j + \rho_j R), \quad j = 1, 2, \ldots, n$$

where P_{n+1} is a price index for an aggregated capital good, δ_j the rate of capital depreciation in sector j, and $\rho_j R$ the rate or real rate of return on capital in sector j. As ρ_j is an exogenously given parameter, the endogenous variable R can be interpreted as an index of the net rate of return on physical capital in the economy as a whole.

It should perhaps be pointed out that the formulation of eq. (8) implies that the composition of the capital stock is the same in all sectors. In the original MSG-model, however, a distinction is made between "Build-ings" and "Other capital goods", and the composition of the capital stock in terms of these two types of aggregated capital goods differs across sectors. However, the input-commodity composition of "Buildings" and "Other capital goods" is the same in all sectors, and is defined by the input-output coefficients of two "bookkeeping" sectors "producing" these capital-goods aggregates.

Dropping the sectoral heterogeneity of capital and letting the input-commodity composition of aggregated capital be determined by one single "bookkeeping" sector leads to the following definition of the price index of capital goods

$$(9) \qquad P_{n+1} = \sum_{i=1}^{n} P_i a_{i,n+1},$$

which completes the description of the supply side of the stylized MSG-model.

Next let us turn to the final-demand side of our model. Following Johansen's original formulation we assume that there is a set of per capita demand funtions such that household demand for commodity group i can be written

$$(10) \qquad C_i = N g_i(P_1, \ldots, P_n, Y/N), \quad i=1,1,\ldots,n$$

where C_i is total household demand for commodity i, N is the number of individuals, and Y is the total disposable income, net of savings, of the household sector.

The per capita demand functions are derived from utility maximization under a budget constraint. Under reasonable assumptions this means that consumption expenditures add up to disposable income (net of savings). Thus the following equation holds

$$(11) \qquad \sum_{i=1}^{n} P_i g_i(P_1, \ldots, P_n, Y/N) = Y/N.$$

It should be pointed out that the constant elasticity type of demand functions used in Johansen's numerical calculations do not identically satisfy eq. (11), a fact that Johansen of course was fully aware of.

Following the original MSG-model where government and net foreign demand for domestically produced goods and services as well as total net investments are exogenously determined, it only remains to specify the equilibrium conditions of our stylized MSG-model. Beginning with the markets for domestically produced commodity groups, these conditions become

(12) $\quad X_i = \sum_{j=1}^{n} a_{ij} X_j + C_i + (G_i + Z_i - M_i), \quad i = 1,2,\ldots,n$

where G_i is government demand, Z_i exports, and M_i imports of commodity group i. Similarly, the equilibrium "production" of the aggregated capital good is given by

(13) $\quad X_{n+1} = I + \sum_{j=1}^{n} \delta_j K_j$

where I is the exogenously given total net investment.

Like the original MSG-model, we take the total labor force and the total stock of capital to be exogenously determined. Consequently, the factor market equilibrium conditions can be written

(14) $\quad L = \sum_{j=1}^{n} L_j$

(15) $\quad K = \sum_{j=1}^{n} K_j$

where L and K are the exogenously given stocks of labor and capital, respectively.

Finally, the use in equilibrium of complementary imports is given by

(16) $\quad \bar{M}_o = \sum_{j=1}^{n} \bar{M}_{oj}, \quad j = 1,2,\ldots,n.$

Table 1 summarizes, in a condensed form, our stylized MSG-model.

Like other neoclassical general equilibrium models, the MSG-model determines only relative prices. Thus, the price system has to be normalized by an appropriate choice of numeraire. In the original MSG-model, the wage index, W, was set equal to unity. Adopting the same normalization here leaves us with $4n+5$ variables and $4n+5$ independent equations.

It should be noted that Y, the total consumption expenditure of the household sector, is implicitly determined by Walras' law. To see this, the producer equilibrium conditions should be multiplied by X_i and added

Table 1. A stylized MSG-model

___

Producer equilibrium

$$P_j = \kappa_j^*(W_j, R_j) + \sum_{i=1}^{n} P_i a_{ij} + \bar{P}_o b_{oj} \;, \quad j = 1, 2, \ldots, n$$

Product market equilibrium

$$X_i = \sum_{j=1}^{n+1} a_{ij} X_j + N g_i (P_1, \ldots, P_n, Y/N) + (G_i + Z_i - M_i), \quad i = 1, 2, \ldots, n$$

$$X_{n+1} = I + \sum_{j=1}^{n} \delta_j \frac{\partial \kappa_j^*(\cdot)}{\partial R_j} X_j$$

Factor market equilibrium

$$L = \sum_{j=1}^{n} \frac{\partial \kappa_j^*(\cdot)}{\partial W_j} X_j$$

$$K = \sum_{j=1}^{n} \frac{\partial \kappa_J^*(\cdot)}{\partial R_j} X_j$$

$$\bar{M}_o = \sum_{j=1}^{n} b_{oj} X_j$$

Definitional equations

$$P_{n+1} = \sum_{i=1}^{n} P_i a_{i, n+1}$$

$$R_j = P_{n+1}(\delta_j + \rho_j R), \quad j = 1, 2, \ldots, n$$

$$W_j = \omega_j W, \quad j = 1, 2, \ldots, n$$

Exogenous variables: $N, K, L, I, G_1, \ldots, G_n, Z_1, \ldots, Z_n, M_1, \ldots, M_n, \bar{P}_o$

Endogenous variables: $X_1, \ldots, X_{n+1}, \bar{M}_o, P_1, \ldots, P_{n+1}, W, W_1, \ldots, W_n,$
$R, R_1, \ldots, R_n, Y$

Number of equations: $4n + 5$

Number of endogenous variables: $4n + 6$

___

over all i, while the product market equilibrium conditions should be
multiplied by P_j and added over j. The results give us two expressions
for the value of total gross output. Since the net unit cost functions $\kappa_j^*(\cdot)$
are linearly homogeneous by assumption, eqs. (3), (4), (6), (9), (10),
(11), and (13) lead to the following representation of the economy's
budget constraint

$$(17) \quad \sum_{j=1}^{n} (W_j L_j + R_j K_j) = Y + \sum_{j=1}^{n} P_j G_j + P_{n+1}(I + \sum_{j=1}^{n} \delta_j K_j) +$$

$$+ \sum_{j=1}^{n} P_j (Z_j - M_j) - \bar{P}_o \bar{M}_o ,$$

where the left-hand side is the gross domestic factor income and the right-
hand side total expenditures on private and public consumption, gross
investments, and net export of goods and services.

A few properties of the MSG-model can be pointed out in connection
with eq. (17). The first is that the current account deficit (or surplus) to
some extent depends on the endogenous variables $\bar{M}_o$, i.e. the so-called
complementary imports. Thus, the economy's budget constraint is not
exogenously given, i.e. the loss (or gain) of foreign reserves is endogenously determined. It is a little hard to see the justification for this property, but given the model's lack of emphasis on foreign trade it is of negligible practical importance.

The second point is that the equality between overall savings and
investment is brought about by a suitable adjustment of the private consumption expenditures, i.e. the variable Y rather than by gross investments, public expenditures, or some combination of these variables. This
way of "closing" the model is somewhat arbitrary, and several other
approaches are conceivable.[2] It should be stressed, however, that the
alternative approaches are equally arbitrary. This of course stems from
the difficulty of incorporating a theory of savings and investment in a
static equilibrium framework.

The third point to note is that the tax and transfer system, as well as
the savings behaviour, is entirely implicit in the model. This approach,
which seems logical given the neglect of financial assets and markets, is
possible because there is only one aggregated household sector in the
model. But that also considerably limits the model's ability to elucidate

income distribution aspects.

Finally a few words should be said about the method used by Johansen for solving the MSG-model. The method essentially amounts to specifying log-linear approximations to the general equilibrium solution, and then solving the resulting linear equations for changes in the endogenous variables as functions of changes in the exogenous variables. This means that the solution does not describe the allocation of resources at a given point in time, but rather the relative rates of change of the endogenous variables from an initial allocation of resources. This way of solving the model, along with a focus on experiments where essentially all exogenous factors are simultaneously changed, gives the MSG-model the flavour of a growth model in spite of the fact that it is basically formulated as a static equilibrium model.

From a technical point of view Johansen's solution procedure has advantages and disadvantages. One advantage of this solution method is that it is very simple and cheap to apply. A disadvantage is that the results are affected by approximation errors, and these errors tend to increase with the magnitude of the changes in exogenous variables.

Considerable efforts have been spent on the development of solution methods for MSG-type models. That work involves elaborations of Johansen's approach as well as the development of algorithms capable of directly solving the model in its non-linear form. In the ensuing exposition, however, I will focus on extensions and applications of the MSG-model as such, and thus not comment further on the development of solution methods.

3.   The MSG-Model and the Development of CGE-Modelling

In recent years numerical models labelled "computable general equilibrium", or simply CGE, have become a widely used tool in quantitative economic analysis. Standard references in the field are Dixon (1982) and Dervis, de Melo and Robinson (1982). The main fields of application are analyses of economic structure and income distribution in developed and developing countries, public finance, energy economics, and international trade. I have already indicated that the MSG-model can be regarded as the first CGE-model. In this section I will try to justify that statement,

and identify some CGE-models which seem to have particularly strong
links to the MSG-model.

The definition of a CGE-model is not obvious, and there is no particular need to make a sharp distinction between CGE-models and other
econometric models except that CGE-models typically are nonstochastic.
There is, however, a number of economy-wide models designed for analysis of resource allocation problems which have so many important features
in common they can be regarded as a particular type of quantitative
economic model. Examples of the type of models I shall denote as "CGE-
models" are presented in Shoven and Whalley (1972), Kelley, Williamson
and Chetham (1972), Taylor and Black (1974), Hudson and Jorgenson
(1974), Whalley (1975), Staelin (1976), Whalley (1977), de Melo and
Dervis (1977), Lloyd (1978), de Melo (1978), Bergman (1978), Adelman
and Robinson (1978), Manne (1978), de Melo (1980), Bergman (1982),
Zalai (1982), Dixon (op.cit.), and Dervis, de Melo and Robinson (op.cit.).

One common feature of these models is their focus on the real side of
the economy and situations where the economy's resources are fully
utilized.[3] Another is that their supply and demand functions explicitly
reflect the behaviour of profit-maximizing producers and utility-maximizing consumers. A third common feature is that both quantities and
relative prices are endogenous to the models, and that the resource allocation patterns determined by the models have a strong flavour of Walrasian general equilibrium. Not all of these models, however, are fully consistent with the textbook general equilibrium model. Shorthand representations and ad hoc assumptions can be found in many of the CGE-models,
which like the MSG-model, primarily are designed for economic forecasting
and planning purposes. Nevertheless most of the authors characterize
their models as computable general equilibrium models.

On the basis of these quite broad and general criteria, the MSG-model
clearly can be classified as a CGE-model. Having established that, it is
natural to ask to what extent Johansen's MSG-model has influenced the
development of CGE-modelling. A question such as this is generally difficult to answer, and I have no intention of trying to give a final judgement. Some rather strong links between the MSG-model and CGE-modelling
can, however, be identified.

First of all it is reasonable to claim that the ORANI model of the
Australian economy (Dixon et.al. (1977) and Dixon et.al. (1982)) is a
very close relative to the MSG-model. This is pointed out by the authors,

and already becomes obvious after a short glance at ORANI. Thus, like
the MSG-model, ORANI essentially is a model of the sectoral allocation of
capital and labor, as well as of the distribution of sectoral outputs
between different uses. It is primarily a tool for economic forecasting and
ex ante evaluations of economic policy measures, and similarly to the MSG-
model has no explicit representation of the tax and transfer system or
the links between factor incomes and the disposable income of the
household sector. Consequently, neither the MSG-model nor ORANI treats
the distribution of income across different types of households. Moreover,
ORANI is solved by means of the linearization procedure which Johansen
used to solve the MSG-model.[4]

In spite of these similarities there are also important differences
between ORANI and the MSG-model. First of all, ORANI provides a lot
more detail, sectoral as well as regional. Thus, while 20 production
sectors are distinguished in the MSG-model, ORANI explicitly treats more
than 100 production sectors in different regions. Another difference is
that ORANI allows for joint production of several outputs in the agricultural sectors. Moreover, several types of labor are distinguished in
ORANI, while there is only one type of labor in the MSG-model. A more
important difference between the models concerns the treatment of foreign
trade. While foreign trade is essentially determined exogenously in the
MSG-model, exports and imports are endogenously determined in ORANI.
Moreover, unlike the MSG-model, ORANI is designed to be a tool for
analysis and evaluation of economic policy, both in the short run and the
long run. None of these differences, however, represent a major deviation from the modelling approach represented by the MSG-model.

On the basis of these observations it is reasonable to characterize
ORANI as a significantly extended and elaborated version of Johansen's
MSG-model. An equally direct influence can be seen on CGE-modelling
in Sweden. For example, the model for long-term economic projections
developed by Restad (1976) is a direct application of the original MSG-
model to Swedish data, although it also incorporated an endogenous
foreign trade sector. A direct influence can also be seen in my own work
on Swedish CGE-models (Bergman (1978, 1982, and 1983)). These models,
designed for analysis of various energy policy issues, contain an elaborate treatment of foreign trade as well as of energy demand. However, for
all the Swedish models except Bergman (1978), numerical solutions are
obtained without making use of Johansen's linearization method.

The models discussed so far are all models of highly developed industrialized economies, but there are also many CGE-models concerned with
developing countries. In that particular branch of the literature, the
models by Taylor and Black (1974) and Staelin (1976) seem to be most
closely related to the MSG-model. In both cases explicit references to
Johansen's MSG-model are made, and numerical solutions are obtained by
means of Johansen's linearization technique. Yet there are important differences. Both Taylor-Black and Staelin, being concerned with the impact
of particular trade policies on an open economy, made foreign trade an
endogenous part of their models. Johansen, on the other hand, took
foreign trade to be essentially exogenous to the model, and refrained from
using the model for policy evaluation. Moreover, while the MSG-model
portrays an essentially competitive economy with mobile labor and capital,
Staelin explicitly incorporated noncompetitive pricing assumptions into his
model while Taylor-Black treated sectoral capital stocks as exogenously
given. Despite the differences these models should still be regarded as
direct extensions of the MSG-model.

In a number of papers Dervis, de Melo and Robinson presented their
own CGE-models of developing countries.[5] Although references to
Johansen are frequent and the influence of the MSG-model is visible,
these models differ considerably from the MSG-model. For example, Dervis
(1975) and de Melo and Dervis (1977) dealt with explicitly intertemporal
models of open economies. In de Melo (1978) several primary factors of
production were distinguished, and as the number of factors exceeded the
number of traded goods with exogenously given prices, the model allows
complete specialization according to comparative advantages. The model
presented in de Melo (1980) focuses on income distribution issues, and
hence incorporates an endogenous determination of the disposable income
of several socio-economic groups.

A common feature of all the aforementioned models, including the
MSG-model, is a focus on future, hypothetical resource allocation patterns
for a national economy. Given an initial point and assuming specific
changes in domestic resources, technology, trade policies, etc., these
models try to determine the resulting resource allocation pattern. From
this point of view the work by Kelley, Williamson and Chetham (1972)
represents a completely different approach. Their model is designed for
counterfactual simulations of Japan's economic development during the
period 1887-1916. Similar approaches are adopted by Kelley and Williamson

(1980), Shishido (1983) in a model of Japan, and Karlström (1982) in a model of Sweden.

The links between these models and Johansen's MSG-model are not very strong, although the authors do make general references to Johansen's original study. Their focus on a historical period obviously leads to particular difficulties, since the model must be able to replicate the actual development of the economy during the period in question, given that the exogenous variables equal their historical values. In contrast, the MSG-model, as well as the other models discussed so far, are only "calibrated" to replicate the state of the economy at one particular point in time, the base year.[6] Moreover, the historical models, for obvious reasons, include a relatively detailed treatment of factor migration and income distribution, i.e. aspects which are not treated in any detail in the MSG-model.

A group of CGE-models even more independent of the MSG-model are presented in Shoven and Whalley (1972), Whalley (1975), Whalley (1977), Feltenstein (forthcoming), and Scarf and Shoven (1983). The modelling tradition represented by these and related models seems to originate in Scarf's algorithm for obtaining explicit numerical solutions to general equilibrium models and Harberger's analyses of the welfare costs of various types of distortions in the functioning of the economy. As a consequence, the formulation of these models very closely follows the "rules of the game" established by Walrasian general equilibrium theory. Johansen, on the other hand, was more concerned about the empirical relevance of the model, and did not hesitate to use shorthand representations of factors and mechanisms that could not be explicitly incorporated into his model.

Still another group of CGE-models has been developed in connection with analyses of the economic consequences of changing energy prices and energy policies. Standard references are Hudson and Jorgenson (1974) and Manne (1978). My own work, referred to above, also belongs to this category of models.

In comparison to the MSG-model, these models have an elaborate treatment of technology. Thus Hudson and Jorgenson make use of translog production functions where capital and labor as well as energy and materials are substitutable factors of production, while Manne represents the substitutability of capital, labor, and energy by means of nested CES/ Cobb-Douglas production functions. In addition, Manne has modelled the technology of the energy supply sector in great detail using an activity analysis type of approach. Moreover, both Manne (1978) and Bergman (1982) make use of a so-called "putty-clay" representation of technology in order to explicitly model the gradual adjustment of factor proportions over time as relative factor prices change.

These energy models represent a variety of modelling traditions. Manne's model can be seen as an elaborate model for technology assessment within the frame of an intertemporal optimization approach. Hudson's and Jorgenson's model, on the other hand, is essentially a medium- and long-term econometric forecasting model which is extended by a submodel of interindustry transactions. In both of these models there are few, if any, direct links to the MSG-model. My own work, on the other hand, is directly based on the MSG-model.

Except for the work by Kelley et al. and similar related approaches, most of the models discussed so far are policy-oriented, i.e. they are intended to be used in connection with analyses of various types of economic policy. The types of policy instruments the authors have in mind are generally indirect measures such as taxes and tariffs. Johansen, on the other hand, seemed to regard the MSG-model also as a tool for economic planning where direct control of resource allocation decisions could be an important ingredient.

The model of the Hungarian economy presented in Zalai (1982) is an extension of the MSG-model in that direction. Drawing on the equivalence between competitive equilibrium and optimum resource allocation, Zalai points out the close relation between MSG-type of models and the programming models traditionally used in Hungarian central planning. He also shows that a suitable reinterpretation of the resource allocation mechanism makes his CGE-model, which is a direct extension of the MSG-model, fit into the central planning framework of the Hungarian economy.

This brief survey is by no means complete. There are many additional CGE-models worth mentioning, and Johansen's MSG-model has influenced economic modelling in other ways than those indicated here. Yet two conclusions seem to be justified on the basis of this discussion. The first is that Johansen very early conceived a modelling approach which now is the basis for a rapidly growing field in economics, i.e. CGE-modelling. The second is that much, although not all, of the work in the CGE-modelling tradition has very strong, direct links to Johansen's MSG-model.

Looking at the development of CGE-modelling and its relation to the

MSG-model, however, also raises a question. Johansen presented his study as early as 1960, yet it appears that CGE-modelling only started in the beginning of the 1970's, not gaining momentum until the end of that decade. Why was the impact of the MSG-model so very limited for more than one decade? Of course one can only speculate about the reasons.

One possible explanation could be that the conditions of stable economic growth prevailing in most countries during the 1960's made the sectoral dimension of economic growth seem relatively unimportant. There were simply too few interesting economic problems which could be analyzed by means of MSG type of models. This explanation is consistent with the rapid growth of CGE-modelling during the latter part of the 1970's when a lot of attention was focused on the resource allocation mechanism in national economies. After the 1973/74 oil price hike, a few years of poor economic performance, and the entrance of the so-called NIC's on international markets where the early industrialized countries had previously dominated, the demand increased for the type of analyses for which CGE-type models are best suited.

Another, perhaps complementary, explanation is that the development of solution algorithms for general equilibrium problems, as well as relatively cheap computers, did not really start until the beginning of the 1970's.

A third explanation could be that economists interested in resource allocation models were too busy with linear programming models to pay any significant attention to Johansen's MSG-model at the time it first appeared. But by the middle of the 1970's the inherent problems of modelling resource allocation in national economies with linear programming models[7] had been well-experienced in practice and were finally understood by many model builders. The time was ripe to look for something else. Thus the lag between the appearance and the full appreciation of the MSG-model might simply reflect Johansen's ability to have conceived the problems with linear programming much earlier than his fellow economic modellers.

4. Extensions of the MSG-model

In the previous section I briefly indicated a number of suggested extensions to the original framework of the MSG-model. For instance, most of the models mentioned have an endogenous foreign trade sector, and some of them distinguish several types of labor, while others include substitutability between primary and intermediate inputs. The purpose of this section is to show how these extensions have actually been carried out, as well as to indicate some problems and alternative approaches.

Our discussion of extensions to the MSG-model will be limited in at least two ways. First we shall confine ourselves to models which are closely related to the MSG-model. On the basis of the discussion in the preceding section, this means that the discussion will concern ORANI, the Swedish models, and the models of developing countries presented by Taylor and Black, Staelin and Dervis, and de Melo and Robinson. Second, our discussion will be limited to extensions of major importance.

Clearly, the relative importance of various extensions of a given modelling approach is a matter of judgement. Some extensions can be quite straightforward from the theoretical point of view, yet still manage to significantly increase the empirical content and practical applicability of the model. A case in point is the increase in scale and detail represented by ORANI. Other extensions might raise difficult theoretical and methodological problems without being particularly demanding in terms of data and computing resources.

The following exposition will focus on a particular extension of the latter type, namely the incorporation of an endogenous foreign trade sector into CGE-type models. This is not only an interesting issue in itself, but also an extension of the MSG-framework which Johansen seemingly found very interesting.[8] In order to make the exposition as clear as possible, I shall make extensive use of the "stylized" MSG-model presented in Section 2.

4.1 Endogenous foreign trade

Given that the stylized MSG-model presented in Section 2 is to be converted into a model of an open economy, the most straightforward way to proceed is by adopting the so-called "small country" assumption. This

means that the goods produced in the economy are perfect substitutes for
goods produced in other countries, and that the prices of tradeables are
assumed to be exogenously given by world market conditions. Assuming
for simplicity that all sectors produce tradeables, the small country
assumption therefore implies

$$(18) \qquad P_j = VP_j^W, \qquad j=1,2,\ldots,n$$

where P_j, as before, is the domestic price of good j, P_j^W is the world
world market price of good j, and V is the exchange rate. To make things
simple, we normalize the domestic price system by setting V equal to
unity. If only eq. (18) is added to the equations in Table 1 the model will
clearly be overdetermined. It is then natural to drop the assumption about
exogenously determined sectoral net exports, i.e. the differences
(Z_j-M_j). Adoption of these changes, however, drastically changes the
properties of the model. The production decisions, as well as the determination of domestic factor incomes, will now be independent of domestic
demand conditions. Moreover, there will be complete specialization in the
domestic production system. This can be explained in the following way.

Due to competition the equilibrium unit production cost cannot be lower
than the exogenously given price of output in any sector. At the equilibrium factor prices, and an arbitrary set of world prices $P_1^W,\ldots,P_n^W$,
some sectors may earn losses. Hence, the producer equilibrium condition
in Table 1 should be written

$$(19) \qquad P_j^W \le \kappa_j^*(W_j,R_j) + \sum_{i=1}^{n} P_i^W a_{ij} + \bar{P}_o b_{oj}, \qquad j=1,2,\ldots,n.$$

However, the equilibrium output level in the sectors where eq. (19) holds
with strict inequality must be zero. With two primary factors and $n \ge 2$,
there will be positive output in at most two sectors, while the equilibrium
output level thus is zero in $n-2$ sectors. This is sometimes denoted as
"the overspecialization problem".

Once the equilibrium factor prices and output levels are determined,
the domestic factor incomes are determined as well. Since the prices of
goods are exogenously given, this means that the domestic demand for
goods also is determined. The domestic demand pattern, however, is most
likely to differ from the domestic output pattern. Consequently there will

be foreign trade; goods in excess supply will be exported and goods in excess demand will be imported. Since domestic spending is constrained by factor incomes and net transfers from abroad, the sum of net foreign factor incomes, net foreign transfers, and export earnings will equal import expenditures. Thus it holds that

$$(20) \qquad \sum_{j=1}^{n} P_j^W (Z_j - M_j) - \bar{P}_o \bar{M}_o = D$$

where D is an exogenously given (positive or negative) current account surplus.[9] Observe that the sector net export, i.e. $(Z_j - M_j)$, is now an endogenous variable in the model.

The overspecialization problem has been handled in many different ways, and there are many different attitudes towards this "problem". The approach adopted by Taylor and Black (1974) and others[10] is to take the allocation of capital as exogenously given. Retaining our earlier assumptions about the sectoral production functions, this means that the technology exhibits decreasing returns to scale in the variable factors. By suitable parametrization there is then, in general, a set of sector production levels at which the marginal cost is equal to the exogenously given product price in each sector. Consequently in equilibrium there will be positive production in all sectors.

In terms of our stylized MSG-model this "solution" to the overspecialization problem means that the profit-maximizing behaviour of the producers is represented by upward sloping output supply functions and downward sloping input demand functions. Thus by Hotelling's lemma we obtain

$$(21) \qquad X_j = \frac{\partial \pi_j (\cdot)}{\partial P_j^W}, \qquad j = 1, 2, \ldots, n$$

$$(22) \qquad L_j = -\frac{\partial \pi_j (\cdot)}{\partial W_j}, \qquad j = 1, 2, \ldots, n$$

where $\pi_j(\cdot)$ is the sectoral profit function, which is well defined once the constant returns to scale assumption is dropped.[11]

With this approach the model produces solutions which are "realistic" in the sense that equilibrium output levels are positive in all sectors. On the other hand it requires that the allocation of capital be exogenously determined. Thus, if one wants to retain the long-run nature of the model, i.e. retain the endogeneity of the sectoral allocation of capital, this is not a very useful approach. This was also pointed out by Johansen.[12]

The studies by Norman and Wergeland (1977) and de Melo (1978) represent another specific approach to the design of long-run CGE-models with endogenous foreign trade. Their models are primarily designed for elucidating the economy's comparative advantages, and consequently, zero equilibrium output levels in some sectors are taken as the logical consequence of the factor endowments and technological constraints of the economy in question. One can remark that these authors essentially base their models on standard Heckscher-Ohlin theory, accepting that the models will have only limited explanatory power with respect to the short- and medium-term allocation of capital and labor across a large number of sectors. In particular, they are not prepared to incorporate ad hoc assumptions in order to secure "realistic" solutions.

Johansen, on the other hand, did not find solutions exhibiting complete specialization in the production system compatible with his vision of the "true", but largely unknown, model. Thus, without proposing a specific modelling approach he pointed out some factors which would prevent "an unrealistic degree of specialization"[13] and which should be taken into account in long-run MSG-type models with endogenous foreign trade. For example, there may be decreasing returns to scale in some sectors, and there may be other sectors facing price-dependent export demand functions rather than parametric world market prices. Moreover, considerations of risk and uncertainty would call for some diversification in the production system.

Later CGE-modellers have to a large extent shared Johansen's concern about "realistic" solutions, and they have also incorporated some of the factors mentioned by Johansen in their models. This applies to the most commonly adopted approach, although the direct inspiration came from Armington (1969).

The hypothesis put forward by Armington is that goods of the same type but with different countries of origin are not perfect substitutes. According to this hypothesis, each country produces a unique set of goods which to a varying degree are substitutes for, but not identical to, goods produced in other countries. In other words the notion of a small, price-taking economy producing goods identical to goods produced in other countries is replaced.

With respect to our stylized MSG-model, the Armington assumption can be represented as follows: Assume for simplicity that all agents, producers as well as consumers, have the same (homothetic) preferences concerning various combinations of imported and domestically produced goods of type i. There is then a single composite of goods demanded by domestic users from the two sources of supply. The price-index of this composite good, P_i^D, can be defined as the unit cost function corresponding to the uniform preference function and written

$$(23) \qquad P_i^D = \psi_i(P_i, P_i^W), \quad i = 1,2,\ldots,n.$$

On the basis of Shephard's lemma, the product market equilibrium conditions of our stylized MSG-model now become

$$(24) \qquad X_i = \frac{\partial \psi_i(\cdot)}{\partial P_i} \left(\sum_{j=1}^{n+1} a_{ij} X_j + C_i + G_i \right) + Z_i, \quad i=1,2,\ldots,n$$

$$(25) \qquad M_i = \frac{\partial \psi_i(\cdot)}{\partial P_i^W} \left(\sum_{j=1}^{n+1} a_{ij} X_j + C_i + G_i \right), \quad i=1,2,\ldots,n$$

while the current account constraint becomes

$$(26) \qquad \sum_{i=1}^{n} P_i Z_i - \sum_{i=1}^{n} P_i^W M_i - \sum_{j=1}^{n} \bar{P}_j \bar{M}_j = D$$

Hence, the Armington assumption leads to the incorporation of price-dependent import demand functions. Nevertheless, the basic question concerns the determination of exports: unless a set of additional equations can be incorporated, the model will be underdetermined. In order to solve this problem, two approaches have been adopted.

The first is to treat the rest of the world in the same fashion as the "home" country. That is, the rest of the world is assumed to have a price-dependent import demand function as well. But from the point of view of the "home" country, that is nothing but an export demand function. Consequently, the model is extended with price-dependent export demand equations.

Indeed CGE-models incorporating the Armington assumption have some nice features.[14] The overspecialization problem is taken care of without arbitrary restrictions on the allocation of capital or other primary resources. In addition, these models incorporate intra-industry trade, a phenomenon which is quite apparent in the real world but difficult to reconcile with the standard small economy model. Yet there are good reasons for being quite critical about the use of price-dependent export demand functions in models of small open economies.

One reason is that the theoretical foundation for the Armington assumption is rather weak. It is true that intra-industry trade can often be observed even at the most disaggregated level of commodity classification, and that "the law of one price" is hard to reconcile with real world observations. It is also true that there exists ample evidence that small countries also produce goods with a considerable degree of uniqueness. Nevertheless these observations are slightly beside the point. The question is not what an economy does produce, but what it could produce. That is, given a suitable time of adjustment and appropriate factor endowments, foreign producers should be able to produce perfect substitutes for the goods produced by domestic producers. Hence, in a long-run CGE-model the best approximation of real world conditions may, after all, be to assume that the goods produced in the small economy are perfect substitutes for the goods produced in other countries.

Another reason for the reluctance to apply Armington export demand functions to CGE-models is that they make the economy's terms of trade endogenous. This means that the home country can make welfare gains by levying taxes on its own exports. Hence, the properties of such a model differ significantly from the properties of the standard small economy model. Moreover, the magnitude of these welfare gains critically depends on the price elasticity parameters of the export demand functions.

The second approach to the determination of exports is to assume that the supply of exports is less than perfectly elastic. With such a specification of the model the assumption about perfectly elastic export demand, and thus exogenously given terms of trade, is retained. From the point of view of modelling, export supply functions can, of course, be derived in many different ways. In de Melo and Robinson (1980), for instance, a market penetration type of argument is offered as a rationale for using logistic functions to determine the ratio of exports to sectoral outputs. On the other hand, Bergman (1983), Condon et al. (1984), and Bergman and Por (forthcoming) derive such ratios as a part of the profit maximization process. The underlying assumption is that domestic sectoral output is a composite of goods for the domestic market and goods for export markets, and that one type of good can be transformed into the other at a diminishing marginal rate of transformation.[15]

In terms of our stylized MSG-model this approach is as follows: Domestic sectoral output, X_i, is made up of goods for the domestic market, H_i, and goods for export markets, Z_i. Assuming that the transformation function is linearly homogeneous, the price of composite output can be written

$$(27) \qquad P_i = \chi_i(P_i^H, P_i^Z), \quad i = 1,2,\ldots,n$$

where $\chi_i(\cdot)$ is the unit revenue function derived from the transformation function, P_i^Z is the world market price of the export good[16], and P_i^H is the endogenous price of goods for the domestic market.

In accordance with Shephard's lemma, the supply of the two types of goods given the supply of the composite goods is determined by the partial derivatives of $\chi_i(\cdot)$. Retaining for the moment the Armington import functions, the product market equilibrium condition of the stylized MSG-model becomes

$$(28) \qquad \frac{\partial \chi_i(\cdot)}{\partial P_i^H} X_i = \frac{\partial \psi_i(\cdot)}{\partial P_i^H} \left(\sum_{i=1}^{n+1} a_{ij} X_j + C_i + G_i \right)$$

while the current account constraint can be written

$$(29) \qquad \sum_{i=1}^{n} P_i^Z \frac{\partial \chi_i(\cdot)}{\partial P_i^Z} X_i - \sum_{i=1}^{n} P_i^W M_i - \sum_{j=1}^{n} \bar{P}_i \bar{M}_i = D.$$

With this specification of the model, determinate solutions exhibiting positive production in all sectors and intra-industry trade will be obtained. Moreover the economy's terms of trade are exogenously given. The real question, however, concerns the economic assumptions behind the transformation function defining the composite output. In a short-run perspective it is quite reasonable to assume that there are minor differences between equally classified goods supplied to different markets, and that producers cannot immediately and costlessly transform one type of good into another. In a long-run perspective, however, the microeconomic

arguments for the existence of transformation functions of the type discussed here are not very strong.

Nevertheless, export supply functions and Armington import demand
functions, can be justified in long-run CGE-models implemented on aggregated data. The argument in favour, however, is not a microeconomic
one. Rather these functions are adopted because of their ability to reflect
changes in the composition of large commodity aggregates across equilibria.
Now, however, the underlying assumptions are: that there are many
goods and many factors, that domestically produced goods are perfect
substitutes for goods produced in other countries, and that domestic
producers face parametric world market prices for tradeables.

For a model builder like Johansen, who primarily is concerned about
the model's ability to replicate the economy's actual development, the
acceptability of the export supply – import demand approach should
essentially be an empirical issue. But for modellers primarily interested in
normative studies, the lack of a solid microeconomic foundation tends to
make this appoach considerably less attractive. Thus there does not yet
seem to be any generally accepted approach for treating foreign trade in
long-run CGE-models.

4.2 Input substitution, heterogeneous labor, and budget constraints

In the literature on CGE-modelling many additional extensions to the
original MSG-framework can be found. It is neither possible nor necessary
to provide a complete survey here. Instead I shall briefly indicate some
of these extensions, and show how they can be incorporated into our stylized MSG-model.

In the original MSG-model Johansen imposed quite strong restrictions
on the substitutability between various inputs. This is demonstrated by
the unit cost function given in eq. (1'). Later CGE-type models have
included less restrictive specifications of technology. For instance Hudson
and Jorgenson (1974) used translog production functions which were
separable into four types of aggregated inputs (capital, labor, energy,
and materials). The technology description in ORANI (Dixon et.al.
(1982)) is quite elaborate, using a nested production function specification which allows substitution within different categories of inputs. Manne

(1978) and Bergman (1978, 1982 and 1983) make use of nested CES/Cobb-Douglas production functions which allow substitution between capital, labor, and energy.[17]

Returning to our stylized MSG-model, these extensions can be represented by a reformulation of eqs. (5) and (6). That is, the constant returns to scale property is retained, but all inputs are in principle substitutable. This means that on the basis of Shephard's lemma the demand for intermediate inputs can be written

$$(30) \qquad X_{ij} = \frac{\partial \kappa_j(\cdot)}{\partial P_j^D} X_j, \qquad i,j = 1,2,\ldots,n$$

$$(31) \qquad \bar{M}_{oj} = \frac{\partial \kappa_j(\cdot)}{\partial \bar{P}_o} X_j, \qquad j = 1,2,\ldots,n.$$

Within the frame of the elaborated description of technology, Dixon et al. (1982), Dervis, de Melo and Robinson (1982), and others distinguish several categories of labor. They assume that the production functions are separable into aggregated labor and other inputs, and that the labor aggregate is defined by a linearly homogeneous function. These models thus contain an endogenous determination of the sectoral wage structure implied by eq. (7) in the stylized MSG-model. Thus, that equation is replaced by

$$(32) \qquad W_j = \phi_j(w_1,\ldots,w_q), \qquad j = 1,2,\ldots,n$$

where $\phi_j(\cdot)$ represents the minimum cost of labor per unit of output in sector j and $w_1 \ldots w_q$ represent the wage rates of different types of labor.[18]

This also means that there will be several different labor markets in the model's economy. The equilibrium condition of these labor markets can be written

$$(33) \qquad L_s = \sum_{j=1}^{n} \frac{\partial \kappa_j(\cdot)}{\partial w_j} \cdot \frac{\partial \phi_j(\cdot)}{\partial w_s}, \qquad s = 1,2,\ldots,q$$

where the first part of the right-hand side represents the cost-minimizing demand for "aggregated" labor per unit of output in sector j, and the

second part represents the cost-minimizing demand for labor of type s per
unit of aggregated labor in sector j.

At this degree of detail it would, at least in principle, be possible to
go one step further and identify different types of households. Households would then differ in terms of their ownership of capital and various
types of labor, and their budget constraints would be determined by the
prices of these factors. A step in that direction is, for instance, taken in
Dervis, de Melo and Robinson (1982). The data problems and the difficulties representing the tax and transfer system without running into too
much detail seem to have discouraged most CGE-modellers from extending
their models in this direction. Major exceptions can, of course, be found
among those CGE-modellers who particularly focus on public finance problems.

In Table 2 an example of an extended version of our stylized MSG-
model is presented. It summarizes the discussion of extensions to the
original MSG-framework.

5. Concluding remarks

This survey could easily be extended by reporting on several other
aspects of the modelling approach represented by the MSG-model. One
obvious topic would be the methods chosen to extend the model to an
explicit time dimension. Another topic would be "global" models designed
to elucidate the pattern of international trade and/or the welfare effects
of various types of trade policies. A third possible topic would be the
models which focus on factor migration, and a fourth would be the attempts
to incorporate disequilibrium phenomena into MSG-type models. However,
the exposition so far should be sufficient to justify my initial statements
that there is indeed a considerable amount of current economic modelling
with very strong links to Leif Johansen's MSG-model.

If one was to proceed a step further and try to estimate the degree of
influence of the MSG-model on the development of various existing CGE-
models, it seems that two broad categories of models should be identified.
One of these categories consists of models primarily aimed at projecting
the actual development of the economy under various assumptions concerning exogenous conditions. Though the authors of these models make

Table 2. An extended version of the stylized MSG model

Producer equilibrium

$$P_j = \kappa_j (W_j, R_j, P_1^D, \ldots, P_n^D, \bar{P}_j), \quad j = 1, 2, \ldots, n$$

$$H_j = \frac{\partial \chi_j(\cdot)}{\partial P_j^H} X_j, \quad j = 1, 2, \ldots, n$$

$$Z_j = \frac{\partial \chi_j(\cdot)}{\partial P_j^Z} X_j, \quad j = 1, 2, \ldots, n$$

Product market equilibrium

a. Domestically produced goods

$$H_i = \frac{\partial \psi_i(\cdot)}{\partial P_i^H} (\sum_{j=1}^{n+1} \frac{\partial \kappa_j(\cdot)}{\partial P_i^D} X_j + N g_i (P_1^D, \ldots, P_n^D, Y/N) + G_i),$$

$$i = 1, 2, \ldots, n$$

b. Imported goods

$$M_i = \frac{\partial \psi_i(\cdot)}{\partial P_i^W} (\sum_{j=1}^{n+1} \frac{\partial \kappa_j(\cdot)}{\partial P_i^D} X_j + N g_i (P_1^D, \ldots, P_n^D, Y/N) + G_i),$$

$$i = 1, 2, \ldots, n$$

c. Capital goods

$$X_{n+1} = I + \sum_{j=1}^{n} \delta_j \frac{\partial \kappa_k(\cdot)}{\partial R_j} X_j$$

Factor market equilibrium

$$L_s = \sum_{j=1}^{n} \frac{\partial \kappa_j(\cdot)}{\partial W_j} \cdot \frac{\partial \phi_j(\cdot)}{\partial w_s}, \quad s = 1, 2, \ldots, q$$

$$K = \sum_{j=1}^{n} \frac{\partial \kappa_j(\cdot)}{\partial R_j} X_j$$

Table 2 continued

$$\bar{M}_o = \sum_{j=1}^{n} \frac{\partial \varkappa_j(\cdot)}{\partial \bar{P}_o} X_j$$

Current account constraint

$$\sum_{i=1}^{n} P_i^Z Z_i - \sum_{i=1}^{n} P_i^W M_i - \bar{P}_o \bar{M}_o = D$$

Definitional equations

$$P_{n+1} = \sum_{i=1}^{n} P_i^D a_{i,n+1}$$

$$R_j = P_{n+1}(\delta_j + p_j R), \quad j = 1, 2, \ldots, n$$

$$W_j = \phi_j(w_1, \ldots, w_q), \quad j = 1, 2, \ldots, n$$

$$P_i = \chi_i(P_i^H, P_i^Z), \quad i = 1, 2, \ldots, n$$

$$P_i^D = \phi_i(P_i^H, P_i^W), \quad i = 1, 2, \ldots, n$$

Exogenous variables: N, K, $L_1, \ldots, L_q$, $G_1, \ldots, G_n$, $P_1^W, \ldots, P_n^W$,

$$P_1^Z, \ldots, P_n^Z, \bar{P}_o, D$$

Endogenous variables: $X_1, \ldots, X_{n+1}$, $H_1, \ldots, H_n$, $M_1, \ldots, M_n$,

$$Z_1, \ldots, Z_n, \bar{M}_o, P_1, \ldots, P_{n+1},$$

$$P_1^H, \ldots, P_n^H, P_1^D, \ldots, P_n^D, W_1, \ldots, W_n,$$

$$w_1, \ldots, w_q, R_1, \ldots, R_n, R, Y$$

Number of equations: $9n + q + 5$

Number of endogenous variables: $9n + q + 5$.

---

extensive use of Walrasian general equilibrium concepts, they often include ad hoc assumptions and shorthand representations, generally with the explicit purpose of improving the model's forecasting ability. In my view, these are the models which have been directly developed in the tradition established by the MSG-model, and these models could clearly be denoted "Johansen models". Obvious examples are the models of Dixon and de Melo, Dervis and Robinson.

The other broad category of CGE-models is made up of models primarily designed for studies of efficient resource allocations and the welfare effects of various economic policies. The model builders of this category, for instance, Norman, Scarf, Shoven, and Whalley, tend to emphasize theoretical consistency rather than forecasting ability, even when their underlying theoretical model is fairly simple. The basic modelling approach adopted in these models has much in common with the MSG-model, but the developments in this category have mainly had other sources of inspiration than Johansen's MSG-model.

Of course the current existence of two separate branches of CGE-modelling is somewhat dissatisfying; ideally models used for normative analyses should also have good forecasting ability. It seems to me that a research enterprise in Johansen's spirit would be to improve the forecasting ability of CGE-models by elaborating their theoretical framework. That is, to build models which to a very large extent are based on economic theory but not necessarily on the static Walrasian model of a competitive economy.

Appendix

Definition of symbols

X_j Gross output in sector j

H_j Output of goods for domestic use in sector j

Z_j Output of goods for export in sector j

M_j Import of goods with the same classification as the domestic goods produced in sector j

$\bar{M}_{oj}$ Complementary imports for direct use in sector j

$\bar{M}_o$ Total complementary imports

I Total net investment

C_j Household consumption of goods with the classification j

G_j Public consumption of goods with the classification j

P_j Price of gross output in sector j

P_j^H Price of output for domestic use, produced in sector j

P_j^D Price of composite goods for domestic use with the classification j

P_j^W World market price of goods with the classification j

P_j^Z World market price of exports with the classification j

$\bar{P}_o$ World market price of complementary imports

$\bar{P}_{oj}$ World market price of complementory imports for direct use in sector j

W_j Wage index in sector j

w_s Wage rate for labor of category s

R Index of the real rate of return on capital

Y Disposable income (less savings) in the household sector

N Number of individuals in the economy

D Current account surplus

Notes

1) The further development and application of the MSG-model itself inside Norway are discussed by Longva, Lorentsen and Olsen (1985) and Larsen and Schreiner (1985) in this volume.

2) See for instance Rattsø (1982) for a discussion of the properties of various "macro closures" in MSG-type models.

3) There are several CGE-models with real wages that are fixed and thus a labor market that does not clear.

4) In the terminology of some authors this means that ORANI is a "Johansen model".

5) Dervis, de Melo and Robinson (1982) to a large extent is a summing up of the experience gained in that work.

6) However, in Johansen (1974) there is a careful evaluation of the MSG-model's ability to replicate the actual development of the Norwegian economy during the period 1950-63.

7) A critical survey of linear programming models of resource allocation can be found in Taylor (1975).

8) See Johansen (1974), p. 184-187.

9) This surplus reflects net foreign transfers and factor incomes in equilibrium.

10) See for instance de Melo and Dervis (1977) and de Melo and Robinson (1980).

11) By assumption the sectoral capital demand functions are dropped.

12) See Johansen (1974), p. 186.

13) See Johansen (1974), p. 187.

14) Examples of such models are ORANI (Dixon (1982)) and the open-economy model presented in Dervis, de Melo and Robinson (1982), ch. 7.

15) In ORANI a similar approach is used to represent the joint output nature of agricultural production.

16) Observe that exports and imports with the classification i are not identical goods. Consequently their prices may differ, although they are both exogenously given.

17) Manne (1978) and Bergman (1982 and 1983) also incorporated the so-called putty-clay hypothesis.

18) It should perhaps be pointed out that Johansen stressed intersectoral differences in working conditions rather than quality differences within the labor force as an explanation for the observed intersectoral wage differentials.

References

Adelman, I. and S. Robinson (1977), Income-Distribution-Policies-in Developing Countries: A Case Study of Korea, Stanford University Press, Stanford.

Armington, P. (1969), "A Theory of Demand for Products Distinguished by Place of Production", IMF Staff Papers 16, 159-178.

Bergman, L. (1978), "Energy Policy in a Small Open Economy: The Case of Sweden", RR-78-16, International Institute for Applied Systems Analysis, Laxenburg, Austria.

Bergman, L. (1982), "A System of Computable General Equilibrium Models for a Small Open Economy", Mathematical Modelling 3, 421-435.

Bergman, L. (1983), "Structural Change and External Shocks: Some Simulations Using a Model of the Swedish Economy", CP-83-48, International Institute for Applied Systems Analysis, Laxenburg, Austria.

Bergman, L. and A. Por (forthcoming), "Computable Models of General Equilibrium in a Small Open Economy", Economic Research Institute at the Stockholm School of Economics, Stockholm.

Condon, T., V. Corbo and J. de Melo (1984), "Growth, Real Wages, the Real Exchange Rate and the Current Account in Chile (1977-1981): A General Equilibrium Analysis", mimeo, The World Bank, Washington D.C.

Dervis, K. (1975), "Planning Capital-Labor Substitution and Intertemporal Equilibrium with a Non-Linear Multi-Sector Growth Model", European Review 6, 77-96.

Dervis, K., J. de Melo and S. Robinson (1982), Planning Models and Development Policy, Cambridge University Press, London.

Dixon, P.B., B.R. Parmenter, G.J. Ryland and J.M. Sutton (1977), ORANI, A General Equilibrium Model of the Australian Economy, Australian Government Publishing Service, Canberra.

Dixon, P.B., B.R. Parmenter, J. Sutton and D.P. Vincent (1982), ORANI: A Multisectoral Model of the Australian Economy, North-Holland Publ. Co., Amsterdam.

Feltenstein, A. (forthcoming), "A Computational General Equilibrium Approach to the Shadow Pricing of Trade Restrictions and the Adjustment of the Exchange Rate with an Application to Argentina", Journal of Policy Modeling.

Hudson, E.A. and D.W. Jorgenson (1974), "U.S. Energy Policy and Economic Growth, 1975-2000", The Bell Journal of Economics Autumn, 461-514.

Johansen, L. (1960), A Multi-Sectoral Study of Economic Growth, North-Holland Publ. Co., Amsterdam.

Johansen, L. (1974), A Multi-Sectoral Study of Economic Growth, Second Enlarged Edition, North-Holland Publ. Co., Amsterdam.

Karlström, U. (1980), "Urbanization and Industrialization: Modeling Swedish Demoeconomic Development from 1870 to 1914", RR-80-44, International Institute for Applied Systems Analysis, Laxenburg, Austria.

Kelley, A., J. Williamson and R. Chetham (1972), Dualistic Economic Development, The University of Chicago Press, Chicago and London.

Kelley, A. and J. Williamson (1980), "Modeling Urbanization and Economic Growth", RR-80-22, International Institute for Applied Systems Analysis, Laxenburg, Austra.

Lloyd, P.J. (1978), "Tax Distortions and the Rate of Economic Growth: A Numerical General Equilibrium Analysis", Keio Economic Studies 2, 33-51.

Manne, A. (1978), "ETA-MACRO: A Model of Energy-Economy Interactions", in Hitch, C.J. (ed.), Modeling Energy-Economy Interactions: Five Approaches, Resources for the Future, Washington D.C.

de Melo, J. and K. Dervis (1977), "Modelling the Effects of Protection in a Dynamic Framework", Journal of Development Economics 4, 149-172.

de Melo, J. (1978), "Estimating the Costs of Protection: A General Equilibrium Approach", Quarterly Journal of Economics, May, 209-226.

de Melo, J., K. Dervis and S. Robinson (1979), "Les modèles d'équilibre général calculables et le commerce international", Economie Appliquée 4, 685-709.

de Melo, J. and S. Robinson (1980), "The Impact of Trade Policies c
    Income Distribution in a Planning Model for Colombia", Journal
    Policy Modeling 2 (1), 81-100.

Norman, V. and T. Wergeland (1977), TOLMOD - A Dual General Equil
    brium Model of the Norwegian Economy, Senter for Anvendt Fors
    ning, Norges Handelshøyskole, Bergen, Norway.

Rattsø, J. (1982), "Different Macroclosures of the Original Johans«
    Model and Their Impact on Policy Evaluation", Journal of Poli
    Modeling 4 (1), 85-97.

Restad, T. (1976), Modeller för samhällsekonomisk perspektivplanering
    Liber förlag, Stockholm.

Scarf, H. and J.B. Shoven (eds.) (1983), Applied General Equilibriu
    Analysis, Cambridge University Press, Cambridge.

Shishido, H. (1983), "Growth, Distribution and Macro Closures:
    General Equilibrium Analysis of Post-World War II Japan", unpublishe
    doctoral thesis, Massachusetts Institute of Technology.

Shoven, J.B. and J. Whalley (1972), "A General Equilibrium Calculatic
    of the Effects of Differential Taxation of Income from Capital in tl
    U.S.", Journal of Public Economics 1, 281-321.

Staelin, C.P. (1976), "A General Equilibrium Model of Tariffs in a Nor
    Competitive Economy", Journal of International Economics 6, 39-63.

Taylor, L. and S.L. Black (1974), "Practical General Equilibrium Estima
    tion of Resource Pulls under Trade Liberalization", Journal of Inter
    national Economics 4, 37-58.

Taylor, L. (1975), "Theoretical Foundations and Technical Implications"
    in Blitzer et al., Economy-Wide Models and Development Planning
    London: Oxford University Press.

Whalley, J. (1975), "How Reliable is Partial Equilibrium Analysis?" Th
    Review of Economics and Statistics LVII, 299-310.

Whalley, J. (1977), "A Simulation Experiment into the Numerical Properties of General Equilibirum Models of Factor Market Distortions", The Review of Economics and Statistics LIX, 194-203.

Zalai, E. (1982), "Computable General Equilibrium Models: An Optimal Planning Perspective", Mathematical Modelling 3, 437-451.

Production, Multi-Sectoral Growth and Planning
F.R. Førsund, M. Hoel, and S. Longva (Editors)
© Elsevier Science Publishers B.V. (North-Holland), 1985

A VERSION OF THE MSG-MODEL WITH
PUTTY–CLAY AND VINTAGE TECHNOLOGY

Håkan Persson
University of Gothenburg and University of Umeå

1. Introduction

In this paper we present a multisectoral growth model, the structure of which is similar to that found in Johansen (1960). More recent applications to the Swedish economy are found in Restad (1976) and Bergman (1978). We shall pay particular attention to certain simplifying assumptions concerning investment and capital that are frequently introduced into this type of model.

In these models, production is limited by the available amount of labour and capital. The latter includes exogenously given investment for the time period considered. The amounts of capital and labour required for the production of each commodity are determined by a production function which is specific to the sector producing the commodity; the production functions are assumed to exhibit unit elasticity of scale. Capital can be moved freely between sectors, and usually, as in Restad (1976) and Bergman (1978), it is of the same composition in all sectors, i.e. there is only one composite capital good in the economy.

In the model presented here, capital is also produced as a composite commodity, but its composition differs depending on where it is employed. We define the productive capacity of each sector and then search for solutions where capacity is not lower than production in any sector. Each sector is characterized by the available capacity embodied in old vintages of capital. Each vintage is described by a production function with fixed

---

This paper is an extended version of Chapter VII of my Ph.D. thesis. I have benefitted greatly from discussions with Morgan Åberg, Åke Andersson, Lennart Hjalmarsson, and Börje Johansson.

factor proportions. New productive capacity is created by investment, and ex ante (before the capital has been committed) substitution is allowed between capital and labour. Within the model all investment levels are determined in such a way that an increase in production requires an increase in productive capacity, which in turn requires an increase in the production of investment goods. Since investment goods are produced within the system, a simultaneous consistency requirement must be fulfilled.

Basically, this is an input-output model where private consumption is determined by prices and disposable income, and where public consumption of goods is given exogenously. Output prices are determined within the system, and are equal to the newly created capacity's unit cost of production.

A simple iterative solution procedure for the model is presented below, followed by some suggestions for further extensions of the model.

2. The framework

The theoretical framework will be outlined by means of a simple model formulation which enables us to concentrate on its basic structure. Later, we shall indicate how other variables and equations may be incorporated into the framework. These extensions will not effect the general setting and instead will lead to models that are comparable with ones found in the literature (e.g. Johansen (1960) and Bergman (1978)).

The model is essentially an input-output model in which net output is divided into private consumption, c, investment demand, z, and public consumption of goods, g. At this stage, the model is simplified by the exclusion of foreign trade. Gross production is denoted by x, and the balance equation of the model is

(1) $x = Ax + z + c + g$

where A is a square input-output matrix and all other variables are column vectors. We assume that there are m production sectors in the economy, which means that the matrix A has m rows and m columns and that all vectors are m-dimensional. The input-output matrix is assumed to be productive and indecomposable. In economic terms this means that it is

possible to simultaneously produce a positive net output of each commodity
and that each commodity is used in the production of every other good
directly, or indirectly.

Prices for individual goods are denoted by a row vector $p = (p_1, \ldots, p_m)$. Public consumption of commodities, g, is given exogenously,
while private consumption is a function of prices and disposable income,
Y, i.e. $c = c(p, Y)$. It is assumed that the demand functions satisfy

(2) $pc(p, Y) = Y$

for each $p > 0$, which means that consumers spend all their income.   For
this type of demand function see e.g. Barten (1977).

2.1 Investment and capital

Productive capacity is created by investment, and the composition of
investment demand determines the aggregate composition of capital. When
making investment decisions, the available choices of technology in each
sector is described by a production function that allows for substitution
between capital and labour.

One unit of capital, K_j, in sector j is defined as a column vector, h^j,
of constants $h_{ij} \geq 0$, $i = 1, \ldots, m$, for which $\sum_{i=1}^{m} h_{ij} = 1$ for each j.
The share of good i in the capital composition of sector j is denoted by
h_{ij}; $\bar{x}_j$ denotes the capacity in sector j, and $\Delta\bar{x}$ the corresponding change
in capacity. The creation of new capacity in sector j consists in choosing
the triplet $(\Delta\bar{x}_j, K_j, L_j)$, where K_j denotes the amount of capital invested
in capacity $\Delta\bar{x}_j$. When capacity $\Delta\bar{x}_j$ is fully used, the required amount of
labour is denoted L_j. The ex ante technology is described by a Cobb–
Douglas production function

(3) $\Delta\bar{x}_j = \gamma_j L_j^{\alpha_j} K_j^{\beta_j}$, $\alpha_j + \beta_j = 1$

where γ_j, α_j and β_j are positive constants.

Ex post production functions are of the Leontief type, and capacity is given by another triplet, $(\Delta \bar{x}_j, a^j, 1_j)$, where a^j is the column vector of sector j in the input-output matrix, A, and 1_j is the constant labour coefficient defined as $1_j = L_j / \Delta \bar{x}_j$. Each investment decision leads to such a triplet, which can be viewed as a specific "plant" or "vintage". Thus we assume that labour requirement coefficients differ among the "vintages" of each sector, whereas input-output coefficients do not. For any sum of utilized capacity of the various vintages, a corresponding average labour requirement coefficient is determined for the sector in question. All techniques embodied in existing "vintages" need not satisfy the production function (3), since this function represents the technology at the time of investment, which may differ from the technology that was available at the time the old "vintages" were created.

For given prices, p, the value of one unit of capital in sector j is

$$(4) \qquad ph^j = \sum_{i=1}^{m} p_i h_{ij}.$$

If we let r denote the rate of interest and δ_j denote the rate of depreciation in sector j, user cost of capital, q_j, becomes

$$(5) \qquad q_j = (r + \delta_j)ph^j = (r + \delta_j) \sum_{i=1}^{m} p_i h_{ij}.$$

In the model the wage, w, and the rate of interest are both uniform throughout the economy, which simplifies the notation. Other assumptions may, of course, be used.

The investment decision which determines ex post factor proportions should take into account the discounted value of future labour costs and the investment cost at present prices, i.e. the value of capital given in (4). For simplicity we assume that investors expect prices, the rate of interest, and the wage to stay constant for all future periods. That is to say knowing present prices is sufficient for determining the optimal choice of technique to be embodied by investment. Relative factor prices can therefore be written

$$q_j / w = (r + \delta_j)ph^j / w.$$

With cost-minimizing investment behaviour at prevailing positive factor prices, factor proportions satisfy

$$wl_j / \alpha_j = q_j k_j / \beta_j$$

where $k_j = K_j / \Delta \bar{x}_j$ is capital per unit of capacity. In connection with (3) this yields the following factor demand functions

(6) $\quad L_j = 1_j \Delta \bar{x}_j = (1/\gamma_j)[(r + \delta_j)ph^j \alpha_j / w\beta_j]^{\beta_j} \Delta \bar{x}_j$

(7) $\quad K_j = k_j \Delta \bar{x}_j = (1/\gamma_j)[w\beta_j/((r + \delta_j)ph^j \alpha_j)]^{\alpha_j} \Delta \bar{x}_j.$

For a one unit increase of capacity in sector j, the demand for investment goods from sector i, b_{ij}, is given by

(8) $\quad b_{ij} = h_{ij} k_j = h_{ij}(1/\gamma_j)[w\beta_j/((r + \delta_j)ph^j \alpha_j)]^{\alpha_j}.$

2.2 Prices

With the above mentioned method determining the techniques to be embodied in the newly created capacity, prices are then determined by the unit costs of production,

(9) $\quad P_j = \sum_{i=1}^{m} P_i a_{ij} + wl_j + q_j k_j.$

These unit costs are for the new "plants" when existing capacity is fully utilized. The price system in (9) has the convenient property that prices do not explicitly depend on production, x. Value-added from each technique is positive since input-output coefficients are common to all techniques in a sector. Thus the positivity of the quasi-rent associated with a specific technique essentially depends on its labour requirement. When prices are given, the amount of old capacity actually employed is determined by the profitability of the various techniques. "Vintages" with negative quasi-rents are not utilized.

The expressions in (6), (7), and (9) together yield

(10) $p_j = \sum\limits_{i=1}^{m} p_i a_{ij} + (w/\alpha_j)^{\alpha_j} ((r + \delta_j)/\beta_j)^{\beta_j} (ph^j)^{\beta_j} (1/\gamma_j).$

For given values of w and r, (10) is a non-linear equation system in p. Obviously, p = 0 is a solution to (10), but since the derivation of (10) explicitly assumed positive factor prices w and q_j, the price equation is not defined for prices where $ph^j = 0$ for some j. On account of the indecomposability of the matrix A, a solution to (10) which is different from the zero vector must be positive in all its arguments. For ease of presentation let us write the price equations as

(11) $p = G(r,w,p),$

where G is assumed to be defined only for r > 0, w > 0, and p > 0. For each value of r, the component function $g_j(r,w,p)$ of G is the unit cost function of commodity j when capital cost is taken into account and when only "new technology" is considered. Each function g_j has all the properties of a cost function; it is concave and homogenous of degree one in w and p and increasing in the sense that

$$(r',w',p') \geq (r,w,p) \Rightarrow g_j(r',w',p') \geq g_j(r,w,p).$$

Looking solely at the price system of the model, unit costs of production satisfy with a slight modification the assumptions used in connection with the so-called dynamic non-substitution theorem (see Mirrlees (1969) and Stiglitz (1970)). To prove the existence and uniqueness of solutions to the system of price equations for fixed values of w and r, we shall refer to the results in the Appendix. We shall also provide an algorithm for the computation of prices.

Proposition 1. Given r > 0 and w > 0, there exists a unique p > 0 satisfying p = G(r,w,p). The solution is the limit of the sequence

(12) $p^{n+1} = G(r,w,p^n), \quad p^o > 0.$

Proof: Define the matrix M(p) with elements

(13) $\qquad m_{ij} = (1/\gamma_j)(w/\alpha_j)^{\alpha_j}((r + \delta_j)/\beta_j)^{\beta_j}(ph^j)^{(\beta_j-1)}h_{ij}.$

The price equation can now be written

(14) $\qquad p = pA + pM(p).$

Let H be the matrix with elements h_{ij}. An inspection of (13) reveals that there exists a constant $\varepsilon > 0$ such that $p > 0$ and $p < \varepsilon$ implies that $H \leq M(p)$. All column sums of H are by definition unity, which implies that one eigenvalue of H is unity. Since A is indecomposable, so is $A + H$. Let $q > 0$ be the eigenvector corresponding to the maximum eigenvalue of $A + H$. Then, $q < q(A + H) \leq q(A + M(q))$ for $q < \varepsilon$. The main conclusion to be drawn here is that for $p > 0$, there exist $q > 0$, such that $q \leq p$ and $q < G(r,w,q)$. An application of Lemma 3 from the Appendix states that there is at most one $p > 0$ for which $p = G(r,w,p)$.

In (13) it is seen that $m_{ij}(p) \rightarrow 0$ for all i and j when $p_i \rightarrow \infty$ for all i. Consequently there exists an eigenvector $\bar{p} > 0$ of A such that $\bar{p} > \bar{p}(A + M(\bar{p})) = G(r, w, \bar{p})$. According to Lemma 1 of the Appendix this proves the existence of a solution.

As proved above, for any $p^o > 0$, there exist $q > 0$ such that $q < p^o$ and $q < G(r,w,q)$. As seen in Lemma 7 of the Appendix the sequence in (12) converges to a solution. Q.E.D.

2.3. Capacity expansion

The model is intended for use as follows: At time $t = 0$, a solution is calculated for a specific future time period, say T units of time ahead, i.e. calculations are made for $t = T$. Productive capacity at T is given by the capacity stemming from investment decisions prior to $t = 0$ and by the capacity created by investment during the forecast period $[0,T]$. The balance equation (1) involves investment decisions and capacity change at $t = T$ only. Somehow, capacity changes at $t = 1,2,\ldots,T-1$ must also be included in the calculations of capacity at T.

In most applications of the MSG-model, capacity or capital at $t = T$ and investment at $t = T$ are given exogeneously. In our model we let capacity in each sector at $t = T$ be an endogenous variabel, and we assume that the capacity increase for the whole period $[0,T]$ is in some way related to

H. Persson

investment at t = T. We make the additional assumption that an increase in capacity growth implies an increase in investment at t = T, and to keep the analysis at a simple and manageable level, we let the capacity change at t = T be the annual average for the whole period, $[0,T]$. Other assumptions may just as well be used, and an example is found in Persson (1983).

Let $\bar{x}_j(t)$ denote productivity capacity in sector j at time t. Then,

(15) $\bar{x}_j(t + 1) = (1 - \delta_j)\bar{x}_j(t) + \Delta x_j(t)$

where $\Delta \bar{x}_j(t) \geq 0$. Let $\bar{x}_j(0)$ denote available capacity at T stemming from investments prior to t = 0. For t = T we have

$$\bar{x}_j(T) = \sum_{t=0}^{T-1} (1 - \delta_j)^{(T-1-t)}\Delta\bar{x}_j(t) + \bar{x}_j(0).$$

This yields

$$\Delta\bar{x}_j(T) = (\bar{x}_j(0))\delta_j/(1 - (1 - \delta_j)^T),$$

since we have assumed that all $\Delta\bar{x}_j(t)$, t = 0,1,...,T are equal, and since

$$1 + (1 - \delta_j) + (1 - \delta_j)^2 + ... + (1 - \delta_j)^{(T-1)} = (1 - (1 - \delta_j)^T)/\delta_j.$$

For efficient use of investment we assume that if production at T $x_j(T)$, exceeds the "old" capacity, $\bar{x}_j(0)$, capacity at T equals production at T. Similarly, the capacity increase is set at zero when production at T is less than the old capacity, $\bar{x}_j(0)$. Hence,

(16) $\Delta\bar{x}_j(T) = (x_j(T) - \bar{x}_j(0))\delta_j/(1-(1-\delta_j)^T)$ for $x_j(T) > \bar{x}_j(0)$

(17) $\Delta\bar{x}_j(T) = 0$ for $x_j(T) \leq \bar{x}_j(0)$.

Since all equations are evaluated at t = T, the time variable can be suppressed, letting the vectors x, $\bar{x}$, and Δx denote production, capacity, and capacity increase at T, respectively.

The amount of old capacity utilized at T depends on prices and the wage rate. Assuming that old "vintages" or "techniques" are not employed when quasi- rents are negative, this means that x_j depends on p and w. Thus (16) and (17) can be written as

(16') $\Delta \bar{x}_j = (x_j - x_j(p, w)) \delta_j / (1 - (1 - \delta_j)^T)$ for $x_j > \bar{x}_j(p, w)$

(17') $\Delta \bar{x}_j = 0$ for $x_j \leq \bar{x}_j(p, w)$.

These equations indicate that capacity changes are a function of production and prices, $\Delta \bar{x} = \Delta \bar{x}(w, p, x)$, and for all values of x, the relation $\bar{x} \geq x$ is satisfied according to the assumptions above.

Investment demand per unit of capacity increase is given by the matrix, $B(r, w, p)$, with elements b_{ij} shown in (8). Thus, investment demand is determined by

(18) $z = B(r, w, p) \Delta \bar{x}(w, p, x)$.

3. The model

The balance equation of the model can now be written as

(19) $x = Ax + B(r, w, p) \Delta \bar{x}(w, p, x) + c(p, Y) + g$.

For given positive values of w and r, prices are uniquely determined by the price equation $p = G(r, w, p)$. It is assumed that prices appearing in (19) satisfy the price equation. For fixed values of r, w, and Y, (19) can be written as

(20) $x = F(x) + y$

where $F(x) = Ax + B(r, w, p) \Delta \bar{x}(w, p, x)$ and $y = c(p, Y) + g$. For ease of presentation we define a matrix $\bar{B}$ with elements, $\bar{b}_{ij}$, defined as

(21) $\bar{b}_{ij} = b_{ij} \delta_j / (1 - (1 - \delta_j)^T)$.

From (16) and (17) it is seen that for fixed r and w, (20) may be written as

(22) $x_i = \sum\limits_{j=1}^{m} a_{ij} x_j + \sum\limits_{j=1}^{m} \bar{b}_{ij} (\max\{0, x_j - \bar{x}_j\}) + y_i .$

Clearly, $F(x)$ is increasing in the sense that

$$x' \geq x \Rightarrow F(x') \geq F(x)$$

and each component $(F_i(x) + y_i)$ of $(F(x) + y)$ is a convex and continuous function.

We can now apply some lemmata from the Appendix to prove that under certain conditions there exists a unique solution to (19).

<u>Proposition 2.</u> Assume that $\delta_j \geq 1 - \alpha_j^{1/T}$ for each j. For fixed positive values of r, w, Y, and prices, p, satisfying $p = G(r,w,p)$, there exists a unique solution to (19). This solution is the limit of the sequence, (x^n), defined by

(23) $x^{n+1} = F(x^n) + y, \quad x^o \geq 0.$

<u>Proof:</u> In (14), the price equation is written as $p = pA + pM(p)$ with the elements, m_{ij}, of the matrix M defined by (13). If we compare the element m_{ij} with b_{ij} defined in (8) we see that

(24) $b_{ij}(r + \delta_j)/\beta_j = m_{ij} .$

From the assumption that $\delta_j \geq 1 - \alpha_j^{1/T}$ we have that $\alpha_j = 1 - \beta_j \geq (1-\delta_j)^T$, i.e.

(25) $\beta_j \leq (1 - (1 - \delta_j)^T).$

For the elements, $\bar{b}_{ij}$, of the matrix $\bar{B}$ defined in (21), we have

$$\bar{b}_{ij} = b_{ij}\delta_j/(1-(1-\delta_j)^T) \leq b_{ij}\delta_j/\beta_j \leq b_{ij}(r + \delta_j)/\beta_j = m_{ij}.$$

The first inequality follows from (25), the second is due to $r > 0$ and the last equality is due to (24). With $r > 0$, $b_{ij} > 0$ implies that $\bar{b}_{ij} < m_{ij}$. Hence $B \leq M$, $B \neq M$. Since A is an indecomposable matrix, we have

$$\lambda(A + \bar{B}) < \lambda(A + M(p)) = 1$$

where $\lambda(\bullet)$ denotes the maximum eigenvalue of the matrix in question. The equality follows from the definition of the price equation stated in (14). Since $A + \bar{B}$ is indecomposable, we can find an arbitrarily large eigenvector, $z > 0$, satisfying $z > (A + \bar{B})z$. This vector can be choosen large enough that $z > \bar{x}$ and

$$z > Az + \bar{B}(z - \bar{x}) + y.$$

From (20) - (22), it follows that for each $x > 0$, there exists $z > x$ such that $z > F(z) + y$. Hence, due to Lemmata 1 and 5, there exists a unique solution $x = F(x) + y$. The convergence of the sequence defined in (23) follows from Lemma 7 of the Appendix.   Q.E.D.

It should be noted that the condition $\delta_j \geq 1 - \alpha_j^{1/T}$ is a sufficient and not a necessary condition. If it holds with strict inequality in some sectors, it may be violated to some extent in others. It can also be replaced or weakened by a positive lower bound on the rate of interest. For example, if we set $T = 10$ and $\alpha_j = 0.7$, we find that the condition yields $\delta_j \geq 0.036$.

It should also be noted that if the forecast period T is shortened, depreciation coefficients must be larger to guarantee the existence of a solution. With high investment requirements per unit of capacity increase and a short time horizon, an increase in capacity may result in increased levels of demand that are higher than the capacity increase supplied by the investments. If investments are made in order to have capacity catch up with demand, additional demand due to investment will always make demand greater than capacity. On the other hand, we can always find a solution for small values of T if the rate of interest is set high enough, thereby lowering investment demand per unit of capacity increase.

The labour requirements in production are determined by the labour requirements per unit of production for "old vintages" and for newly created capacity. The labour requirements for old capacity are given exogenously, while the labour coefficients for new capacity are determined by factor prices according to (6). Thus labour demand, L, is a function of factor prices and productions, and a full employment solution satisfies

$$L(r, w, p, x) = \bar{L}.$$

To close the model we need two additional conditions. First, the wage rate is set equal to unity,

$$w = 1.$$

Secondly, a prescribed level, $\bar{s}$, is imposed on the rate of saving,

$$\bar{s} = pB(r, w, p)\Delta\bar{x}(w, p, x)/(px - pAx).$$

This second condition reflects the desirability of consumption beyond the forecast period T.

With $w = 1$, the model can now be summarized by four expressions:

(26) $x = Ax + B(r, p)\Delta\bar{x}(p, x) + c(p, Y) + g$

(27) $p = G(r, p)$

(28) $L(r, p, x) = \bar{L}$

(29) $s = pB(r, p)\Delta\bar{x}(p, x)/(px - pAx) = \bar{s}.$

There is a certain hierarchy among the variables of the model. The rate of interest alone uniquely determines prices as seen in (27). Numerically, we can solve prices by the iterative procedure in (12).

When both the rate of interest and disposable income, Y, are given, production is also determined as seen in (26). To compute production numerically we may use the algorithm found in (23). For given values of r and Y, employment and the rate of saving can also be determined, but obviously these values need not satisfy (28) and (29) for arbitrary r and Y.

An increase in the rate of interest will increase prices as noted above. Consequently, user cost of capital in all sectors increases and production with new techniques becomes more labour intensive. The elements of the investment matrix, $B(r, p)$, will decrease and thus lower investment demand at a given level of production. Increasing prices will also lower private consumption if nominal disposable income, Y, is kept constant.

Although a change in relative prices might increase the private consumption of some goods, aggregate consumption will always decrease. Due to
the shifts in both private consumption and investment demand, there will
be a decrease of production in (26) at least on the aggregate level.

As for employment, an increase in the rate of interest results in the
choosing of new technology that is more labour intensive with a subse-
quent tendency towards increasing employment. However, this tendency
is counteracted by the decrease in production, as shown above, which in
turn tends to reduce the effect on employment. Hence, the compound
effects on employment of a change in the rate of interest is not determined
a priori. Observe that the forces increasing labour act only with respect
to new technology, i.e. on a part of the production system, whereas the
other mentioned effects concern all final demand components except public
consumption of goods. The smaller the public share of consumption is and
the smaller the increase in new capacity is, the more significant the
employment reducing effect on the increase in the rate of interest will be.

A change in the rate of interest will also influence the rate of saving
as expressed in (29). With constant investment demand, i.e. with
$z = B(\cdot, \cdot)\Delta x(\cdot, x)$ fixed, changing prices appear both in the numerator
and denominator of (29); the direct price effect is therefore ambiguous.
This is also the case for the price effect in $\Delta \bar{x}(p, x)$. Still, these effects
may be of minor importance, since all prices change in the same direction
as the reaction to changes in the rate of interest. As mentioned above, an
increase in r decreases investment demand per unit of capacity change,
i.e. the elements of the investment matrix decrease, and production also
decreases. Moreover, since the capacity change per unit of production in
each sector j, $\Delta \bar{x}_j(p, x_j)/x_j$, increases with production, an increase in r
will most likely imply a decrease in the rate of saving, s.

The effects on various variables of a change in disposable income can
be determined more directly. At a constant rate of interest, prices are
constant. An increase in disposable income, Y, increases private consumption if the income-elasticity is nonnegative for each commodity. Even
if some of the income-elasticities are negative the condition $pc(p, Y) = Y$
nevertheless implies that aggregate private consumption will increase.
Consequently, investment, production, and employment will increase. The
rate of saving also increases due to the change in $\Delta \bar{x}_j(p, x)/x_j$ mentioned
above.

It is now possible to solve for the remaining variables for given

values of the rate of interest and disposable income. Numerically, equality
in (26) and (27) is established by means of two iterative procedures described in (12) and (23). In order to obtain a solution for the complete
model, we need to find certain values of r and Y that also yield equality
in (28) and (29). Once r and Y are given, employment can be expressed
as a function of just these two variables. A similar argument applies to
the rate of saving: with implicit solutions for prices and production which
satisfy (26) and (27), the model can be written as

$$(30) \qquad L(r, Y) = \bar{L}$$
$$\qquad\qquad {\scriptstyle -?\ \ +}$$

$$(31) \qquad s(r, Y) = \bar{s}$$
$$\qquad\qquad {\scriptstyle -?\ \ +}$$

where the signs below the equations refer to the effects of changes in the
two variables r and Y.

To prove that there is a solution to (30) and (31) we need two additional assumptions. As described above, old vintages are not employed if
quasi-rents are negative. This means that old capacity, $\bar{x}(r,p)$, is a
discontinuous function. If we assume, however, that old techniques are
taken out of use or added in a continuous manner as quasi-rents change,
then old capacity becomes a continuous function in r since p(r) is continuous.

With Cobb-Douglas technologies for new techniques, capital income,
$(r + \delta_j)\Sigma_i p_i b_{ij}$, is a constant fraction of value added per unit of the new
technique's output. Hence, $pB(r,p)\Delta\bar{x}/(p(I-A)\Delta\bar{x})$ tends to zero for fixed
$\Delta\bar{x}$ as r approaches infinity. For full employment solutions, $x = \bar{x} + \Delta\bar{x}$
satisfying (28), and value-added, $p(I - A)(\bar{x} + \Delta\bar{x})$, is bounded below
by some positive number. Then, s as defined in (29) clearly approaches
zero as r tends to infinity.

Our continuity assumption regarding $\bar{x}(r,p)$ implies that $\bar{x}$ and $\Delta\bar{x}$,
satisfying (26)-(28), changes continuously with r, which in turn implies
that s in (29) is a continuous function of r.

Regarding our second assumption we assume that the vector g in (26)
is small enough so that (26)-(28) can be solved for each $r \geq 0$. We further
assume that for r = 0, Y satisfying $L(0, Y) = \bar{L}$ fulfills $s(0, Y) \geq \bar{s} > 0$.

As r increases from r = 0, s changes continuously for solutions satisfying (26)-(28), and approaches zero as r tends to infinity as noted

above. The function s is then bound to equal $\bar{s}$ for some value of r, which proves that there is a solution to the model.

We shall not try to prove uniqueness of solutions, but will provide some arguments in favour of such a conjecture. Note that an increase in r implies that user cost of capital increases, which then leads to increasing labour requirement coefficients, l_j, for the new techniques. With fixed labour coefficients in old vintages and input-output coefficients common to all vintages in each individual sector, profitability of old vintages improves as r increases up to the limit at which all old techniques are fully employed. Employment, L_n, in new techniques is thus non-increasing with respect to r. Since employment in the new techniques satisfies $L_n = \Sigma_j l_j \Delta \bar{x}_j$ and since L_n is non-increasing and each l_j is increasing, we expect reductions in most $\Delta \bar{x}_j$. As r increases, all prices will increase with relatively higher increases in sectors with high capital costs relative to labour costs. We can thus expect private consumption to change in favour of commodities that directly or indirectly utilize less of commodities with high capital costs. Therefore, the compound effect is that $\Delta \bar{x}_j$ decreases for sectors with high captial costs and may increase for sectors with high labour costs.

As noted above in the proof of existence of a solution, the value of investment, $\Sigma_i p_i b_{ij}$, per unit of capacity decreases as a fraction of value-added per unit. With the conjectured changes in $\Delta \bar{x}_j$, we have that $pB(r,p)\Delta \bar{x}$ decreases as a fraction of total value-added, which is to say that the function s decreases as a function of r for solutions satisfying (26)-(28). If this is true, the solution to the model is unique and our second assumption above is not only a sufficient but also a necessary condition for the existence of a solution.

Solving the model is now essentially a problem of solving an equation system in two unknowns and two equations. By means of iterative procedures this can be done in a number of ways. The idea is to apply some numerical algorithm that systematically change the values of r and Y so as to construct a sequence of L(r,Y) and sequence of s(r,Y) which converge to $\bar{L}$ and $\bar{s}$ respectively. One way to proceed is to find approximate values of the relevant derivatives and then use a version of the Newton method. Another method – that might work – is to iteratively find the value, $\bar{Y}$, of Y that satisfies $L(r,\bar{Y}) = \bar{L}$ for a given value of r. The next step should then be to calculate $s(r,\bar{Y})$ and compare this value with $\bar{s}$. If $s(r,\bar{Y}) > \bar{s}$, r is set at a new value, $\bar{r} > r$, and if $s(r,\bar{Y}) < \bar{s}$, the rate of interest is lowered. The condition in (31) is not fulfilled in each single step. Each step merely gives an indication of the appropriate change for r. In the next round of calculations, $L(\bar{r}, Y) = \bar{L}$ yields a new value of disposable income, and hopefully, a repetition of this process will yield an approximate solution.

The equation system defined by (30) and (31) is also a relevant tool when determining how a change in various variables are affected by a change in the supply of labour or a change in the rate of saving. If precise statements are to be made, additional assumptions are required due to the uncertainty surrounding the various magnitudes involved in (30) and (31). Naturally, numerical estimates of such changes are determined in empirical applications of the model.

4. Some extensions

Within the given framework it should not be difficult to create alternative formulations of the model. In empirical work some trivial modifications must be included, i.e. numerical specifications of the model (such as trends of parameters entering the various expressions and different fixed wages in different sectors).

Another kind of modification is to include factors of production other than capital and labour as choice variables in the ex ante selection of "new technology". Such extensions fit nicely into the framework described here. For example, one such factor of production that could be included is energy, treated as a composite commodity of, say electricity, oil and other fuels. With this modification energy is produced within the system and as such it differs from labour which is a primary, non-produced input. It also differs from capital in that it is a flow-variable. In technical terms, such an introduction of energy implies that some of the elements in the input-output matrix for "new technology" are now functions of prices for the average technique, input-output coefficients also depend on the distribution of production between "old" and "new" techniques. However the principal structure of the model described by the four equations (26) (29) is not altered.

Another extension, which must be made in applied analysis, is to incorporate export and import relations into the framework of the model. For the sake of simplicity assume that exports, e, of the various commo-

dities are functions of domestic and world market prices, denoted by p
and p^w, respectively. Import, m, apart from being a function of prices,
can also be assumed to depend on production, x. This gives us two
column vectors of volumes written as $e = e(p, p^w)$ and $m = m(p, p^w, x)$.
Assuming that our model describes "a small open economy", which means
that world market prices are fixed and independent of the other variables
of the model, we can suppress the variable p^w in our expressions and
write $e = e(p)$ and $m = m(p, x)$.

The model in (26)-(29) can now be modified so that (26) is replaced
by

$$x = Ax + B(r,p)\Delta\bar{x}(p,x) + c(p,Y) + g + e(p) - m(p,x).$$

One further modification may also be appropriate. The condition $w = 1$
may be replaced by a balance of trade condition

$$\beta \equiv p^w(e(p) - m(p,x)) \equiv \sum_{i=1}^{m} p_i^w(e_i(p) - m_i(p,x)) = \bar{\beta},$$

which states that the difference, β, between export and import at world
market prices should satisfy a certain value, $\bar{\beta}$.

The extended model is now:

$$x = Ax + B(r,w,p)\Delta\bar{x}(w,p,x) + c(p,Y) + g + e(p) - m(p,x)$$
$$p = G(r,w,p)$$
$$L(r,w,p,x) = \bar{L}$$
$$s = pB(r,w,p)\Delta x(w,p,x)/(px - pAx) = s$$
$$\beta = p^w(e(p) - m(p,x)) = \bar{\beta}.$$

As for the original model, with given values of r, w, and Y, all other
variables are determined, which means that with implicit solutions for
prices and production, three equations and three unknowns remain

$$L(r,w,Y) = \bar{L}$$
$$s(r,w,Y) = \bar{s}$$
$$\beta(r,w,Y) = \bar{\beta}.$$

Appendix

In this appendix we prove some statements regarding increasing functions that are used in the propositions above.

We assume that f is a function mapping the nonnegative orthant of R^m into itself and that f is an increasing function in the sense that

(A1) $x' \geq x \Rightarrow f(x') \geq f(x)$,

The function f is also assumed to be continuous.

Lemma 1. Assume that there exist vectors z and y such that $z \geq y \geq 0$, $z \geq f(z)$, and $y \leq f(y)$. Then there exists a fixed point of f, $x = f(x)$, such that $y \leq x \leq z$, and there exist a sequence, (x^n), defined by

(A2) $x^{n+1} = f(x^n)$

with either $x^o = y$ or $x^o = z$ converging to a fixed point of f.

Proof: Consider the sequence, (x^n), defined by (A2) starting at $x^o = y$. Assume by induction that $x^n \leq x^{n+1} \leq z$. Then, due to (A1) and the assumption that $z \geq f(z)$ we have $f(x^n) \leq f(x^{n+1}) \leq f(z) \leq z$. This means that $x^{n+1} \leq x^{n+2} \leq z$ due to (A2). With $x^o = y$, we have by assumption that $x^o \leq f(x^o) \leq z$. This implies that $x^n \leq x^{n+1} \leq z$ for all n. In each component, the sequence (x^n) is increasing and bounded from above. The sequence thus converges to some vector x, and due to (A2), the sequence $f(x^n)$ also converges to x. Since f is continuous, $x^n \to x = f(x)$. We have thus proved the existence of a solution, and the convergence of the sequence defined in (A2), starting at $x^o = y$. The convergence of the sequence starting at $x^o = z$ is proved in a similar way.   Q.E.D.

It will be of interest to consider functions f(x) such that each component function, $f_i(x)$, is a concave function, and to consider the case in which each component function is convex. We say that f is concave if each function f_i is concave, and that f is convex if f_i is convex for each i.

Starting with the concave case, it is well-known that a concave function is continuous on the interior of its domain and that left-hand side and right-hand side partial derivatives, defined as limits of increasing and decreasing sequences respectively, exist everywhere on the same set. For the function $f_i(x)$, these partial derivatives with respect to x_j are denoted by

$$f_{ij}^- = \partial^- f_i(x)/\partial x_j$$

$$f_{ij}^+ = \partial^+ f_i(x)/\partial x_j$$

respectively.

The following inequality for concave functions can be interpreted as a mean value property

$$(A3) \qquad f_i(x) \leq f_i(\bar{x}) + \sum_{j=1}^m f_{ij}^-(\bar{x})(x_j - \bar{x}_j).$$

The inequality is valid if $f_{ij}^-(\bar{x})$ is replaced by $f_{ij}^+(\bar{x})$ or any constant b_{ij} for which $f_{ij}^-(\bar{x}) \geq b_{ij} \geq f_{ij}^+(\bar{x})$. If we denote the matrix of elements $f_{ij}^-(\bar{x})$ by $J^-(\bar{x})$, (A3) can be written as

$$(A4) \qquad f(x) \leq f(\bar{x}) + J^-(\bar{x})(x - \bar{x}),$$

since each function $f_i(x)$ is concave.

Since $f(x)$ is increasing, all partial derivatives will be nonnegative and the matrix $J^-(\bar{x})$ in (A4) is a nonnegative square matrix. The maximum eigenvalue of J is denoted by $\lambda(J)$; the following lemma states that $\lambda(J^-(x))$ is less than unity for a solution $x = f(x)$ if f is concave and if there exist $y \geq 0$ such that $y < f(y)$.

Lemma 2. Assume that f is concave and that there exist $y \geq 0$ such that $y < f(y)$ and $y \leq x = f(x)$. Then, $\lambda(J^-(x)) < 1$. Furthermore, $y < x$.

Proof. Due to monotonicity of $f(x)$, $y \leq x \Rightarrow f(y) \leq f(x)$. Then, $y < f(y) \leq f(x) = x$, proving that $y < x$. From (A4) it now follows that

(A5) $J^-(x)(x - y) \leq f(x) - f(y) < x - y$

where the latter inequality follows from $x = f(x)$ and $y < f(y)$. Since $J^-(x) < 0$, there exist a row vector $p \geq 0$, $p \neq 0$ for which $\lambda p = pJ^-(x)$, $\lambda = \lambda(J^-(x))$. From (A5) it now follows that

$$\lambda p(x - y) = pJ^-(x)(x - y) < p(x - y)$$

which implies that $\lambda(J^-(x)) < 1$ since $p(x - y) > 0$.   Q.E.D.

With the aid of Lemma 2, we can now prove a lemma that will be useful when proving uniqueness of prices in our model. If we interpret x as a vector of prices and $f(x)$ as unit cost functions, Lemma 3 in fact provides the proof of a slightly generalized version of the nonsubstitution theorem found in Stiglitz (1970).

Lemma 3. Assume that f is concave and that there exist $y \geq 0$ for which $y < f(y)$. Assume further that there exist $x = f(x) \geq y$. Then, x is the only fixed point of f for which $x \geq y$.

Proof. Assume that there are two solutions, $x = f(x)$ and $\bar{x} = f(\bar{x})$. From (A4) it follows that for the two solutions x and $\bar{x}$, $x - \bar{x} \geq J^-(x)(x - \bar{x})$, which can be written as $(I - J^-(x))(x - \bar{x}) \geq 0$. The inverse matrix $(I - J^-(x))^{-1}$ is nonnegative, since $\lambda(J^-(x)) < 1$ according to Lemma 2, which implies that $x - \bar{x} \geq 0$. Changing the roles of x and $\bar{x}$ leads to $\bar{x} - x \geq 0$. Hence, $x = \bar{x}$.   Q.E.D.

If the function f is convex, then the function $-f$ is concave, which implies that if f is convex the inequality (A4) is replaced by

(A6) $f(x) \geq f(\bar{x}) + J^+(\bar{x})(x - \bar{x})$.

If slightly different assumptions are stated, corresponding versions of Lemma 2 and 3 are available for convex functions.

Lemma 4. Assume that f is convex and that for each $x \geq 0$, there exists a vector $z > x$ for which $z > f(z)$. Then, for each solution $\bar{x} = f(\bar{x})$, $\lambda(J^+(\bar{x})) < 1$.

Proof: For $\bar{x} = f(\bar{x})$, there exist $z > \bar{x}$, $z > f(z)$. (A6) then implies that

(A7) $z - \bar{x} > f(z) - f(\bar{x}) \geq J^+(\bar{x})(z - \bar{x})$.

Since f is increasing, $J^+(\bar{x}) \geq 0$, and thus there exists a row vector $p \geq 0$, $p \neq 0$ such that $\lambda p = pJ^+(\bar{x})$, $\lambda = \lambda(J^+(\bar{x}))$. (A7) yields

$$p(z - \bar{x}) > pJ^+(\bar{x})(z - \bar{x}) = \lambda p(z - \bar{x}),$$

which implies that $\lambda(J^+(\bar{x})) < 1$ since $p(z - \bar{x}) > 0$.   Q.E.D.

Lemma 5.   Assume that f is convex and that for each $x \geq 0$ there exist $z > x$ such that $z > f(z)$. Then there is a unique solution $x = f(x)$.

Proof: Since f maps the nonnegative orthant into itself, $f(0) \geq 0$. Setting $y = 0$ into Lemma 1 then proves the existence of a solution. Assume that there are two solutions $x = f(x)$ and $\bar{x} = f(\bar{x})$. (A6) now yields $\bar{x} \geq J^+(\bar{x})(x - \bar{x})$, i.e. $(I - J^+(\bar{x}))(x - \bar{x}) \geq 0$. The inverse matrix $(I - J^+(\bar{x}))^{-1}$ is nonnegative since $\lambda(J^+(\bar{x})) < 1$ due to Lemma 4. This implies that $x - \bar{x} \geq 0$. Changing the roles of x and $\bar{x}$ leads to $\bar{x} - x \geq 0$. Hence $x = \bar{x}$.   Q.E.D.

Our final aim is to prove convergence of a numerical procedure used in the model. To do this we need a lemma for the case where f is concave.

Lemma 6.   Assume that f is concave and that there exist $y \geq 0$ such that $y < f(y)$. Assume also that there exists a solution $\bar{x} = f(\bar{x})$. Then, for each $x > y$, there exist $z > x$ such that $z > f(z)$.

Proof: Let $\bar{x} = f(\bar{x})$. From (A4) it follows that $f(\bar{x}) - f(x) \geq J^-(\bar{x})(\bar{x} - x)$. Thus $y < f(y)$ implies that $\bar{x} - y > J^-(\bar{x})(\bar{x} - y)$, and according to Lemma 2, $\bar{x} - y > 0$. For $x \geq y$, there exists a constant $\gamma > 0$ such that

$z \equiv \bar{x} + \gamma(\bar{x} - y) > x$. This definition of z also reads $z - \bar{x} = \gamma(\bar{x} - y)$ implying that $z - \bar{x} > J^-(\bar{x})(z - \bar{x})$. This inequality together with (A4) yields

$$f(z) - f(\bar{x}) \leq J^-(\bar{x})(z - \bar{x}) < z - \bar{x},$$

i.e. $z > f(z)$ since $\bar{x} = f(\bar{x})$.   Q.E.D.

Lemma 7. Assume that there exist $y \geq 0$ such that $y \leq f(y)$, and assume that for each $x \geq y$ there exist $z \geq x$ such that $z \geq f(z)$. If there exists a unique fixed point $x = f(x) \geq y$, then the sequence, (x^n), defined by

(A8) $x^{n+1} = f(x^n), \quad x^o \geq y$

converges to the fixed point $x = f(x)$.

Proof: Assume that x^o satisfies $x^o \geq y$ and let $z \geq x^o$ satisfy $z \geq f(z)$. Define the two sequences, $(\bar{x}^n)$ and $(\underline{x}^n)$, by $\bar{x}^{n+1} = f(\bar{x}^n)$, $\bar{x}^o = z$ and $\underline{x}^{n+1} = f(\underline{x}^n)$, $\underline{x}^o = y$, respectively. Due to Lemma 1, both sequences converge to $x = f(x)$.

Assume that for the sequence, (x^n), defined in (A8), we have $\underline{x}^n \leq x^n \leq \bar{x}^n$. Then, due to (A1), $f(\underline{x}^n) \leq f(x^n) \leq f(\bar{x}^n)$, i.e. $\underline{x}^{n+1} \leq x^{n+1} \leq \bar{x}^{n+1}$.   Clearly, $y = \underline{x}^o \leq x^o \leq \bar{x}^o = z$ and by induction $\underline{x}^n \leq x^n \leq \bar{x}^n$ for all n. Since both $\bar{x}^n \to x$ and $\underline{x}^n \to x$, we have $x^n \to x = f(x)$.   Q.E.D.

If Lemmata 5 and 7 are applied, we see that for f convex and for $x \geq 0$ there exist $z > x$ such that $z > f(z)$, then the sequence defined in (A8) converges to the unique solution $x = f(x)$.

Similarly, from Lemmata 6 and 7, it follows that for f concave and for $y < f(y)$, the sequence defined in (A8) converges to the unique solution, $x = f(x)$, if it exists. In this case, regarding x as a vector of prices and $f(x)$ as a vector of corresponding unit cost functions, Lemmata 6 and 7 generalize the main results of Chander (1978).

References

Barten, A.P. (1977), "The Systems of Consumer Demand Functions Approach: A Review", Econometrica 45, 23-51.

Bergman, L. (1978), "Energy Policy in a Small Open Economy: The Case of Sweden", RR-78-16 International Institute of Applied Systems Analysis, Laxenburg, Austria.

Chander, P. (1978), "The Computation of Equilibrium Prices", Econometrica 46, 723-726.

Johansen, L. (1960), A Multi-Sectoral Study of Economic Growth, (Second enlarged edition 1974). North-Holland, Amsterdam.

Johansen, L. (1972), Production Functions, North-Holland, Amsterdam.

Lahiri, S. (1977), "Efficient Investment and Growth Consistency in the Input-Output Frame: An Analytical Contribution", Econometrica 45, 1823-1834.

Mirrlees, J.A. (1969), "The Dynamic Nonsubstitution Theorem", Review of Economic Studies 36, 67-76.

Nikaido, H. (1968), Convex Structures and Economic Theory, Academic Press, New York.

Persson, H. (1983), Theory and Applications of Multisectoral Growth Models, Ph.D. thesis, University of Gothenburg.

Restad, T. (1976), Modeller för Samhällsekonomisk Perspektivplanering, SOU 1976:51, Stockholm.

Stiglitz, J.E. (1970), "Non-Substitution Theorems with Durable Capital Goods", Review of Economic Studies 37, 543-553.

Production, Multi-Sectoral Growth and Planning
F.R. Førsund, M. Hoel, and S. Longva (Editors)
© Elsevier Science Publishers B.V. (North-Holland), 1985

THE MULTI-SECTORAL GROWTH MODEL MSG-4
FORMAL STRUCTURE AND EMPIRICAL CHARACTERISTICS

Svein Longva
Central Bureau of Statistics of Norway

Lorents Lorentsen
Central Bureau of Statistics of Norway

Øystein Olsen
Central Bureau of Statistics of Norway

1. Model background and history

The macroeconomic model known as the MSG-model (abbreviated from Multi-Sectoral Growth) was first presented in Johansen (1960). This work represented the first successful implementation of an applied general equilibrium model without the assumption of fixed input-output coefficients (cf. Jorgenson (1982)). Johansen assumed fixed coefficients in modelling demands for intermediate goods, but applied Cobb-Douglas productions functions in modelling the substitution between labour and capital services. Neutral technical change was assumed by adding time trends to the linear logarithmic production functions. Johansen replaced the normally applied assumption of fixed coefficients in household demand by a system of demand functions based on Frisch (1959). Both producer and household behaviour were thus dependent on relative prices. The total supplies of capital and labour were assumed to be inelastic, i.e. exogenous, and the equilibrium solution to Johansen's original 20-sector model was simultaneous in prices and quantities.

The Johansen study was an attempt to construct a model which covered important aspects of the process of economic growth, with particular

The authors would like to thank Petter Frenger, Michael Hoel, and Dale W. Jorgenson for useful comments to an earlier draft.

emphasis on explaining the differences in growth rates between various
sectors of the economy. It was the explicit intention of the model's orgina-
tor that the theoretical content should be kept simple enough for the
model to be implemented by existing statistics and solved by means of
computational equipment available around 1960. Linear logarithmic functions imply that the parameters describing substitution between labour
and capital can be estimated as factor shares from a single data point.
The price elasticities of the Frisch demand system can also be determined
from a single data point, given the expenditure elasticities and the elasticity of the marginal utility of total expenditure, which must be estimated
econometrically. As a concession to computational difficulties, the original
study only included calculations of growth rates from a starting point,
obtained by neatly partitioning and manipulating the matrix formulation of
the model. During the sixties and early seventies, Johansen's MSG-model
gave impetus to an extensive research effort at the Institute of Economics
at the University of Oslo. For complete references, see Johansen (1974),
which also presents a survey of general equilibrium modelling up to that
date.

    Some years after the original presentation, the Norwegian Ministry of
Finance launched a project to revise the model and to develop adequate
computational and administrative routines so that the model could be used
in long-term economic planning. Larsen and Schreiner (in this volume)
contains a detailed account of the introduction of the MSG-model into the
Norwegian planning system. This revised version of the model, called
MSG-2F, became operational in 1968, and is described by Schreiner (1972)
and Spurkland (1970). MSG-2F was extensively used for some years,
mainly to calculate growth paths for the economic development five to thirty
years ahead, but also to solidify government reports and for ad hoc
analyses.

    In the early seventies another revision of the model became necessary
mainly due to the introduction of a new system of national accounts, but
also on account of the growing magnitude of the Norwegian petroleum
activities. This work was undertaken by the Central Bureau of Statistics
in 1974-75 with the close cooperation of the Ministry of Finance. This
third generation of the MSG-model, MSG-3, is presented in Lorentsen and
Skoglund (1976). Since MSG-3's introduction, the Central Bureau of
Statistics has been responsible for maintenance and further development
of the model along with other models originated to aid government plan-

ning in Norway.

The fourth and latest version, MSG-4, presented below, appeared in 1980. Through many years of administrative use the MSG-models have proved to be useful not only for elaborating long-term perspectives of macroeconomic trends, but also to some extent for sectoral planning. In addition to its traditional applications, MSG-4 was designed specifically to incorporate the interactions between economic growth and energy production and demand (see Longva, Lorentsen and Olsen (1983)). This fourth generation of the model includes alternative assumptions for the capital market, new elements from the neo-classical theory of production, some sector models that are partly based on an engineering approach, the greater application of econometric methods in assessing model parameters, and the introduction of a powerful and flexible computer system that greatly facilitates the computational work.

With these four major revisions, the size of the model has increased somewhat (the present version has 32 production sectors) and a number of changes have been made. However, the main theoretical content and structure of the original model have to a great extent been preserved from the original version. The pragmatic usefulness of Johansen's approach is underlined both by the continuous use of the model for more than 15 years in Norwegian economic planning (see Larsen and Schreiner in this volume), and through the international proliferation of the model. Gradually, the MSG type of model has become a concept in the literature on economic growth and planning, embracing a variety of multi-sectoral, neo-classical, long-term equilibrium models (cf. Bergman in this volume).

2. Choice of theoretical content in an equilibrium model to be used in long-term macroeconomic planning

2.1 Macroeconomic planning, theory, and practice

The concept macroeconomic planning has been defined differently by different authors. Johansen (1977) arrived at the following eclectic definition:

Macroeconomic planning is an institutionalized activity by, or on behalf

of a Central Authority for (a) the preparation of decisions and actions
to be taken by the Central Authority, and (b) the coordination of
decisions and actions by lower-order units of the economy, as
between themselves and vis-a-vis the Central Authority, for the
purpose of governing the development of the whole economy and its
constituent parts so as to achieve certain (more or less detailed and
more or less explicitly specified) goals for the economy and harmonize
the development of the economy with broader non-economic goals.

At the most advanced level this concept of planning would imply the
elaboration of strategies, i.e. sets of plans to meet different situations
where the actions would be conditional upon the future outcome of uncon-
trolled variables. The longer the planning horizon, the more important
becomes the strategy element. A theoretically satisfactory treatment of the
planning problem would require the use of intertemporal optimization
models, where the time profiles of the implemented political instruments
are determined by maximizing some time dependent welfare function. So
far such models have only been used for illustrative purposes in academic
settings rather than for decision making. The reasons are obvious: an
intertemporal optimization model with an adequate representation of the
economy and a maximand with several (conflicting) target variables is at
present unmanageable. And even if it was to become technically manageable, the model would probably not be transparent enough to be accepted
by decision makers. However, an iterative process between simple intertemporal optimization models and more traditional macroeconomic models is
manageable and an attractive compromise. In practice, models used for
planning purposes have been of the instrument-target type, operated by
assessing time paths for instruments and other variables exogenous to the
model. The preferable or optimal solution is then drawn from a mapping of
several alternative developments generated by the model. In most models
adapted for long-term macroeconomic planning, including MSG, the
instruments are represented only indirectly and in aggregate terms. The
main concern is to select feasible solutions; the issue of future implementation problems is often paid little attention or left aside. Nevertheless,
the implicit economic policy constraints necessary to attain the development paths generated by the model should be derived in order to evaluate
the results.

Even if we limit ourselves to the traditional instrument-target models,

there are still some fundamental choices to be made concerning the theoretical content of a long-term general equilibrium model used in a planning
process. These choices influence not only the model results but also their
proper interpretations. Broadly classsified, there are two basic model
approaches:

The first approach is to try to model what is actually going to happen
the next 10 to 20 years. In this case, if the model is to be realistic, it will
have to include some explicit or implicit elements of disequilibrium, which
taken together, result in discrepancies between potential and actual
growth, i.e. it must allow for low capacity utilization, delays of adjustments, probably some mismanagement, etc. This does not mean that the
model will have to trace business cycles, but that on average it will
account for some opportunities foregone.

The second approach is to try to model what would happen if every-
thing was working smoothly, i.e. to model potential growth or steady-
state growth. The Cambridge Growth Project originally adapted this
approach, using one model to describe the movement of the economy from
an initial situation towards a steady-state path and another model to
describe the steady-state path (see Stone (1964)). This method has the
advantage of being theoretically satisfactory, but the policy conclusions
one can draw from it depend on the realism of the steady-state path as a
preferable and "achieveable" goal.

Within the Norwegian context of long-term economic planning, the
MSG simulations have normally been considered as "neutral projections."
Although the intentions have not always been clearly stated, these simulations have been interpreted as projecting how the economy actually will
work and are normally not consistent with steady-state paths. The idea
has been to prolong the short- and medium-term trends, assuming that
external and internal conditions are not radically changed and that economic policies are reasonably successful.

In this approach, the relationship between the long-term path
depicted by the model and the transition path on which current policy
must be based is of course very important. As stressed by Bjerkholt and
Tveitereid (in this volume) the underlying logic of the long-term path is
that medium-term policy should be transitory and directed towards
reaching the long-term path. In the short-term and medium-term planning
of the Norwegian economy, the multi-sectoral input-output based models,
MODIS and MODAG, play a central role (see Bjerkholt and Longva (1980)

and Cappelen and Longva (1984)). These models are oriented towards demand management and incomes policy, combining certain elements from the Scandinavian model of inflation and Keynesian macrotheory. This is a contrast to the MSG-model where the factors of growth (growth in labour force, capital accumulation, and technical progress), i.e. supply side factors, are the driving forces. The separate modelling approaches for long-term planning and for short- and medium-term planning partly reflect the fact that the explicit policy instruments in Norway are mostly related to demand management and incomes policy, while the instruments affecting the supply side are more indirect and have a longer time perspective. However, it also reflects the fact that coordination between medium- and long-term planning and policy is hard to achieve. The "technical" solution adopted is either to let the medium-term projection approach the long-term path, or to "force" the long-term path through the last year of the current medium-term projection.

It is important to note that the projections produced in the Norwegian planning process have never been simple presentations of model calculations. Published projections, normally included as addenda to the government long-term programs, are the result of an iterative process, drawing on the information and experience of various agencies and experts. Once reliable base projections have been drawn, they serve as starting points for alternative projections, and they are extensively used in more detailed analyses - elaborating energy programs, deducing environmental consequences, analyzing regional effects, etc.

2.2. The modelling of labour and capital markets and of external trade

In the actual formulation of a general equilibrium model for the Norwegian economy there are some modelling issues that deserve special attention, namely how to model the labour and capital markets and how to model external trade.

In most economic growth models the total supply of labour is exogenous, i.e. inelastic. Hence, a change in the use of material input, energy, or capital must change the equilibrium price of labour in real terms. This approach seems appropriate as an approximation to the long-run equilibrium in the Norwegian labour market, or in any economy where full employment is the first priority target, and therefore has been chosen for the MSG-4 model.

The choice of an approximation for the long-run equilibrium in the capital market is less obvious. Two extreme alternatives emerge as convenient simplifications (Hogan (1979)):

i)   A fixed total input of capital, i.e. inelastic supply (MSG-4S).
ii) Fixed real rate of return to capital, i.e. perfectly elastic supply (MSG-4E).

In case i) changes in other inputs – materials, labour, or energy – will change the marginal productivity of capital. With a given total stock of capital the equilibrium rate of return to capital in real terms must also change. This may, over time, affect the willingness to save and invest, and the assumption of inelastic supply of capital may turn out to be implausible without some compensating capital policy or without some iterative mechanisms influencing the capital supply. While with inelastic supplies the interplay of labour and capital at the macro level is trivial, the equilibrium factor prices will need to be checked for realism.

In case ii) capital input is adjusted to changes in materials, labour or energy inputs so that the marginal productivity of capital is maintained. With this approximation of the long-run equilibrium in the capital market, a change for instance in the price of energy will change the total use of capital, materials and energy, the real price of labour and energy, and gross output.

A constant real rate of return to capital is characteristic of steady-state growth in a neo-classical growth model (i.e. an elastic supply of capital) while the assumption of an inelastic supply of capital is an appropriate short-run specification for such a model. Even though the MSG-model is not used to trace out steady-state paths in any strict sense, the steady-state results indicate that the assumption of perfectly elastic supply of capital is most suitable when studying the long-run tendencies of the economy. When studying the transition path, the assumption of inelastic supply of capital may be the most appropriate specification.

The two extreme methods of modelling the capital market have been embedded in two versions of the present MSG-model. Previous MSG-models featured an exogenous total supply of capital; this tradition is continued in a version called MSG-4S. In addition a new version with elastic supply of capital, called MSG-4E, has been developed. Except for this difference in the philosophy and modelling of the capital market, the two MSG versions are identical.

In academic models and textbooks, a (small) open economy is normally assumed to face a perfectly elastic supply of imports and a perfectly elastic demand for exports at given world market prices. If the economy consumes and is able to produce n different tradeables by means of m factors of production at constant returns to scale (where n>m), equilibrium conditions commonly imply that at most m goods will be produced and possibly exported. In such models only net exports of tradeable goods are determined (see Samuelson (1953)). This theory is, of course, not meant to be applied straightforwardly in an empirical model like MSG with only two primary production factors and 32 domestic production sectors of which around 20 produce tradeables. The theory reveals some equilibrium or optimum features of trade liberalization and specialization, but there are many good reasons for empirically rejecting it. In the model a production sector includes many different activities, some of which will survive facing international competition, many others which will not. Consequently the production technology of the sector will change due to changes in the activity composition, but the remaining (and possibly expanding activities) may still be within the old sector classification. Assuming only a small number of different production factors is also a simplification. More realistically there are specific types of capital and skilled labour in each production sector. Although an equilibrium solution may imply a specialization in the long run, immobility and different expectations will prevent it. For some sectors there may be nonproportionate returns to scale, in which case changes in scale will keep the rate of return to factors at the required level. Technological improvements will do the same.

Similarly, if Samuelson's stylized small country assumption is replaced by the assumption of country-specific goods, i.e. the Armington assumption of price dependent exports and imports, adaption along demand and supply curves may allow for more than m survivors. However, the assumption that foreign goods are imperfect substitutes to domestically produced tradeables may be difficult to accept in a long-term context, and the estimated elasticities will most probably be rather unreliable. Considerations of risk and uncertainty will also lead to hedging or diversification, even if calculations based on expectations suggest specialization.

As pointed out by Johansen (1974), these complicated problems of trade are not artifical difficulties created by the formal representation of the economy in a model. They represent real problems that are difficult to model adequately. Again, the MSG solution is a compromise. In MSG-4S and MSG-4E export volumes, noncompetitive import prices, and market shares of imports (estimated by commodity and receiving sector) are exogenous, while prices of competitive imports and exports are endogenous and cost determined. In MSG-4E one can optionally apply a balance of trade restriction, in which case export volumes and import shares are scaled proportionately from initially assessed developments to provide a given balance of trade at every point of time. This option is convenient in the actual use of the model, but the procedure is theoretically dubious unless the exogenous assessments of export volumes and import shares are based on support models or other supplementary information. The idea is that if the relative composition of production of tradeables can be determined by specific market analyses, the exchange rate policy and incomes policy must secure a competitiveness which scales the production of tradeables to a required level. This also means that the price levels of Norwegian tradeables, generated by MSG, are assumed to correspond to the inter-national equilibrium levels.

3. Economic and formal structure of MSG-4

The fourth generation of the MSG-model was constructed in order to study the overall long-term prospects of the Norwegian economy and also more specifically the long-term interactions between economic growth and energy supply and demand. The model is mainly used by the Ministry of Finance as a quantitative tool in macroeconomic planning, but other govern-ment bodies and research institutes also make use of it. The dimensions of the model, 32 production sectors and 42 commodities, reflect a compromise between the ambition to produce and to apply detailed sector information with the Ministry's need for a manageable model. In most industries the input aggregates - labour, capital, energy, and materials - are substitutable according to neo-classical production functions. In addition, interfuel substitution is assumed within the energy group of each sector. In the terminology of the model these input aggregates of commodities or primary inputs define activities, i.e. aggregates with fixed relative proportions. Thus, the model is based on an input-output description of the economy, where the substitution possibilities are defined between activities comprising aggregate inputs. Labour and capital are assumed to be freely moveable and malleable, i.e. unconstrained in the allocation between sectors.

As discussed in Section 2 there are two versions of the present MSG model, MSG-4S where total capital is exogenous and MSG-4E where the real rate of return to capital is exogenous. The development of the total production capacity of the economy is determined by the exogenous growth of total labour force, sectoral assessments of technical change, and total supply of capital (MSG-4S) or the rates of return to capital (MSG-4E). In addition, the composition of production influences total productive capacity since sectors are not equally efficient.

The model is closed by letting the level of household consumption be determined endogenously such that full capacity utilization is ensured. By omitting the macro consumption function, household consumption is determined by allocating to consumer activities what is left of production capacity over gross investments, government consumption, and net exports. The model calculates the corresponding equilibrium prices for commodities, real wages, and in the case of the MSG-4S version also the equilibrium real rate of return to capital. This does not necessarily mean that the model must show an economy running at "full employment" or at full capacity utilization or with general equilibrium prices - labour supply can be set below the available labour force, sectoral capacity utilization indices below one, or mark-up rates different from one. The model will, however, trace out paths of balanced growth in the sense that there is a continuous balance between supply and demand of goods and factors of production within the limits of available capacity. Some price indices such as nominal wages, the prices of non-competitive imports, oil, gas, electricity, government fees, and commodity taxes are exogenous to the model and determine the nominal price level.

By manipulating exogenous demand assessments, sector specific rates of technical change, parameters for capacity utilization, and mark-up rates, the model can be calibrated to coincide neatly with actual figures for one year or with period averages. From a disequilibrium starting point, the model can either be steered towards the long-term equilibrium (i.e. simulating the transition path) by normalizing parameters and exogenous growth rates, or it can be used to simulate a prolonged, partly malfunctioning, actual development.

Such long-term equilibrium paths depicted by the model also show many important deviations from uniform and constant growth rates. Partly this is due to formal properties of the model such as exogenous supply, demand and price assessments, different demand elasticities for different goods, and different rates of Hicks neutral technical change in production sectors. It may also be argued that 10 to 30 years is too short a period to impose steady-state growth properties when the focus is on "neutral projections".

The substitution parameters of the model are most properly interpreted as long-term elasticities. In an equilibrium model with no lags, as in MSG, agents react immediately to adjust their allocations to changes in prices or other incentives. In the real world, it necessarily takes time for economic agents to adapt to changed incentives. The MSG-model therefore "over-substitutes" in its predictions of year-by-year fluctuations caused for instance by significant changes in input prices. The model more adequately predicts the average development over a period where changed incentives have persisted long enough to allow agents to adjust.

A simplified structure of the MSG-4E version of the model is depicted in Figure 1. The MSG-4E version is easier to describe than MSG-4S, since the outside assessment of both wages and returns to capital, and the assumption of constant returns to scale (or exogenous prices or exogenously determined production) makes the model neatly recursive in a price model and a quantity model.

When examining Figure 1, assume that all industries produce at constant returns to scale, minimize costs, and set prices equal to unit costs. Start in the upper part of the diagram and assume given wage rates, returns to capital, trends of technical change, and capacity utilization indices. The intersectoral price-cost relations, mark-up indices, and the price dependent input demand functions then simultaneously determine the cost-minimizing techniques in terms of input coefficients (labour, capital, materials and energy per unit of output) and the commodity prices that cover calculated costs. The capacity utilization and mark-up indices are used to adjust for deviations from normal or long-run equilibrium behaviour.

Given the cost-minimizing techniques and prices, the quantity side of the model may be solved as a traditional input-output model with fixed coefficients. The scale of production by industry is determined by demand assessments - which are partly exogenous such as exports and govern-

198   Longva et al.

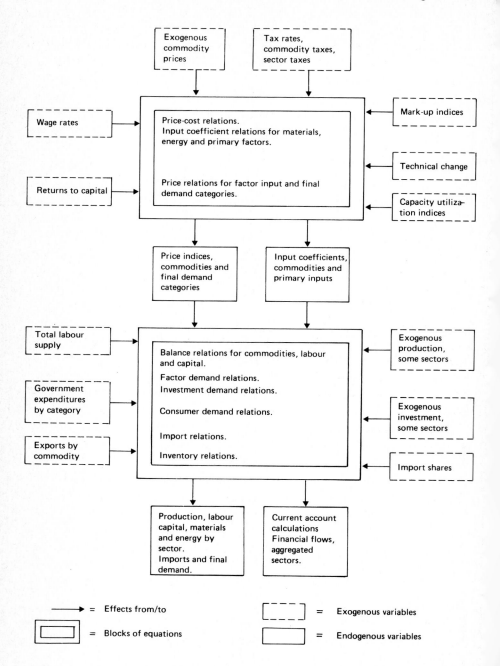

Figure 1. Structure of MSG-4E

ment expenditures, and partly endogenous such as private gross investments and household consumption - and by imports for intermediate and
final use which are calculated from import shares and specified by
commodity and purchasing sector. Private gross investments are determined in a closed loop with the scale of production by industry. The scale
of production by industry determines the demand for capital services and
thereby capital stock specified by industry and by kind of capital good.
This again determines private gross investments specified by commodity.
For given prices the commodity composition of household consumption
depends only upon total household consumption expenditure, which is
determined such that the specified labour force is fully employed.

In MSG-4E the productive capacity of the economy as a whole is
determined by the exogenous total labour force, technical change, the
capital stock consistent with the exogenous rate of return to productive
capital, and the distribution of production between sectors.

With an inelastic supply of capital in the MSG-4S version of the model,
there is a crucial link between the price and quantity side of the model
represented by the overall level of return to capital. Given the resource
restriction on capital, the level of return to capital has to be determined
endogenously. The equation systems of the two versions are equal, but
MSG-4S is simultaneous in prices and quantities.

The MSG-model also includes equations and special features not indicated in the figure, such as submodels for capital depreciation, indirect
taxes, government consumption, energy supply and demand, etc. Special
options to "control" the model's results for the balance of trade by adjusting the exogenous import shares and export volumes are introduced.

A number of support routines and models are also linked to MSG.
These models are either pre-calculations providing exogenous estimates
(e.g. labour force, population growth, oil investment and production
profiles, etc.) or post-calculations (e.g. demand for different types of
skilled labour, industry pollution, financial variables, etc.).

3.1 Basic concepts and balance equations for commodities and prices [1]

The Norwegian national accounting system, which very closely
adheres to the revised SNA (see the United Nations (1968)), forms the
conceptual framework for the MSG-model. The main model includes an

accounting system, i.e. balance equations and definitional relations, which to a great extent are identical with the real flows of the national accounts. The financial flows are not included in the main model except for some aggregated current account figures. However, a "post model" for financial flows has been constructed (cf. Section 3.6).

The commodity flows of the MSG-model can be described as flows between (functional) sectors. The interindustry transactions of the economy form a central component of the model, and the sector concept is first of all used for the classification of establishments and similar economic units into production sectors. The model has 32 production sectors, i.e. 27 industries and 5 general government production sectors. In addition to a classification of establishments, the sector concept is also applied to broad categories of goods and services classified by origin or use, i.e. sectors for imports, exports, household consumption, general government consumption, private investments, and general government investments.

The commodity classification is arrived at by adopting the "main producer" principle, i.e. letting all goods and services with the same industry as the main producer form one commodity. The classifications of industries and commodities are thus closely related. If strictly followed, this procedure will give the same number of domestically produced commodities as the number of industries.[2] Commodities representing imports for which there is no domestic production (noncompetitive imports) and marketed government services are included as separate commodities. Altogether there are 42 commodities in the model.

In addition to commodities, each production sector absorbs primary factors, i.e. labour and capital services. At present there is just one category of labour input, while the model distinguishes between three categories of capital goods ("buildings and constructions", "machinery" and "transportation equipment").[3]

The rather disaggregated representation of the commodity-by-sector flows makes it possible to focus both on the industrial and final demand structure, and on the industrial interdependences in a growth process. However, with respect to the specification of behavioural relations in the model it is hardly possible, nor essential for the quality of the model results, to introduce substitution possibilities between all inputs and outputs in each sector. To simplify the model, the detailed set of commodity and primary input flows in each sector is partitioned into mutually exclusive and exhaustive subsets. Each subset defines an aggregate of input or output commodities or of primary inputs. Substitution possibilities in the production or utility functions are introduced only between aggregates, i.e. activities.[4] Within each aggregate, fixed proportions are assumed, i.e. the aggregator functions are simple Leontief functions. In the model these fixed coefficient commodity and primary input aggregates within each sector are called activities.

In each production sector, commodities and primary inputs are aggregated into five input activities, namely one for capital services (three types of capital goods), one for labour (one type only), one for materials (all non-energy commodities), one for electricity (electricity and distribution services), and one for other energy inputs (petrol and fuel oil), for short called fuels. In the household consumption sector the individual input commodities are aggregated into 18 activities.

The different value concepts adopted are essential in the modelling of the interindustry transactions and in the modelling of substitution induced by changes in relative prices. The fixed coefficients within each activity are estimated from the national accounts for the base year of the model. This means that the quantities of commodity flows are measured in unit prices of the base year, i.e. constant unit values. The principal concept for evaluating commodity flows in the model is (approximate) basic values.[5] The basic value concept is preferred to producer value or purchaser value because the trade margins (including transport charges) and commodity tax rates may vary between receiving sectors of the same commodity, and thus may cause a discrepancy between calculated total supply and total demand in constant unit values in producer or purchaser prices.[6]

The activities, however, are evaluated in market values, computed as producer value of commodity outputs and as purchaser value of commodity inputs or primary inputs. The rationale behind this choice is that the substitution possibilities within each sector are specified between activities not between commodities. Market prices of activities have therefore been selected as the most relevant price concept when modelling producer and consumer behaviour.

In matrix notation, the commodity balance equation in the MSG-4 model, which includes the assumption of fixed activity coefficients, is given by

(3.1) $\Lambda_I I + \Lambda_X X = \Lambda_M M + \Lambda_E E + \Lambda_F F + \Lambda_C C + \Lambda_J J + \Lambda_A A.$

In relation (3.1) the Λ's are matrices of commodity-by-activity coefficients, where the elements are commodity flows relative to corresponding activity levels. The commodity flows are measured in basic value and the activity levels in producers' or purchasers' value. On the left hand side of (3.1) the Λ's are combined with (column) vectors of activity levels for imports (I) and domestic production (X) to give total supply of goods. On the right hand side the commodity demand is separated into intermediate inputs of materials (M), electricity (E) and fuels (F) (input activities for commodities in production sectors, see Section 3.2), and the final demand categories household consumption (C), gross investments (J) and exports (A).

With respect to the price side of the model, the separation of commodity flows into activities implies that the following set of activity price indices may be defined:

(3.2) $P_i = \Lambda_i' B$ $i = I, X, M, E, F, C, J, A$

where the P's are (column) vectors of price indices for the commodity activities specified in (3.1), and B is a vector of commodity basic price indices, i.e. prices of commodity flows (superscript ' denotes transposed matrix).

(3.2) is the dual relation to (3.1), with the number of equations corresponding to the number of activities in the commodity balance equation. To simplify the specification of (3.2) we have omitted the commodity taxes, which are specified in rather great detail in the actual equations of the model.

3.2 The submodel for production [7]

While substitution possibilities in earlier versions of the MSG-model were restricted to the primary inputs labour and capital, a more general specification of the production structure has been selected for MSG-4. The model of producer behaviour includes substitution possibilities between the input activities labour (L), capital (K), electricity (E), fuels (F), and materials (M), while fixed coefficients are assumed within the activities.

The substitution responses are formally represented by Generalized
Leontief (GL) cost functions, interpreted as second-order approximations
to the "real" production structure (Diewert (1971)). In most industries the
production functions are linearly homogeneous in the aggregate inputs, and
technical change is assumed to be Hicks neutral.[8]

In addition to the separation of the industry inputs into activities, a
further separability condition is introduced restricting the substitution
properties of the two energy inputs. Electricity and fuels are assumed to
be weakly separable from the other aggregate inputs, implying that the
energy goods are only substituted against other inputs via an aggregate
for total energy input, denoted by U in the following.

Restricting this aggregate function so as to be linearly homogeneous,
the overall cost function will be separable in the corresponding price
indices (Berndt and Christensen (1973)), and the dual to the energy
activity aggregate may be interpreted as a price index for energy
(denoted by P_U). A GL unit cost function is selected as an approximation
also for this relation.

For industry j the unit cost structure is represented by the following
relations:

$$(3.3) \qquad \frac{Q_j}{X_j} = h_j(t) \sum_k \sum_\ell \alpha_{k\ell} (P_{kj} P_{\ell j})^{\frac{1}{2}} \quad ; \qquad k,\ell = K,L,U,M$$

$$(3.4) \qquad P_{Uj} = \sum_k \sum_\ell \beta_{k\ell} (P_{kj} P_{\ell j})^{\frac{1}{2}} \quad ; \qquad k,\ell = E,F$$

where the P's are prices of the input activities, Q_j denotes total costs,
$h_j(t)$ describes Hicks neutral technical change, and the α's and β's are
parameters.

The estimation of the cost functions is based on time series of national
accounting figures for the five aggregate inputs labour, capital, materials,
electricity and fuels, and price indices for the same inputs.

Applying "Shephards lemma" (Shephard (1953)), the factor demand
system in terms of factor input coefficients may be derived as

$$(3.5) \quad Z_{kj} \equiv \frac{\partial \frac{Q_j}{X_j}}{\partial P_{kj}} = h_j(t) \sum_\ell \alpha_{k\ell} \left(\frac{P_{\ell j}}{P_{kj}}\right)^{\frac{1}{2}}, \quad k,\ell = K,L,U,M$$

$$(3.6) \quad Z_{Ukj} \equiv \frac{\partial P_{Uj}}{\partial P_{kj}} = \sum_\ell \beta_{k\ell} \left(\frac{P_{\ell j}}{P_{kj}}\right)^{\frac{1}{2}}, \quad k,\ell = E,F$$

$$(3.7) \quad Z_{kj} = Z_{Ukj} Z_{Uj}, \quad k = E,F$$

where the Z_{kj}'s are input coefficients measuring aggregate input per unit of output, and the Z_{Ukj}'s are energy coefficients measuring the input of electricity and fuels respectively per unit of total energy use.

The factor demand relations of industry j may then be written as

$$(3.8) \quad \begin{matrix} K_j \\ L_j \\ M_j \\ E_j \\ F_j \end{matrix} = Z_{kj} X_j; \quad k = K,L,M,E,F.$$

The producers are assumed to be profit maximizers, which implies that marginal costs equal the output price, i.e. for industry j:

$$(3.9) \quad P_{Xj} = \frac{\partial Q_j}{\partial X_j}.$$

However, when the production function is linearly homogeneous, profit maximization fails to determine a unique supply curve. In these industries it is assumed that output is priced such that the price just covers average costs (equal to marginal costs). This means that (3.9) can be interpreted as a competitive market equilibrium condition rather than as a supply function. Cost minimization is then, together with this equilibrium condition, sufficient as a description of producer behaviour.[9)]

With the notation introduced above the price-cost relation for industry j may be written as

(3.10) $P_{Xj} = Z_{Lj}P_{Lj} + Z_{Kj}P_{Kj} + Z_{Mj}P_{Mj} + Z_{Ej}P_{Ej} + Z_{Fj}P_{Fj}$

where P_{Lj} is an index of wage costs per unit of labour input and P_{Kj} is the user cost of capital.[10)]

For each industry, (3.10) gives the relation between the activity price indices defined in (3.2) and the production structure as measured by the input coefficients Z; (3.10) is the dual relation to (3.8). For given prices of the primary inputs (P_{Lj} and P_{Kj}), the relation expresses that the output prices are determined from the cost side.

While the wage rates (P_{Lj}) are actually exogenous variables, the model contains expressions for user cost of capital that are non-trivial. Capital stock is assumed to follow an exponential survival curve (geometric depreciation). With the assumption of a constant composition of capital equipment within each industry, the user cost of capital in industry j is expressed as

(3.11) $P_{Kj} = \sum_{i=1}^{m} \kappa_{ij}(R_j + \delta_{ij})P_i$

where R_j is the rate of return to capital, the κ's are fixed industry capital structure coefficients, the δ's are the fixed rates of depreciation specified by kind of capital and industry, and m is the number of capital categories (three in most industries).

3.3 Labour and capital markets

As discussed in Section 2 the total supply of labour is exogenous, i.e. inelastic. The supply of labour, defined as man hours, is derived from estimates of population development and changes in working force participation rates by sex and age, and from assumed changes in normal working hours. The development of the nominal wage rate in each industry is also determined exogenously. This allows for wage differentials between industries even in long-run equilibrium. When using the model, the historical wage differentials, which have been rather stable in Norway, are normally assumed to prevail also in the future. This means that the (common) change in wage rates may be interpreted as the "numeraire" of the model.

The rate of return to capital in industry j is given by the equation

(3.12) $R_j = \rho_j \bar{R}$

where ρ_j is the relative rate of return of industry j and $\bar{R}$ is the rate of
return to capital in the economy as a whole. The ρ's are exogenous variables, while $\bar{R}$, as mentioned in Section 2, is exogenous in the model
version with perfectly elastic supply of capital (the price-quantity recursive version), but is endogenous in the version with inelastic supply of
capital (the price-quantity simultaneous version). The assumption of
return differentials between industries is explained by traditional differences in profit requirements, investment risks, average size of the firms,
degree of monopolization, etc., within the various industries (Johansen
(1960)). Relative rates of return for the different industries are actually
estimated from national account data of operating surplus (the residually
determined capital income). Following Strøm (1967) it is assumed that
there is not a divergent development in the observed relative rates of
return, and base year values for the ρ's are calculated as the steady state
solutions of these magnitudes.[11]

3.4 The submodel for household consumption [12]

As in the original version of the MSG-model developed by Leif
Johansen, there is no aggregate consumption function in MSG-4. Total
consumption is determined residually as what is left of total capacity output over gross investments, government consumption, and net exports.
Nevertheless, a system of household demand functions is a central part of
the model, determining the commodity composition of household demand
from relative prices and the level of total consumption. More precisely,
the demand system determines the allocation of demand between consumption activities, while commodity demand follows from the assumption of
fixed coefficients within each of these aggregates.

The chosen system of demand functions has been directly specified
rather than derived from an explicit specification of either the direct or
the indirect utility function. It is important that the system have reasonable long-run properties. For reasons of transparency it is advantageous

that the parameters of the demand functions have fairly straightforward interpretations.

The demand for consumption activity (category) i is written as

$$(3.13) \qquad C_i = \eta_{Ci} (\Theta V)^{\xi_i} \prod_j P_{Cj}^{\gamma_{ij}}$$

where V is total expenditure, Θ is an auxiliary variable, P_{Cj} is the price of consumption activity j, and η_{Ci}, ξ_i and γ_{ij} are parameters. The system can be interpreted as a first-order logarithmic approximation of any complete system of demand functions. The auxiliary variable Θ is introduced to insure that the budget constraint

$$(3.14) \qquad \sum_i P_{Ci} C_i = V$$

is fullfilled for every combination of prices and demand. The specification of Θ into the demand system (3.13) is commonly denoted "horizontal adjustments of Engel curves." If the demand system is adjusted to fit the data in a base year (i.e. Θ is normalized to one), the ξ's and γ's have straightforward interpretations as Engel and Cournot elasticities, respectively.

In the estimation of the demand system (3.13-3.14), which is based on national accounting data, rather strong restrictions are placed on the underlying utility function. The "complete scheme" approach of Frisch (1959) assumed "want independence" (an additive utility function), i.e. strong separability between every single consumption good. In MSG-4 the energy orientation of the model structure has led us to introduce want dependence within two groups of consumption activities, housing and transportation services, where energy use is strongly related to the consumption of other goods. The assumption of strong separability between these two groups and the other consumption activities is retained.

3.5 Other main parts of the model

Private investments

Optimal capital stock per unit of output in each industry is determined by the cost-minimizing procedure underlying the (unit) input demand functions (3.5) and (3.6). The MSG-4 model thus includes relations describing neo-classical investment behaviour. In deriving investments and commodity demand from changes in capital stocks, the model distinguishes between a number of capital/investment categories. For each category an investment activity, J_i, is defined, "demanding" deliveries of commodities in constant proportions. The activity level of investment activity (category) i is determined by the relations

$$(3.15) \qquad J_i = \sum_{j=1}^{n} \kappa_{ij} \left[(K_j - K_j(-1)) + \delta_{ij} K_j \right]$$

where n is the number of industries. As mentioned in Section 3.2, the fixed κ's indicate the assumed constant composition of the capital equipment within each industry.

External trade

Export activities - one for each commodity of which there is domestic production - are exogenously determined. Import activity levels are derived from simple import demand relations, with import shares specified with respect to the various intermediate and final demand activities (categories). The import relations are thus written as

$$(3.16) \qquad \Lambda_I I = (S_M \circ \Lambda_M) M + (S_E \circ \Lambda_E) E + (S_F \circ \Lambda_F) F$$

$$+ (S_C \circ \Lambda_C) C + (S_J \circ \Lambda_J) J + (S_A \circ \Lambda_A) A$$

where the S's are import-share matrices (the symbol 'o' denotes matrix multiplication element by element). In the present versions of the model changes in the import shares by commodity are exogenous variables.

In MSG-4E and MSG-4S, the balance of trade is endogenously deter-mined (endogenous prices, but exogenous export volumes and import shares assessed by the model user). In a special version of MSG-4E, MSG-4ET, the user's preliminary assessments of export volumes and the import volumes implied by the import shares are endogenously scaled to achieve a given target path for the balance of trade. Some commodities are excepted from the scaling procedure in MSG-4ET. For example, the export assessments for oil, gas, and shipping services are retained at the user determined values. Thus, in MSG-4ET, the traditional export/import industries have to restructure to attain the required external balance. The balance of trade restriction in MSG-4ET first of all provides a convenient procedure for fine-tuning a model run. It does not provide a procedure for determining the composition of tradeables.

Government consumption and investments

In the present version there are five government production sectors. In these sectors gross investments (and thereby capital stock), and employment, material, and energy inputs are determined exogenously. Government consumption is calculated as gross total wages, material expenditures and depreciation less marketed government services, i.e. in accordance with the national accounting practice.

3.6 Special features of the MSG-4 model

The above description of the formal structure outlines the main features and economic content of the MSG-4 model. However, from this outline have been excluded a number of details in the actual equation system, exceptions from the general treatment of sectors and commodities, and other specific properties. The omittance of commodity taxes in equa-tion (3.2) and industry taxes in equation (3.10) has already been mentioned. To complete the presentation of the model the most important of these special features will be discussed below.

Net additions to stocks

Relations describing net additions to stocks specified by commodity are included in the model structure. Changes in stocks are related to changes in supply by a vector of fixed coefficients. Net additions to stocks are then of course also included in the commodity balance equation (3.1).

The specification of electricity flows

As emphasized above, the principal concept for evaluating commodity flows in the model is basic values. However, in the MSG-4 model special attention is given to the specification of value flows for electricity. In the national accounts the basic value flows for electricity are divided into two model commodities, electricity and distribution services, with two corresponding production sectors. The two commodities are constructed by deducting distribution costs and calculated rates of price differentiation, specified with respect to user, from the basic value flows in the accounts. The resulting constant value flow defines the volume concept for electricity in the model, referred to as "constant standard value." The price differentiation terms are specified explicitly in the model as artifical "taxes" or "subsidies" with differentiated rates. On the demand side of the model the two commodities, electricity and distribution services, are assumed to be used in fixed but purchaser differentiated proportions. In the model language they thus constitute one commodity activity in each sector.[14]

Furthermore the specification of the production structure in the two "electricity supply sectors" differs from the general formulation outlined above. The cost structure is specified in order to benefit from calculations of future long-term marginal costs in electricity supply. This kind of data is provided by the Norwegian Water Resources and Electricity Board.[15]

Oil activities and ocean transport

Crude oil and gas production and ocean transport are large and important sectors in the Norwegian economy. Their activity levels have a particularly important impact on the trade balance. These industries are completely "exogenous sectors" in the present MSG-model, as investments (and thereby capital stock), employment, production, and material input requirements must be given by the model user. For the oil sector, the exogenous treatment is justified by the dominating role of the government in oil related activities and by the limited number and diversity of oil and gas fields in actual production or to be developed in the next 20 years. The activity level in ocean transport is clearly dependent on international trade, and exports of these services are exogenous in MSG-4.

Industries with decreasing returns to scale

As noted in the description of the general production model, the production technologies in most sectors are assumed to be homogeneous of degree one in the specified inputs. Exceptions from this specification - in addition to the two electricity sectors - are agriculture, fishing, and mining. Retaining the general formulation of GL cost functions, these three sectors are assumed to exhibit decreasing returns to scale based on the argument that they are extractive activities. The exogenous determination of the production levels is justified on account of the strong government influence on the development of these industries.[16]

Corrections for disequilibrium

MSG-4 is formulated as an equilibrium model. Perfect mobility and given utilization rates of capital and labour are assumed, and the prices may be interpreted as equilibrium prices. The estimated parameters of the model are supposed to be long-run parameters. However, the economy itself is normally not in equilibrium and there is therefore no reason to expect that a simulation on the model would automatically result in endogenous variables that coincide with actual figures for either the past or the future.

Since the MSG-model is a model for practical use, some of the main "sources" of discrepancies between long-run equilibrium and actual performance are identified and parameterized in the model. The most important of these adjustment parameters are

- capacity utilization rates (short-run demand fluctuations)
- mark-up rates on prices (price setting or monopoly behaviour in the short run)
- "temperature-corrections" for energy use (climatic conditions)
- differences between long- and short-run demand adjustments (partial adjustment or price-lags in the demand relations in the short run).

From the estimations of the submodels for producer behaviour and household consumption, these adjustment parameters normally can be derived for past years including the base year of the model. Given the base year estimates of these adjustment parameters, the model may then – from a disequilibrium starting point – be steered towards an equilibrium path by normalizing these parameters.[17]

Calculations of financial flows

MSG-4 contains relations between real flows of the economy. These flows are traced between functional sectors. Perfect mobility and a given utilization of labour and capital are assumed, and the model then calculates the long-run development of volume figures such as production by industry, household consumption, investment, and the corresponding equilibrium prices. Equations describing financial flows between institutional sectors and relations between income and demand (i.e. a "Keynesian" consumption function) are not explicitly specified in the main model. A common rationale for this is that an equilibrium path traced by the MSG-model tacitly assumes that incomes and financial flows between different sectors are distributed in such a way that the calculated development can be realized.

However, from a user point of view calculations of incomes and financial flows are very useful for evaluating the realism of an economic development (in real terms) simulated by MSG-4. In addition to MSG's

calculation of national account figures in constant and current prices, a
"post model" (called MINK) which calculates financial flows has been
constructed and linked to the MSG-model (Bergan (1984)). The MINK
model contains relations between six institutional sectors of the Norwegian
economy. The equations in the model may be interpreted as simplified
income and capital accounts for these sectors. Starting out from calculations of incomes and expenditures (including transfers), total savings for
each sector are estimated. Financial investments are defined as the difference between total savings and real investments. Accumulating the figures
for financial investments, the development of the stock of financial assets
in the various sectors may be calculated.

Income and expenditure figures used as input to the financial calculations are partly taken from a simulation of the MSG-model (e.g. wages,
operating surplus, and indirect taxes) and partly exogenously (e.g.
transfers and direct taxes). In distributing various income flows from
MSG-4 to the six (institutional) sectors in the MINK model, fixed coefficients are applied. Incomes/expenditures in terms of interest flows are
dependent, however, on the stocks of finanical assets.

As mentioned above, the MINK model may be used to examine the
consistency between the development of real values from the MSG model
and the corresponding financial flows. In addition to a comparison between
figures for household consumption (from MSG) and disposable income and
savings by households (from MINK), the balance of current accounts,
government incomes and expenditures, and the relationship between
savings and investments in private enterprises are evaluated.

4.   Empirical characteristics of MSG-4 illustrated by long-term total elasticities

The MSG-4 model is meant to be a practical tool in the long-term
planning process. Both the formal structure and the empirical content are
decisive for the actual usefulness of the model. The close conceptual and
empirical links to the national accounts are, as already mentioned, a main
feature of the model. The parameters of the production and consumption
submodels are estimated econometrically from national accounts, time
series. The fixed coefficients of the activities, i.e. the input-output

coefficients, are estimated from the national accounts for the base year of
the model. The model is regularly updated; normally the base year lags
only one or two years behind the present year.

The submodels for production and consumption are presented in
Longva and Olsen (1983a, 1983c) and Bjerkholt and Rinde (1983),
respectively. Instead of repeating the discussion of these empirical
findings we shall present the empirical characteristics of the complete
model through estimates of long-term total elasticities.

All model-builders have to cut some corners in order to keep their
model at a manageable level. As clearly indicated in the discussion in
Section 3, the MSG-model is not a complete model of the working of the
economy. Several important groups of variables, which obviously are
endogenous to the economy are treated as exogenous in the model. This
means that the model will, at least for some types of sensitivity analysis,
yield unrealistic, counterintuitive, or even adverse results. A
presentation of the empirical characteristics of MSG-4, as given below,
will only illustrate the functioning of the model as such and not
necessarily the working of the economy. The actual usefulness of MSG-4
can therefore only be reviewed when the model is regarded in its proper
setting, i.e. as a tool in a planning or a policy analysing process. An
example of the utilization of the model as a tool for describing and
understanding how the economy actually works and to make projections is
given by Bjerkholt and Tveitereid (in this volume).

4.1 Some elasticity concepts [18)]

Elasticities can only be given a precise interpretation with reference to
a specified model. In general, elasticities refer to measures of the respon-
siveness of the endogenous variables to changes in the exogenous variables. The most common and well-known examples are the elasticities
defined from a single demand equation (partial elasticities). In this case
the own-price elasticity is the percentage change in quantity demanded
resulting from a one percent change in the price of the good in question,
assuming that all other (specified) determinants of demand remain constant. Elasticities with respect to other prices (cross-price elasticities) or
with respect to income or output (income or output elasticities) are similarly defined. In simultaneous models one can also define elasticities from

a single equation as the percentage change in one endogenous variable resulting from a one percent change in one of the exogenous variables, assuming all other exogenous - and all other endogenous variables - remain constant. However, in a simultaneous model a change in one of the exogenous variables will in general affect all endogenous variables. An initial shock in equation j will have repercussions through the model system back to the endogenous variables in equation j. The total elasticity may then be defined as the percentage change in an endogenous variable resulting from a one percent change in one of the exogenous variables, assuming that all other exogenous variables remain constant - but allowing all endogenous variables to attain their new equilibrium values.

The magnitudes of partial and total elasticities defined in the same model may be strikingly different. Consider for instance the impacts of an increase in the electricity price on electricity demand in a MSG production sector. The partial elasticity, derived from a factor demand function, may be low if the elasticities of substitution for electricity against other input factors are low. The total elasticity, derived from solving the whole model, may on the other hand be quite high, since low substitution elasticities on the input side mean that the increasing energy cost to a great extent is passed over to the output prices, reducing demand, and hence scaling down both the output level and energy use of the sector.

In static, linear models the total elasticities follow straightforwardly as the elasticities of the reduced form model. In dynamic, non-linear models the total elasticities are clearly both dependent on time and on the reference scenario. The classic example is the effects on consumption from increasing investments in a growth model of the MSG type. The short-term effect is a reduction in consumption, but as investments accumulate the productive capacity of the economy increases and allows for both higher investments and consumption than in the reference scenario. The short-term elasticity is thus negative, the medium-term elasticity passes through zero, and the long-term elasticity is positive. Furthermore, if the return to capital is a decreasing function of the stock of capital, the magnitude of the elasticity is at each point of time dependent on the initial stock of capital (or in general dependent on all of the variables in the reference scenario).

Elasticities as defined above are single measures of how a specific model is working. Keeping in mind that the elasticities may be defined in several ways, that they change signs and magnitudes over time, and are dependent on the reference scenario, a set of total elasticities may be of great value to the model user. In addition to the instructive or pedagogical value of the elasticities, they give useful information when preparing new rounds of model calculations. The availability of total elasticities may even save rounds of full numerical recalculations, since elasticities may be used to approximate new solutions by adjusting a reference scenario. This procedure is particularly useful when the model is (close to) static and linear, in which case the reduced form coefficients give a full set of (approximately correct) elasticities or table of effects (cf. Cappelen, Holm and Sand (1980)).

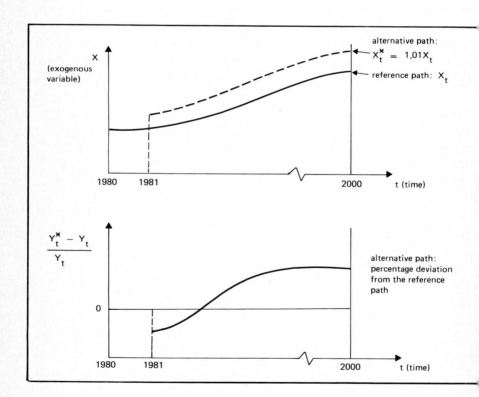

Figure 2. Procedure for estimating long-term total elasticities

4.2 Elasticities with respect to changes in the growth potential

Most of the MSG elasticities reported below are long-term total elasticities. They are calculated by increasing the value of one exogenous variable one per cent at each point of time compared to a reference scenario, and then calculating the deviations in the resulting endogenous variables at a terminal point where the model is assumed to be in long-term equilibrium. The reference scenario for the elasticity below covers the period 1980 to 2000. The procedure is illustrated in Figure 2.

Where relevant the elasticities are calculated for all three versions of the MSG-4 model, i.e. the simultaneous version, MSG-4S, the price-quantity recursive version, MSG-4E, and the trade balance restricted version of MSG-4E, MSG-4ET.[20] This comparison of elasticities reveals important differences in the theoretical contents of the three model versions although their equation systems are – with minor exceptions for MSG-4ET – exactly the same.

The elasticities for some key economic aggregates with respect to changes in main economic growth factors (employment, technical change, and capital stock) are displayed in Table 4.1 for the three models. Table 4.2 gives some specific elasticities for labour and capital input by industries, and illustrates in more detail the substitution effects of the model. The comments below are grouped by kind of exogenous change.

Increased total employment

An increase in total employment increases the productive capacity of the economy. Thus, gross domestic product (GDP) increases in all three model versions. There is, however, a marked difference between the impact on the activity level in MSG-4S (i.e. with a completely inelastic supply of real capital assumed) and the corresponding effects calculated when using the MSG-4E or the MSG-4ET version (where the supply of capital is assumed to be infinitly elastic). In the latter cases a one per cent increase in total employment leads to increases in GDP and total capital stock of approximately the same magnitude. The reason is rather obvious. In most of MSG industries the input coefficients – and thus the relations between labour and capital – are functions only of prices (as the production functions are linearly homogeneous). In MSG-4E as well as in

MSG-4ET, where prices are independent of quantity variables, the input coefficients are not influenced by changes in total employment; in each industry the capital stock changes proportionally to the change in employment. The fact that both the elasticity of the total capital stock and the GDP-elasticity with respect to employment slightly exceeds one in the simulation on the MSG-4E model is a result of a change in the composition of industries in favour of relatively capital-intensive consumer good industries.

In the simultaneous version of the model (MSG-4S), total capital stock is exogenous and thus unaffected by the increase in total employment. This is sufficient to explain why the impact on total output of the economy is markedly less in this case than when the change in employment is accompanied by a corresponding change in the capital stock. The input structure in industries changes, and the production techniques become more labour intensive and less capital intensive. Changes in the input structure require, as mentioned above, changes in (relative) input prices. Since wage rates are exogenous, other prices must increase in order to make labour relatively cheaper. It is seen from Table 4.1 that the most important effect on prices is a significant increase in the rate of return to capital. This makes labour input relatively cheaper, thus motivating the producers to apply more labour-intensive techniques, and at the same time counteracting the increased demand for capital caused by the higher activity level in the economy. The implicit elasticity for total labour input with respect to the real product wage (nominal wage deflated by the GDP deflator) is slightly above -2. With respect to the real wage (nominal wage deflated by consumption prices) this elasticity is considerably lower in absolute terms (close to -1.2). The interpretation is that along this growth path the real wage will have to decrease by 2 per cent (alternatively 1.2 per cent) to absorb a 1 per cent increase in labour supply.

Turning to the effects on final demand categories it is seen from Table 4.1 that the strongest impact of increasing total employment is an increase in private consumption. This applies both to the simultaneous version and the price-quantity recursive version, particularly when no restriction on the balance of trade is imposed. The highest elasticity for private consumption is reasonably enough derived from the MSG-4E version since this model involves the strongest long-run impact on the

Table 4.1. Effects of changing the growth potential of the economy: impacts on main economic aggregates and corresponding prices derived from simulations on different model versions. Elasticities

MSG-4S: The price-quantity simultaneous version
MSG-4E: The price-quantity recursive version
MSG-4ET: The price-quantity recursive version with restricted trade balance

Growth factors:	Total employment			Technical change			Total capital stock	Rate of return	
Model version:	MSG-4S	MSG-4E	MSG-4ET	MSG-4S	MSG-4E	MSG-4ET	MSG-4S	MSG-4E	MSG-4ET
V O L U M E S									
GDP	0.6	1.1	1.0	1.5	2.2	2.1	0.4	-0.07	-0.06
Export surplus[*]	-1.0	-1.8	0.0	-1.6	-2.9	-0.6	-0.6	0.12	0.02
Domestic use	1.0	1.9	0.9	2.1	3.4	2.3	0.6	-0.12	-0.07
Private consumption	2.1	3.1	1.4	4.2	6.0	3.7	0.8	-0.17	-0.07
Investments	-0.1	1.0	0.8	-0.1	1.5	1.3	0.9	-0.11	-0.11
Government cons. ..	-0.1	-0.1	-0.1	-0.1	-0.2	-0.1	-0.1	0.01	0.01
Total employment	1.0	1.0	1.0	-	-	-	-	-	-
Total capital stock .	-	1.3	1.0	-	2.1	1.7	1.0	-0.19	-0.17
Total energy demand .	1.4	2.4	1.5	2.3	3.9	2.8	0.7	-0.16	-0.09
P R I C E S									
GDP ....:..	0.5	-0.1	-0.1	-0.9	-1.7	-1.7	-0.4	0.07	0.07
Domestic use	0.6	0.0	0.0	-0.9	-1.9	-1.9	-0.5	0.08	0.08
Private consumption	0.8	0.0	0.0	-0.9	-2.1	-2.1	-0.6	0.11	0.11
Investments	0.5	0.0	0.0	-1.5	-2.2	-2.3	-0.4	0.08	0.06
Government cons. ..	0.2	0.0	0.0	-0.6	-0.9	-0.9	-0.1	0.03	0.03
Real product wage ...	0.5	-	-	0.9	1.7	1.7	0.4	-0.07	-0.07
Returns to capital ..	7.2	-	-	11.6	-	-	-5.6	1.00	1.00
Real energy price ...	-0.5	-	-	0.9	1.7	1.7	0.4	-0.07	-0.07

*) Change in export surplus in constant prices relative to total export in the reference scenario.

Table 4.2. Effects of changing the growth potential of the economy: impacts on employment and capital stock in various industries. Elasticities

Growth factors: Model version:	Relative shares*)	Total employment		Technical change		Total capital stock	Rate of return
		MSG-4S	MSG-4E	MSG-4S	MSG-4E	MSG-4S	MSG-4E
EMPLOYMENT							
Primary industries	5.9	2.9	0.1	1.3	-3.0	-2.1	0.4
Energy intensive industries ..	2.0	0.7	0.1	-1.6	-2.6	-0.5	0.1
Other industries and mining ..	15.3	1.3	0.9	-0.8	-1.4	-0.3	0.0
Construction	6.6	0.7	1.5	-1.7	-0.7	0.6	-0.1
Electricity supply	2.0	1.0	1.9	1.1	2.7	0.7	-0.1
Domestic transportation	11.3	0.8	1.3	0.2	1.0	0.3	-0.1
Private service industries ...	32.6	1.4	1.7	0.4	1.0	0.3	-0.1
Public service industries	22.2	0.0	0.0	0.0	0.0	0.0	0.0
Ocean transport	1.5	0.0	0.0	0.0	0.0	0.0	0.0
Oil- and gas production	0.6	0.0	0.0	0.0	0.0	0.0	0.0
All industries	100.0	1.0	1.0	0.0	0.0	0.0	0.0
CAPITAL STOCK							
Primary industries	5.8	-1.4	0.1	-2.1	0.3	1.2	-0.2
Energy intensive industries ..	1.9	-0.7	0.1	-1.7	-0.4	0.6	-0.1
Other industries and mining ..	7.7	-1.2	0.9	-1.7	1.7	1.7	-0.3
Construction	1.1	-1.3	1.5	-1.0	3.4	2.2	-0.3
Electricity supply	9.2	1.1	2.2	0.4	2.2	0.8	-0.2
Domestic transportation	5.7	-0.1	1.3	-0.5	1.7	1.1	-0.2
Private service industries ...	31.2	0.3	2.9	0.9	5.0	2.0	-0.4
Public service industries	20.4	0.0	0.0	0.0	0.0	0.0	0.0
Ocean transport	5.6	0.0	0.0	0.0	0.0	0.0	0.0
Oil- and gas production	11.4	0.0	0.0	0.0	0.0	0.0	0.0
All industries	100.0	0.0	1.3	0.0	2.1	1.0	-0.2

*) Relative shares in the year 2000 in the reference scenario.

activity level. In the two model versions with no restriction on the trade balance (MSG-4S and MSG-4E) the increased domestic use of goods and services - particularly private consumption - leads to increased imports (determined by exogenous import shares). With export volumes kept unchanged, this implies a deterioration of the balance of trade. When the trade balance (in current prices) is assumed to be kept unchanged from the reference scenario (i.e. the simulation from the MSG-4ET version), imports are reduced and exports are increased. The main impact is a reduction of total domestic use revealed through the elasticity for private consumption, which decreases markedly (from 3.1 in MSG-4E to 1.4 in MSG-4ET). Real resources will have to be allocated from production of consumption goods to production of tradeables to meet the balance of trade constraint imposed on MSG-4ET.

Commodity prices are influenced by changes in employment only in the simulation with the MSG-4S version where there are two-way links between the price and quantity sides of the model. (The minor changes in the price deflators of economic aggregates also observed in Table 4.1 for the simulations of the price-quantity recursive versions are caused by changes in the composition of these aggregates.) The most important price effect in the simultaneous version is the significant increase in the rate of return to capital. The impacts on the price deflators for GDP and total domestic use measured by elasticities are both close to 0.5. The impact on the price index for private consumption is stronger than the relative change in the price deflator for investments and government consumption, reflecting partly the relatively higher capital intensity in important consumer good industries than in industries producing investment goods.

Increased Hicks-neutral technical change

A one per cent increase in total productivity in all private industries (except ocean transport and oil and gas production) reduces proportionally the input requirements per unit of output for every given combination of factor prices. Thus, more outputs can be produced with the same amounts of inputs, which means that the production potential is increased. A general increase in productivity has a direct effect on price levels as unit costs of production are reduced. An important implication for relative prices is that real wages increase since the prices of produced goods decrease. This effect, in combination with the assumption of a given supply of labour that must be absorbed in production activities, imply that the total demand for real capital is increased.

In the various simulations with increased productivity it is seen from Table 4.1 that the expansive effects on main economic aggregates such as GDP, total domestic use, and private consumption have close to twice the impacts obtained in corresponding simulations with increased labour supply. For GDP the elasticity exceeds 2 in both simulations of the price-quantity block recursive model where the capital stock is determined from the demand side, while the elasticity is reduced to 1.5 when the growth path is restricted by exogenously given capital. The stronger impact of increased productivity as compared to increased labour supply is due to the fact that technological progress is assumed to be Hicks-neutral. This means that all inputs - including raw materials, labour, and capital - immediately become more "productive". Following the growth process step by step, there is a "first-order direct effect" on output in each sector of one per cent and on GDP by more than one per cent even with the input levels unchanged. However, since the productivity increase also affects sectors producing intermediate inputs and capital goods, the situation cannot represent a new equilibrium solution; a second-order effect of increased efficiency in the supply of productive resources gives over time an additional expansion of the economy.

The most significant long-run impact of higher productivity is its effect on the volume of private consumption, which increases by 3.7 per cent even when domestic expenditure is restricted so as to maintain the balance of payments. Also in these simulations, the long-run changes in investments are somewhat less than the corresponding changes in capital stocks, reflecting that the composition of the capital stock is figures) calculated by the various model versions when productivity is increased are approximately the same as in the case of changed employment, and the differences may also be explained by the same mechanisms: in MSG-4S total capital supply is predetermined. In MSG-4E the increased activity levels and the change in relative prices induced by employment or productivity growth imply that the demand for capital is also increased, and consequently the impacts on production and expenditure are stronger than in MSG-4S. Applying the MSG-4ET model with a restriction on the development of the trade balance increases the export surplus and decreases the impact on private consumption as compared to MSG-4E. The elasticities for GDP and investments/capital stock are also higher in MSG-4E than in MSG-4ET, reflecting the relatively high capital intensity in some industries producing private consumption goods.

The increased productivities in private industries lead to reductions in unit costs of production and consequently to lower prices of produced goods and services. The impacts on prices are obviously strongest when the returns to capital are frozen and the increased productive capacity is followed by an increased demand for capital. In the simultaneous version, MSG-4S, where the capital stock is assumed to remain unchanged, the capital demand is restricted by a strong increase in the rates of return and thus in the user cost of capital. This counteracts the downward pressure on price levels caused by the increased productivity.

Increased total capital stock

The effects of increased total capital supply is, of course, only simulated in the MSG-4S version. An increase in the total capital stock implies a rise in the productive capacity of the economy. It is seen, however, that for the economy as a whole the marginal elasticity of capital is less than the marginal elasticity of labour (the total GDP elasticities are 0.4 and 0.6 respectively). The impacts on the domestic expenditures also differ compared to the simulations with changes in labour supply and productivity. Since the capital stock is increased (by one per cent) for every year in the simulation period, a corresponding effect is reflected in

The increased supply of capital implies that the "price" of capital services is reduced; from Table 4.1 it is seen that the rate of return to capital decreases by 5.6 per cent. This implies a substitution towards more capital intensive techniques. In combination with the increased activity levels in production sectors these substitution effects ensure that the new capital stock is fully utilized in the economy.

The decrease in the rate of return to capital furthermore causes a downward pressure on commodity prices in the model. From Table 4.1 it is revealed that on average the price indices for domestic use decrease by nearly 0.5 per cent, the price impacts being strongest for (capital intensive) consumption goods also in this simulation.

Increased rate of return to capital

An increase in the overall rate of return to capital in the MSG-4E version has the effect that real capital becomes relatively more expensive, the total capital stock demanded by industries is decreased, and the productive capacity of the economy reduced. The elasticity for the total capital stock with respect to the rate of return to capital is estimated at -0.2, and consequently the impact (in absolute values) on other main variables such as GDP, private consumption, and investments are markedly weaker in this simulation than when the capital stock is increased exogenously by one per cent in the MSG-4S version. It may be noted that the proportions between the elasticities are very much the same.

The reduced activity level involves an increase in the export surplus (imports are reduced) in the simulation with the MSG-4E model. When the effect on the trade balance (in current prices) is restricted to zero, as is the case in MSG-4ET, export volumes are reduced and more real resources are left for the production of consumption goods.

The magnitudes of the elasticities derived by changing the rate of return by one per cent should not be compared with the elasticities derived from a corresponding change in, for example, total employment. From the elasticities presented in Table 4.1 one may deduce - assuming that the elasticities are approximately constant over some range of variation in the rate of return - that in order to obtain the same impacts on the economy with a change in the rate of return (in the MSG-4E version) as with the case of an increase in the total capital stock of one per cent (in the MSG-4S version), the rate of return must be lowered by 5 per cent. As the rate of return may be interpreted as an interest rate, which itself is commonly expressed in per cent, this may correspond to a reduction from e.g., 7.0 to 6.6 per cent.

4.3 Energy demand elasticities

Several recent empirical studies have addressed the question of the relation between economic growth, energy prices, and the demand for energy. MSG-4 is meant to be a tool also for analysing this type of question. In this section we shall illustrate how the interactions between the energy demand and the rest of the economy are depicted by the MSG-model. Energy demand elasticities are only calculated for the price-quantity recursive versions of the model, i.e. the versions with perfectly elastic capital supply (MSG-4E and MSG-4ET). As argued by Hogan (1979), a general equilibrium model with inelastic supply of labour and elastic supply of capital seems to be the most appropriate approach when studying long-term energy-economy interactions.

Changes in the activity level of the economy induced by one of the main "growth factors" of Table 4.1 imply changes in the energy demand of the economy. The implicit energy/GDP-elasticities (impacts on energy demand normalized by changes in GDP) estimated from the various simulations of price-quantity recursive versions of MSG-4 are presented in Table 4.3. These results serve to illustrate that the relation between energy demand and economic growth is highly dependent on how this growth arises.

A general feature of the estimated energy/GDP-elasticities is that they exceed one. This means that when the total activity level of the economy increases, total energy demand increases more than proportionately. The explanation is obviously that in all simulations private consumption increases more than GDP (cf. the discussion above), and thus strongly affects the energy use in the household sector.

The highest energy/GDP-elasticity (in absolute value) is obtained when the rate of return to capital is changed in the simulation with the MSG-4E version.

Table 4.3. Energy/GDP elasticities caused by (one per cent) changes in the various growth factors.

Growth factors:	Total employment		Technical change		Rate of return to capital	
Model version:	MSG-4E	MSG-4ET	MSG-4E	MSG-4ET	MSG-4E	MSG-4ET
Total Energy	2.1	1.5	1.7	1.4	2.4	1.5
Electricity	2.0	1.6	1.3	1.1	2.4	1.7
Fuels	2.2	1.5	1.9	1.5	2.3	1.3

Since energy and capital are complements in most industries, less energy intensive techniques are applied in the production sectors. The lowest energy/GDP-elasticities are obtained, as is rather obvious, in the cases where the increased activity level (measured by GDP) is caused by a general increase in productivity. As mentioned above, technical change in the MSG-model is assumed to be "neutral" and therefore all input coefficients - including the inputs of energy per unit of outputs - are reduced when productivity increases. Another interesting feature of the results in Table 4.3 is the differences in the impacts on electricity and fuel demand between simulations with the MSG-4E version and simulations with the MSG-4ET version. When restricting the trade balance by running the latter model, the demand for both electricity and fuels is reduced compared to the MSG-4E version as a result of the dampened effect on private consumption in these simulations (for electricity this effect is counteracted by increased electricity demand in the production sectors due to the relative increase in exports and the production of energy intensive goods).

When analysing energy-economy interactions the effects of price changes on energy demand are also of general interest. We shall therefore conclude this section by studying how the MSG-model visualizes the effects of changes in energy prices on the energy markets themselves and on the rest of the economy. This may be viewed as an example of how the model can be used as an applied general equilibrium model in policy oriented analysis, in addition to its use for studying the more traditional growth oriented questions already addressed above.[21]

In the MSG-model the price of crude oil (and natural gas) as well as the electricity price is specified as an exogenous variable. More specifically, the basic prices (see Section 3.1) of these commodities are exogenous. In a report from Energy Modeling Forum (1980), it is stressed that demand choices are made at the retail level and that it is therefore desirable to measure price elasticities as close to consumption as possible. The energy price elasticities presented below are therefore measured relative to changes in purchasers' prices of energy.

In analysing price sensitivity the substitution responses are of course of central interest. However, in the case of Norway, induced income effects may be very important when studying changes in the prices of crude oil and natural gas since the production of these goods amount to about one fifth of the Norwegian GDP.

In Table 4.4 we present estimates of energy price elasticities, both for energy demand and main economic aggregates. When there are no restrictions imposed on the balance of payments, i.e. when possible effects of changes in terms of trade are not accounted for (MSG-4E), we see from Table 4.4 that the overall energy-capital complementarity causes a reduction in the total production level and total capital stock. GDP is thus slightly reduced compared to the reference scenario. Since electricity has little weight both in exports and imports, the main effect of a partial increase in the electricity price is a fall in investments, implying that more real resources are available for private consumption. When the crude oil price is raised and the increased revenues from exports are not injected into the economy, a negative real income effect causes a reduction in domestic demand and production while the balance of payments is

Table 4.4. Effects of changes in energy prices on volumes of main economic aggregates and energy demand. Elasticities

Increase in:	Electricity prices		Prices of crude oil and natural gas	
Model version:	MSG-4	MSG-4ET	MSG-4E	MSG-4ET
GDP	-0.02	-0.02	-0.01	0.01
Domestic use	-0.02	-0.02	-0.02	0.13
Private consumption	0.06	0.05	-0.04	0.22
Investments	-0.13	-0.13	-0.03	0.07
Total capital stock	-0.10	-0.10	0.00	0.03
Total energy demand	-0.16	-0.17	-0.21	-0.05
Electricity demand	-0.55	-0.56	0.13	0.24
Industries	-0.65	-0.64	0.02	-0.21
Households	-0.53	-0.54	0.27	0.80
Fuels demand	0.13	0.12	-0.46	-0.27
Industries	0.04	0.03	-0.42	-0.49
Households	0.24	0.23	-0.68	-0.11

considerably improved.

The estimates based on MSG-4ET presented in Table 4.4 show that the effects of a change in the price of electricity are approximately the same with and without restrictions on the balance of payments. This simply reflects the fact that changes in the electricity price does not significantly influence the terms of trade.[22] However, when the price of crude oil is increased, the change in terms of trade allows for an increase in domestic demand and particularly private consumption rises. The reallocation of resources is also seen to have a positive effect on GDP.

For energy demand we see that the direct price elasticity for electricity is close to -0.5 in both model versions. The cross-price elasticities are also practically identical.

The fuel price elasticities are, however, markedly different in the two model versions. For households the very strong terms of trade effects in MSG-4ET reduce considerably the absolute values of the elasticities of fuel and increase markedly the elasticities of electricity demand as compared to the results of MSG-4E. Furthermore, the terms of trade effects induce changes in the production structure as resources are reallocated from the energy intensive export oriented manufacturing industries to industries producing consumption goods and services. As a consequence energy demand - and particularly the demand for electricity - in the total enterprise sector is reduced.

4.4 Transition paths and long-run properties

The numerical estimates presented above are calculated for a simulation period of 20 years. It may therefore be of some interest to study how the elasticities change over time, i.e. the transition path, and whether the "final" elasticities actually represent long-run properties of the model. In the following, some examples of time profiles for elasticities are presented. The chosen examples have all been calculated on the MSG-4ET model, i.e. the model with fixed real rate of returns to capital and a balance of trade restriction. This model version may be regarded as a long-term neoclassical general equilibrium growth model.

In Figure 3, time profiles for the elasticities of GDP, consumption, investments, and capital stock are drawn with respect to employment. The figure illustrates how the relative impacts on consumption and investments

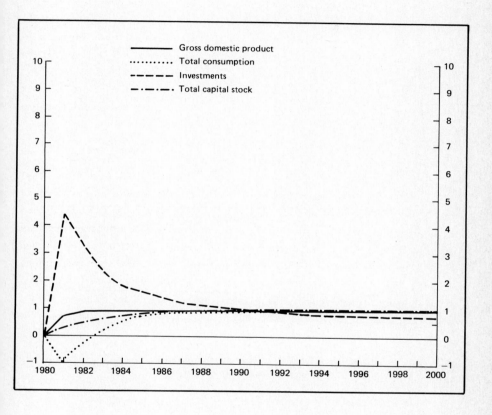

Figure 3.   Total elasticities MSG-4ET. Transition paths and long-run
              values. Increased total employment

change markedly from the year when employment is increased (1981) to the
year when the elasticities presented in the previous tables are measured
(2000).   It may be noted that the elasticities do not reach their "long-run
equilibrium values" until after at least 10 to 15 years into the simulation.

    The strong, immediate effect on investments occurs as a result of the

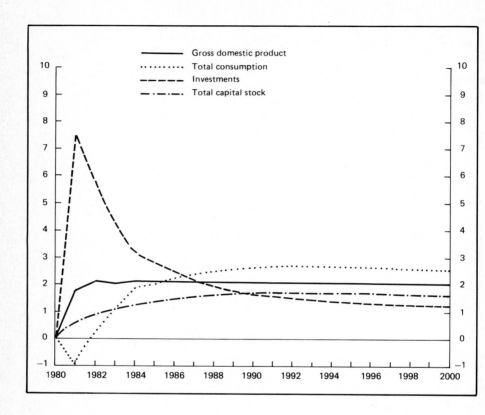

Figure 4.   Total elasticities MSG-4ET. Transition paths and long-run
             values. Increased technical change

fact that capital stocks in each production sector must increase proportionally to the labour inputs. In order to reach the new equilibrium levels
for the capital stock the increase in labour supply will have to be engaged
for some years mainly in increased production of investment goods.
Therefore, during the first couple of years there are no real resources
available for increased consumption (cf. that the elasticity is close to zero
in 1981). As capital stocks are gradually built up, real resources (labour
input) are removed from the investment good sector to the production of
consumption goods.   As opposed to the impact on the expenditure variables, the elasticity for GDP reaches its long-run level almost immediately.

The variation over time in this elasticity is only a result of differences in efficiency and primary input returns between the various industries.

After 20 years, the relative increases in both GDP, capital stock, investments, and the consuption potential are (somewhat below) 1 per cent, i.e. close to the increase in labour supply. For the main aggregates the elasticities are approximately constant and uniform in the long run. When changing the growth potential by increasing labour supply, the "long-run" macroeconomic developments depicted by the model resembles that of steady-state growth.

The development over time of the elasticities for main economic variables when simulating effects of technical change is rather similar to the development in the case of increased employment. In Figure 4 we present time profiles for technical change elasticities. As for changes in employment, the figure illustrates that it is essential for the measurement of long-run model properties to simulate the model some years ahead and have the elasticities approach constant values. The deviations from uniform rates are mainly due to the assumption of Hicks-neutral technical change.

Appendix

A simplified equation system of MSG-4

In this appendix a simplified version of the equation system of the MSG-4 model is presented. The equation system is structured in accordance with Figure 1 of Section 3.

The relations are formulated in matrix notation, refering to the equations of the various submodels presented in the main text. All vectors are column vectors. To simplify we

(i) assume the same number of commodities and industries

(ii) ignore government consumption and investment

(iii) assume the same number of import - and export activities - as commodities

(iv) ignore all the special features of the model discussed in section 3.6.

The price block

Price-cost relations by industries (equation 3.19)):

(A1) $P_X = \hat{Z}_L P_L + \hat{Z}_K P_K + \hat{Z}_M P_M + \hat{Z}_E P_E + \hat{Z}_F P_F$; n_X equations

Factor input coefficient relations by industry written in general form (equations (3.5), (3.6) and (3.7)):

(A2) $Z_i = Z_i(P_K, P_L, P_M, P_E, P_F; t)$; i=K,L,M,E,F,
$5\, n_X$ equations

Factor input prices for capital services by industry (user cost of capital, assuming only one capital (and investment) category, equation (3.11)):

(A3) $P_K = (\hat{R+\delta}) P_J$; n_X equations

Relations for relative rates of return to capital by industry (equation 3.12))

(A4) $R = \rho \bar{R}$; n_X equations

Factor input prices for labour by industry (wage rates)

$P_L = P_L^*$;   i.e. exogenously given wage rates

Prices of imports, production, commodity input and final demand categories (commodity activity prices, equation (3.2)):

$$P_I = \Lambda_I' B$$
$$P_X = \Lambda_X' B$$
$$P_M = \Lambda_M' B$$
$$P_E = \Lambda_E' B$$
(A5)
$$P_F = \Lambda_F' B \; ; \qquad 6n_X + n_C + n_J \text{ equations}$$
$$P_C = \Lambda_C' B$$
$$P_J = \Lambda_J' B$$
$$P_A = \Lambda_A' B$$

The quantity block

Factor demand relations by industry (equation (3.8)):

$$K = \hat{Z}_K X$$
$$L = \hat{Z}_L X$$
(A6)
$$M = \hat{Z}_M X \; ; \qquad 5n_X \text{ equations}$$
$$E = \hat{Z}_E X$$
$$F = \hat{Z}_F X$$

Commodity balance relations, i.e. the dual of the commodity activity price relation (equation 3.11)):

(A7)
$$\Lambda_I I + \Lambda_X X = \Lambda_M M + \Lambda_E E + \Lambda_F F + \Lambda_C C + \Lambda_J J + \Lambda_A A;$$
$$n_X \text{ equations}$$

Import relations by commodity (equation (3.16)):

(A8)
$$\Lambda_I I = (S_M \circ \Lambda_M) M + (S_E \circ \Lambda_E) E + (S_F \circ \Lambda_F) F$$
$$+ (S_C \circ \Lambda_C) C + (S_J \circ \Lambda_J) J + (S_A \circ \Lambda_A) A; \quad n_X \text{ equations}$$

Household consumption demand by consumption activity, written in general form (equations (3.13) and (3.14)):

$$C = C(P_C, V)$$

(A9) n_C (independent) equations

$$P'_C C = V$$

Private investment demand, assuming only one capital (and investment) category (equation (3.15)):

(A10) $J = K - K(-1) + \hat{\delta} K;\ n_J$ equations

Exports by commodity

$$A = A^*; \text{ i.e. exogenously given exports}$$

Primary factor balance relations

(A11) $e' L = \bar{L}^*;$ i.e. exogenously given total supply of labour

(A12) $e' K = \bar{K}$

(i)   In MSG-4S $\bar{K}$ is exogenously given, while $\bar{R}$ is endogenously determined (inelastic supply of capital)

(ii) In MSG-4E $\bar{R}$ is exogenously given while $\bar{K}$ is endogenously determined (perfectly elastic supply of capital).

The MSG-4 model above has $21n_X + 2n_C + 2n_J + 2$ independent equations between the same number of endogenous variables. In this simplified model only P_L (wage rates), L (labour), $\bar{K}$ (capital stock) or $\bar{R}$ (rate of return to capital), and A (exports) are exogenously given.

Notes

1) A more comprehensive discussion of these concepts is given in Bjerkholt and Longva (1980) and Longva, Lorentsen and Olsen (1983).

2) This does not mean that there is a one-to-one correspondence between commodities and industry outputs. At the chosen level of aggregation there will still be significant non-zero off-diagonal elements in the commodity-by-industry output matrix, i.e. multiple output in industries.

3) In addition, capital in shipping and three kinds of capital in crude oil production form separate categories.

4) Formally this means that these functions are assumed to be weakly separable in the defined subsets, see Berndt and Christensen (1973).

5) The Norwegian national accounting system includes a set of value notions, as recommended in A System of National Accounts, United Nations (1968).

6) Note that, apart from trade margins and commodity taxes, there may be genuine price differentiation in the base year. This bias in the base year weights may be a source of error in the model computations. Price differentiation is however explicitly corrected for in the case of electricity, See Section 3.6.

7) For a more detailed and complete presentation, including estimation methods and numerical results, see Longva and Olsen (1983a, 1983c).

8) In the estimation of the cost functions the less restrictive assumption of a homothetic production structure was imposed.

9) Alternatively, producer equilibrium under constant returns to scale may be said to define a "horizontal" supply function.

10) To simplify, the terms for industry taxes, rates of capacity utilization, and mark-up indices are omitted.

11) Since estimated rates of return in general will deviate from the observed rates of return in the base year, total incomes will not be equal to total costs, i.e. relation (3.10) will not automatically be fullfilled in the base year. In the model structure this is solved by introducing mark-up indices and capacity utilization rates in these equations (see also Section 3.6). The difference between observed and estimated (expected) rates of return are therefore assumed to have been caused partly by less than full capacity utilization and partly by deviation between actual prices and (long-run) marginal costs.

12) For a more detailed presentation of this submodel, including a description of estimation procedures and estimation results, see Bjerkholt and Rinde (1983).

13) A further understanding of this correction method may be gained from

the general expression of Engel elasticities, E_i derived from (3.13 - 3.14), i.e. $E_i = \xi_i / \underset{j}{\Sigma} a_j \xi_j$, where the a's are budget shares.

14) For a further discussion of the specification of value flows for electricity, see Longva and Olsen (1983b).

15) Two different marginal cost functions have been estimated: one is based on a ranking of projects according to their succession in the official plans, while the other is based on a ranking of projects according to increasing costs (see Rinde and Strøm (1983)). To facilitate the use of the model to study various alternatives, marginal input coefficients for real capital are exogenous in the model.

16) The decreasing returns to scale would also otherwise have introduced a linkage between the "price" side and the "quantity" side of the model.

17) As mentioned in Section 2 the equation system of the model also contains a set of parameters that may (and most commonly are) residually determined in such a way that the model "passes through the base year." These parameters correct for stochastic disturbances and base year changes (rebasing of the variables) in the econometrically estimated relations.

18) A more comprehensive discussion of the elasticity concepts presented below is given in Longva, Olsen and Rinde (1983).

19) A more detailed presentation of elasticity calculations from MSG-4 is given in Offerdal (1985).

20) Obviously a "trade balance version" of the MSG-4S model might have been specified. However, at present no such operational model version exists.

21) More detailed and comprehensive discussions of these issues are given in Longva, Olsen and Rinde (1983) and Longva, Olsen and Strøm (1985).

22) Electricity intensive products are important export commodities. However, the induced increases in the prices of these products are very moderate.

References

Bergan, R. (1984), "MINK. En finansiell ettermodell til MSG. En MSG-rapport", Reports from the Central Bureau of Statistics, No. 84/23, Oslo.

Bergman, L. (1985), "Extensions and Applications of the MSG Model; a Brief Survey", this volume.

Berndt, E.R. and L.R. Christensen (1973), "The Internal Structure of Functional Relationships: Separability, Substitution and Aggregation", Review of Economic Studies 40, 403-410.

Bjerkholt, O. and S. Longva (1980), MODIS IV. A Model for Economic Analysis and National Planning, in Social Economic Studies from the Central Bureau of Statistics, No 43, Oslo.

Bjerkholt, O. and J. Rinde (1983), "Consumption Demand in the MSG Model", in Bjerkholt et al. (eds.) (1983), 84-107.

Bjerkholt, O. and S. Tveitereid (1985), "The Use of the MSG Model in Preparing a 'Perspective Analysis 1980-2000' for the Norwegian Economy", this volume.

Bjerkholt, O., S. Longva, Ø. Olsen and S. Strøm (eds.) (1983), Analysis of Supply and Demand of Electricity in the Norwegian Economy, Social Economic Studies from the Central Bureau of Statistics, No. 53, Oslo.

Cappelen, Å., I. Holm and P. Sand (1980), "MODIS IV. Virkningstabeller for 1978", Articles from the Central Bureau of Statistics, No. 124, Oslo.

Cappelen, Å. and S. Longva (1984), "MODAG A. A Medium Term Model of the Norwegian Economy", paper presented at "Nordisk modellseminar om utvikling og anvendelse av makromodeller", Oct. 8-9, 1984 in Lyngby, Central Bureau of Statistics, Oslo.

Diewert, W.E. (1971), "An Application of the Shephard Duality Theorem: A Generalized Leontief Production Function." Journal of Political Economy 79, 481-507.

Energy Modeling Forum (1980), "Aggregate Elasticities of Energy Demand", EMF Report 4, Vol. 1, Stanford University.

Frisch, R. (1959), "A Complete Scheme for Computing all Direct and Cross Demand Elasticities in a Model with Many Sectors", Econometrica 27, 177-196.

Hogan, W. (1979), "Capital-Energy Complementarity in Aggregate Energy-Economic Analysis", Resources and Energy, 2, 201-220.

Johansen, L. (1960), A Multi-Sectoral Study of Economic Growth, North-Holland Publishing Company, Amsterdam.

Johansen, L. (1974), A Multi-Sectoral Study of Economic Growth. Second Enlarged Edition, North-Holland Publishing Company, Amsterdam.

Johansen, L. (1977), Lectures on Macroeconomic Planning. Vol. I. North-Holland Publishing Company, Amsterdam.

Johansen, L. (1978), Lectures on Macroeconomic Planning. Vol. II. North-Holland Publishing Company, Amsterdam.

Jorgenson, D.W. (1982), "An Econometric Approach to General Equilibrium Analysis", Paper presented at the International Symposium on Development in Econometrics and Related Fields, Rotterdam, January 12-15, 1982.

Larsen, K.A. and P. Schreiner (1985), "On the Introduction and Application of the MSG Model in the Norwegian Planning System", this volume.

Longva, S. and Ø. Olsen (1983a), "Producer Behaviour in the MSG model", in Bjerkholt et al. (eds.) (1983), 52-83.

Longva, S. and Ø. Olsen (1983b), "The Specification of Electricity Flows in the MSG Model", in Bjerkholt et al. (eds.) (1983), 108-133.

Longva, S. and Ø. Olsen (1983c), "Price Sensitivity of Energy Demand in Norwegian Industries", Scandinavian Journal of Economics 85, 17-36.

Longva, S., L. Lorentsen and Ø. Olsen (1983), "Energy in the Multisectoral Growth Model MSG", in Bjerkholt et al. (eds.) 1983), 27-51.

Longva, S., Ø. Olsen and J. Rinde (1983), "Energy Price Sensitivity of the Norwegian Economy", in Bjerkholt et al. (eds.) (1983), 161-179.

Longva, S., Ø. Olsen and S. Strøm (1985), "Total Elasticities of Energy Demand Analysed within a General Equilibrium Model", Discussion Papers from the Central Bureau of Statistics, Oslo, forthcoming.

Lorentsen, L. and T. Skoglund (1976), "MSG-3. A model for Analysis of the Long Term Economic Development", Articles from the Central Bureau of Statistics, No. 83, Oslo.

Offerdal, E. (1985), "Hovedtrekk ved MSG-4 beskrevet ved totale langtidselastisiteter", Reports from the Central Bureau of Statistics, Oslo, forthcoming.

Rinde, J. and S. Strøm (1983), "Cost Structure of Electricity Production", in Bjerkholt et al. (eds.) (1983), 134-150.

Samuelson, P.A. (1953), "Prices of Factors and Goods in General Equilibrium," Review of Economic Studies 21, 1-20.

Shephard, R.W. (1953), Cost and Production Functions, Princeton University Press, Princeton, N.J.

Schreiner, P. (1972), "The Role of Input-Output in the Perspective Analysis of the Norwegian Economy", in A. Brody and A.P. Carter (eds.), Input-Output Techniques, North-Holland Publishing Company, Amsterdam, 449-487.

Spurkland, S. (1970), "MSG - a Tool in Long-Term Planning", Mimeographed, Norwegian Computer Centre, Oslo.

Stone, R. (1964), "British Economic Balances in 1970: A Trial Run on a Rocket", in Econometric Analysis for National Economic Planning, Colston Papers No. 16, Butterworths, London.

240   Longva et al.

Strøm, S. (1967), "Kapitalavkastning i industrisektorer, struktur og tidsutvikling", Memorandum from the Institute of Economics, University of Oslo, 10 July 1967.

United Nations (1968), A System of National Accounts, United Nations, Studies in Methods, Series F, No. 2, Rev. 3, New York.

Production, Multi-Sectoral Growth and Planning
F.R. Førsund, M. Hoel, and S. Longva (Editors)
© Elsevier Science Publishers B.V. (North-Holland), 1985

ON THE INTRODUCTION AND APPLICATION OF THE MSG–MODEL
IN THE NORWEGIAN PLANNING SYSTEM

Per Schreiner
Ministry of Finance

Knut Arild Larsen
Institute for Studies in Research and Higher Education

1. Institutional background

1.1 Historical background

Economic planning has been an integral part of Norway's institutional structure and government policy since the end of World War II (see Bjerve (1976)). During that time it has enjoyed broad political support. While there are differences among the political parties in Norway as to the use and tuning of the instruments of economic policy, all parties when in power make full use of the planning machinery.

During the immediate post war years the Labour government, in power with a solid majority in the Storting (Parliament), chose to keep in place the extensive spectrum of direct instruments inherited from the war economy (e.g. rationing and regulation). The planning system which grew up to administer all these instruments had few ideological overtones; rather it had the pragmatic goal of providing a numerical basis for, and a coordination of, the many decisions which by necessity had to be delegated to a wide range of various government bodies.

This administrative approach has also characterized the later development of Norwegian planning. It can be distinguished from macroeconomic planning in most other countries, which to a large extent has developed

The authors want to thank Sverre Munck, Svein Longva, Steinar Strøm, and Sigurd Tveitereid for helpful comments and suggestions on earlier drafts of this paper.

outside or parallel to the traditional decision making bodies for economic policy.

The early integration of sectoral analysis and decision making into the macroeconomic planning system of Norway is also worth noting - especially if one wants to understand the roots and preconditions for Leif Johansen's later MSG-model.

Developments in economic theory and economic statistics just before and during the war led to efforts in many countries to develop a complete overview of the economy in the form of a detailed national accounting system. Norwegian economists, the students of Ragnar Frisch, were pioneers in developing the national accounting system, both theoretically and empirically. Their efforts were always closely linked to practical policy making. Aukrust and Bjerve (1945) in their book Hva krigen kostet Norge ("What the War cost Norway"), used national accounting estimates to give advice on how to direct the reconstruction of the Norwegian economy. Bjerve was also responsible for the elaboration of the first "National Budget" in 1946.

In the post-war years the provision of detailed and updated national account figures became part of the current production of economic statistics. The availability of national account figures, together with the concern for sectoral coordination, clearly both facilitated and stimulated the development and use of models in Norwegian policy making.

Formal econometric models based on the national accounting system are now extensively employed in Norwegian macroeconomic decision making. The two main models are MODIS, MOdel of a DISaggregated type, (see Sevaldson (1964), and Bjerkholt and Longva (1980)), and MSG, Multi-Sectoral Growth, (see Johansen (1960a, 1974) and Longva, Lorentsen and Olsen (in this volume)). MODIS is used in the preparation of short-term and medium-term analysis and plans, while MSG is used as an aid in the elaboration of long-term perspectives.

The first model that was actually used in the administrative planning process, and which still is in use today, was the MODIS-model. Although not put into effective operation until 1960, the construction of MODIS stretched all the way back to the immediate post war years. The fact that from the beginning the national accounts were designed with the construction of such a comprehensive model for national economic planning in mind also facilitated the conceptual and empirical development of the MSG-model. MODIS is a static model around an extensive input-output table and with an emphasis on definitional or accounting relationships. Except for the consumption functions and a classification of different types of price setting by industry, there is no behavioral content in MODIS.

1.2 Economic planning and policies in Norway

Six main characteristics of national economic planning in Norway can be distinguished:

-   Planning is the responsibility of the constitutional political authorities. Plans are prepared in the name of the government and are discussed in the Parliament.

-   The planning units are integral parts of the government administration proper, not separate agencies. This reduces the risk of duplication, rivalry, and blurred lines of responsibility. Macroeconomic planning is performed within the Ministry of Finance.

-   The plan documents contain not only forecasts, but to a large extent actual government programmes.

-   The plans are prepared within the framework of national accounts and are supported by disaggregated econometric models.

-   Central government targets for economic development are not highly detailed, but rather conceived in broad terms. However, sectoral consistency is provided by disaggregated analysis.

-   The main policy instruments for implementing the plans are fiscal and monetary policies, although in some areas regulatory laws are also used.

There are three main national economic planning documents:

-   The annual fiscal budget for the central government and for the social security system: The budget document includes a four-year fiscal budget for the central government and the social security system. This "long-term budget" is updated yearly and is presented in a more aggregated form than the annual budget.

- The annual plan called "the National Budget," a term coined by Frisch as the logical extension of national accounts: It presents the economic policy of the government based on a detailed analysis of the current economic situation, and it provides directives for the State banks.

- The four-year program, "the Long-Term Programme": Normally presented in full detail only once every four years, it covers the next 4-year parliamentary period. This program also contains perspectives for the ensuing 15 to 25 years.

In addition to these documents, macroeconomic planning documents covering subjects receiving particular political attention are presented by the Ministry of Finance from time to time. These documents are presented by the government as white papers to the parliament, and they form a basis both for major economic policy decisions and for bringing sectoral policies in line with macroeconomic goals. All ministries are involved in preparing these documents, with the Ministry of Finance as the coordinating body.

The private sector participates in preparing the economic plans of the government in a rather limited and informal way, mainly through the ministries responsible for the different sectors (agriculture, manufacturing industry, etc.). Over the last 20 years, however, an extensive cooperation has developed between the government and the labour market organizations in connection with the settlement of income negotiations. The analysis provided for these negotiations relies fundamentally on macroeconomic models, and this has contributed to a general recognition and acceptance of the usefulness of such models.

1.3 Models and plans

Norway has an open and decentralized economy. The government sector is comparatively small with municipalities and counties constituting the larger part. Large transfers inflate public expenditure, but government ownership of industry is limited and where it exists it is not used to direct day-to-day business affairs. Still Norway is considered by many as a planned economy. The reason may be partly historical, related to the dependence in the early post war years on extensive use of war time regulatory instruments.

Another explanation may be the tradition in Norway of considering a wide set of various government decisions within an overall setting. That is, the planning does not address itself so much towards directing the private sector as to keeping track of governmental decision making. Furthermore, Keynesian thinking, with its view of government activity as an important instrument of aggregate demand management, has been widely accepted.

The Norwegian models, both MODIS and MSG, are disaggregated into more sectors than corresponding models in other countries. This should not be interpreted, however, as a desire to direct the development in each single sector. It merely reflects one particular approach to establishing autonomous relations. Sectorial disaggregation is seen as giving a better understanding of the institutional or behavioral mechanisms behind the development of macro variables than aggregated relationships with coefficients established on a time series basis.

In addition, there is probably no way around some sectoral detail if one wishes to obtain consistency and coordination between the institutions responsible for the preparation of macro analysis and those responsible for regional or sectoral analyses and plans. As mentioned, the Norwegian planning system is an integral part of government decision making and the models play an important part in improving communication and understanding within the bureaucracy. The degree of sectoral detail together with the flexibility of the models make them useful as instruments or frameworks for organizing analyses of a wide spectrum of subjects and for facilitating the information flows between such analyses.

1.4 The economic triangle

The "economic triangle" is an important feature of the development of economic planning in Norway. By the "economic triangle" we mean the link between:

- The Department of Economics at the University of Oslo,
- the Central Bureau of Statistics with its Research Department and

its national accounting office, and
-   the ministry responsible for economic policy, presently the Ministry of
    Finance.

This link is a key to understanding how the now fairly extensive model
network has been developed with quite small resources as compared to
similar efforts in other countries (see Johansen and Strand (1981), and
Ministry of Finance (1984)).

During the 1930s through the 1950s at the University of Oslo's
Department of Economics, Professor Ragnar Frisch was the central person-
ality, and by his teaching and research he contributed tremendously to
the theoretical foundations of economic policy making. Through his own
research and through the work of his students, he had a profound influence on the development of applied Norwegian planning. But his own
development of decision models, which was pioneering and well ahead of
its time, had little impact on model building for applied planning and still
is not applied to any extent. His greatest achievement with respect to
planning was the inspiration he gave to generations of students, research
assistants, and teachers, and the sense of purpose which he implanted in
them and with which they approached their later tasks. Two of his
promising students were Trygve Haavelmo, later professor of the
University and who was responsible for the elaboration of one of the first
"National Budgets" in 1948, and Leif Johansen, who was also very early
active as an adviser to the government.

The Central Bureau of Statistics has a long tradition of considering
statistical data and statistical publications as elements of policy making
and as a means of promoting a more general understanding of the society
-statistics are to be used, not only to be gathered. One factor which may
have contributed to this management philosophy, which is not prevalent in
all countries, is that its directors for a long period of time have had close
ties to the political community, some even serving as Ministers of Finance
or Central Bank governors.

The Ministry of Finance has had on its staff economists with a firm
academic training, often with a university or research career before they
entered the Ministry. They have been willing to communicate with economists at the university and in the research department of the Central
Bureau of Statistics.

Over the years the personalities and the ideas have changed, but the

close relationships within the triangle have remained. One formalized
aspect of the triangle is the "Model Development Committee". It is an
advisory body appointed by the Ministry of Finance to handle questions
related to the formal institutional framework for economic planning and
economic policy making. In later years it has been supplemented with
representatives from the Bank of Norway and from universities outside
Oslo, but the basic set-up has remained the same - as a meeting place
between parties involved in research, statistics, and policy making. The
committee now meets six to eight times a year. Leif Johansen was a regular member from the founding of the committee in 1963 until his death in
December 1982.

In addition to this permanent committee several other temporary ones
have been formed, with representatives from the same institutions but
with more specific mandates. They have given advice on the development
of different models for long-term planning, as well as models which might
assist the MSG-model in developing its long-term perspectives for the
Norwegian economy. Leif Johansen took part in most of these groups -
either as a member or as an adviser. Our impression is that he took part
not only to help with his advice, but also because he found involvement in
the practical problems of policy making and model building stimulating and
useful for his own theoretical work.

2.   The first steps in applying the MSG-model

2.1 The beginning

On March 14, 1957 Leif Johansen presented a research proposal to
develop "the model basis for a study of the relationships between production sectors under economic growth," with the intention of constructing a model that could perform calculations "with numbers which in order
of magnitude correspond to Norwegian conditions". The outcome of this
proposal was Leif Johansen's September 1959 doctoral thesis, titled "A
Multi-Sectoral Study of Economic Growth", which was first published by
North-Holland in 1960, and which later was enlarged (1974).

2.2 From research to administrative instrument

The original MSG-model was not designed for specific tasks within the national economic planning administration as was the case with the MODIS-model developed at the same time. On the other hand it was not merely an empirical illustration of a theoretical and methodological approach. Leif Johansen formulated his purpose quite succinctly in the introductory chapter of his book (Johansen (1960, p. 3)):

Again it has beome a habit among economists who are quantifying their models to say something like the following: "The principal aim of the present study is methodological. The statistical data are very scanty and unreliable. The quantitative analaysis should therefore be considered merely as an illustration of the method." Having given this statement, the author would hardly be blamed for using the statistical data uncritically.

I should therefore like to characterize the quantitative analysis contained in this study in a way which differs somewhat from the usual one: The data and the quantitative analysis do serve the purpose of illustrating the method and the model. But, at the same time, if I were required to make decisions and take actions in connections with relationships covered by this study, I would (in the absence of more reliable results, and without doing more work) rely to a great extent on the data and the results presented in the following chapters.

When the members of the group responsible for the Long-Term Programme 1962-1965 became aware of the MSG-model early in 1960, they were naturally eager to inquire whether they could benefit from this model in their work. As a response, Johansen prepared a note to the Ministry (May 6, 1960) in which he explained how his model could be used in the preparation of a government economic programme. At that time there was no scope for updating the model, and one question was the relevance of computations of growth rates in 1960 with a model using 1950 as a base year. Johansen concluded and later repeated in the introductory chapter of his book quoted above that he himself, if he were to have the responsibility, would use the model as a support but without feeling constrained by its results.

His colleagues and the staff at the Department of Economics at the

University of Oslo were considerably more sceptical. The scepticism was not related to the relevance of the model, but to the interim group's ability to exploit the potential of the model.

Even if the MSG-model throws light on possible directions for the economy, a good working knowledge of the model is required to be able to interpret and discover the relevance of the model results. It is not possible to use a large economic model, and particularly not the MSG-model, by relying on a set of independent assumptions for the exogenous variables and then just applying the "answers" directly. To become relevant, the analysis based on such a model must be related to and contrasted with other approaches, and it must be integrated into the administrative and political process. Therefore, at the time, the opinion of Johansens's colleagues was that the model calculations made by outside researchers would be of little use to a temporary planning group. This was also the conclusion of the group itself, and the model was not used then.

However, when a Planning Department was created within the Ministry of Finance in 1963, a permanent staff came into existence with responsibility for medium- and long-term macroeconomic analysis and planning. This was partly in response to the emergence during the preceding years of sectoral planning, i.e. the development of plans for roads, schools, energy, hospitals, etc., which tended to be prepared with insufficient concern for consistency with the broader economic development.

With this permanent department and with a concern about the insufficient coordination of sectoral plans, the situation was ripe for the practical application of the MSG-model. In the mid-1960s the Department of Economics at the University of Oslo and the Planning Department of the Ministry of Finance started to update and develop MSG further (see Alstadheim (1968), and Johansen (1968), which also includes a comparison with the observed developments in 1950-1963). The Central Bureau of Statistics was also involved, particularly with the sector specifications and with the aggregation of data from the national accounts. The Norwegian Computation Centre developed a new algorithm for solving the model and in the process provided substantial feedback to the formulation of the model.

2.3 Integration of the model into the administrative system

Norwegian macroeconomic planning and model building have been developed in an atmosphere of pragmatism. The initiatives have come from professionals and bureaucrats who have had to demonstrate, step by step, the advantages of the new methods as compared with the traditional procedures of analysis and decision making.

The first version of the MSG-model prepared for application in the planning process was called MSG-2F. It was ready for use in 1968 and was extensively used in the years immediately thereafter (see Schreiner (1972)). The first official presentation of its results was a "Perspective analysis" in an annex to the white paper on the Long-Term Programme 1970-1973 (see Ministry of Finance (1969)). In a more informal report the analysis was elaborated and extended by a working group with representatives from industry and interest-organizations (see Ministry of Finance (1970)).

Whereas MODIS and related models were developed and operated by the Research Department of the Central Bureau of Statistics, this department played only an auxiliary role in the original development and the initial applications of the MSG-model.

The early experience with the MSG-model demonstrated the need for substantial on-going computational and data support to keep the model operational. Neither the University nor the Ministry had the required computational competence and capacity. The Norwegian Computation Centre, which was in charge of operating the model during the first years, was mainly a research body, not well-organized to supply continuous upgrading of the model. Also the distance from the production (and the updating) of data was inconvenient. Therefore the responsibility for the operation and maintenance of the model was transferred to the Central Bureau of Statistics in 1974.

At the same time, and in connection with the adaption of the Norwegian national accounts to the new system of national accounts (SNA), the model was further developed and adapted so as, among other things, to be more compatible with the sector specifications of the MODIS-model. The new version of the model, called MSG-3, became operational in 1975.

Since then improvements of the model, the algorithm, and the more practical operational features have been going on continuously. However, some changes are of a more fundamental character, making it possible to distinguish "generations" of the model. The present version called MSG-4 was completed in 1980 (see e.g. Longva, Lorentsen and Olsen (in this volume)).

The MSG-model is well adapted for use by the government ministries. It is available on-line through terminals operated by the professional staff. Great efforts have been made to obtain flexibility and simplicity in the interaction with the model, particularly as regards the handling of input and output data sets. These aspects, while they may seem trivial from an analytical point of view, are very important to the integration obtained between the model analysis and the other aspects of the planning process.

The use of the MSG-model has now moved well beyond macroeconomic planning proper. One particular version, called MSG-4E as it is used to study energy questions within a macroeconomic context, was developed with support from the Ministry of Energy (see Bjerkholt et al. (1983)).

For some applications, the model itself is not changed but rather the ministries develop either ex ante models with computational routines for preparing estimates of the exogenous variables, or ex post models for further elaboration of the model results. With the appearance of programming languages like TROLL, the distinction between the model proper and additional support models tends to become blurred (see Ministry of Finance (1984a)).

In spite of this flexibility the operation of the model still demands money, time, and experience. The model requires a high number of exogenous variables, and the meaningfulness of the model results depends on both the quality of the input and the previous experience with interpreting the results. Therefore, up to now only the Ministry of Finance and the Central Bureau of Statistics have directly applied the model.

To stimulate interest in analyses based on the MSG results within a wider set of institutions, print-outs or tapes are made available to research organizations. In addition, special runs have been prepared on occasion. However, the Ministry is careful to require that such model results not be presented as official forecasts of economic development even though the estimates of the exogenous variables have been made within the Ministry.

Table 1. Perspective analyses on the Norwegian economy published
          in official documents and prepared on the basis of
          MSG-computations

Year	Type of document	Time period	Number of paths
1969	Annex to government white paper on the Long-Term Programme 1970-1973 Ministry of Finance (1969)	1963 - 1990	1
1970	Report from a working group Ministry of Finance (1970)	1966 - 1990	4
1973	Part of government white paper on the Long-Term Programme 1974-1977 Ministry of Finance (1973)	1980 - 2000	2
1975	Part of government white paper on Natural Resources and Economic Development Ministry of Finance (1975)	1980 - 2000	3
1977	Annex to government white paper on the Long-Term Programme 1978-1981 Ministry of Finance (1977)	1981 - 2000	5
1981	Annex to government white paper on the Long-Term Programme 1982-1985 Ministry of Planning (1981)	1985 - 2000	3
1983	Report from a Royal Commission on the Future of the Petroleum Industry, NOU (1983a)	1980 - 2010	7
1983	Report from a Working Group on the Perspectives of the Norwegian Economy to the Year 2000 NOU (1983c)	1980 - 2000	10
1984	Report from a Royal Commission on the Future of the Social Security System NOU (1984a)	1980 - 2010	
1984	Part of government white paper on the Future of Petroleum Activities Ministry of Oil and Energy (1984)	1980 - 2010	2
1984	Report from a Royal Commission on Instruments for Regional Development NOU (1984b)	1980 - 2000	1

3.   A short survey of applications

3.1 Perspective analyses in official documents based on MSG

Since 1969, macroeconomic perspectives based on the use of the MSG-model have been regularly published in government documents (see Table 1). All the Long-Term Programmes since 1969 have contained MSG-based macroeconomic calculations. Mostly, the longer term perspectives have been presented as annexes to the programme document in order to underline the background nature of these calculations. However, in the Long-Term Programme for 1974-1977 the paths generated by the model were to a large extent used in the programme. Moreover, the reports of the Royal Commissions and working groups previously refered to also indicate explicit long-term perspectives within their main text.

3.2 Special studies based on MSG

Over the years there have been many special studies based on MSG calculations. In Table 2 the more important ones are listed. In some cases such special studies have been part of a further development of MSG to cover areas of special interest. With respect to manpower analysis the potential long-term employment in different sectors was made in Kobberstad (1976). For the latest MSG-related model development in this field, see Larsen (1985). In the studies of regional development, a regional input-output model named REGION (see Skoglund (1980)) has been formalized. This model is used as an ex post model to MSG.

The latest version of MSG, MSG-4, was specifically constructed to study the long-term interaction between economic growth, relative prices, and energy supply and demand. These modelling aspects are further discussed in Longva et.al. (1980) and Bjerkholt et.al. (1983).

The first studies based on MSG did not draw much attention from politicians and the general public. To the extent that they did, the focus was upon the macro features of the projections, e.g. GNP growth and consumption per capita in the future, where the MSG-model had few advantages over simpler macro growth models. Instead the interest and support for the model came from colleagues in government agencies and from technocrats in private firms searching for general background mate-

Table 2.   Special studies published on the basis of
           MSG-computations

Type of study	References	Time period
Employment and education studies	Thonstad (1969)	1963 - 1990
	Kobberstad (1976) and Eriksen (1978)	1973 - 1990
	Eriksen and Kjølberg (1981)	1975 - 2000
	Larsen (1982)	1980 - 2000
	Institute for Studies in Research and Higher Education (1983)	1980 - 2010
Employment and structural change studies	Larsen (1976)	1980 - 2000
	Gjærum and Holm (1982)	1980 - 2000
	Larsen (1981)	1975 - 2000
	NOU (1983c)	1980 - 2000
Regional development	Ministry of Finance (1970)	1966 - 1990
	Directorate of Labour (1971)	1966 - 1990
	Transportøkonomisk institutt (1983)	1973 - 2000
	Schreiner and Skoglund (1984a)	1980 - 2000
	Schreiner and Skoglund (1984b)	1980 - 2000
Environmental studies	Førsund and Strøm (1973)	1970 - 1990
	Førsund and Strøm (1974)	1970 - 1990
Oil related studies	Bjerkholt et al. (1981)	1980 - 1990
	NOU (1983a)	1980 - 2010
	Ministry of Oil and Energy (1984)	
Energy studies	Lorentsen, Strøm and Østby (1979)	1977 - 1995
	Longva, Olsen and Rinde (1983)	
	Longva, Lorentsen, Rinde and Strøm (1983)	1980 - 2000
	Dale et al. (1985)	1980 - 2000
Studies of working environment and unionization	Eriksen, Thonstad and Qvigstad (1978)	1975 - 2000
	Colbjørnsen and Larsen (1985)	1980 - 2000
Industry related studies	Borg (1979, 1983)	1980 - 2000
	Norwegian Research Institute of Commerce (1979, 1982)	1980 - 2000
	Vannebo (1981)	1980 - 2000
	NOU (1983b)	1980 - 2000
Resource policy studies	Dale et al. (1984)	1980 - 2000

rial for their own forecasting and strategic planning.

But in later years there have been signs that an appreciation of the relevance of the analyses has penetrated beyond this small group of specialists. For instance, the Norwegian Federation of Trade Unions and the Federation of Norwegian Industry have cooperated in a study, "Norway as an Industrial Nation," (Foundation of Industrial Development (1984)), which draws heavily on the projections in NOU (1983c) to advocate an active national industrial policy.

4. Political and administrative aspects of utilizing the MSG-model

4.1 General properties of the model

The MSG-model is an open model in the sense that the model results are controlled to a great extent by the user. The main accomplishment of the model is that given the growth potential of the economy it yields insights into how the different industries grow or decline, e.g. as a result of differential technical progress, changing domestic consumption patterns, or the assumed development of exports. With these fundamental factors exogenous, the usefulness of final outcomes depends on the user's judgement. While the model thereby makes demands upon the user, it also stimulates systematic thinking about long-term development.

The experience of those who have used the model over several years is that, in addition to serving as a computational device, it structures their thinking on growth problems and helps to distinguish factors and relationships which are important for the results from those which can be changed without large consequences. This pedagogical effect may be as important as the actual results of the computations.

Attempts are made to decentralize the generation of exogenous inputs for the model and the evaluation of the results of the computations. This is not only cost efficient, but it has the additional benefit of improving the rapport between different agencies and between the individual members of the ministry staff, since by this procedure they get an opportunity to see their own particular task or activity in a broader setting.

In the same way the model constitutes a useful framework for organizing economic research. Probably all of those who have been involved in economic policy making have been frustrated at times by their lack of knowledge in fields related to their activity. A model like the MSG-model is very useful in deciding priorities for research efforts and for accumulating and organizing new insights.

The MSG-model is not a decision or planning model; it could rather be conceived of as a "decision support" model. Basically it computes the endogenous variables from assumptions about the exogenous variables. But, as is often the case in model work, variables which are exogenous in the model are not always exogenous in the economy. Therefore a typical computation includes several rounds in which the exogenous variables are adjusted in light of preliminary results. Some of these iterations are performed by the operator at the terminal, while others are part of a broader process involving various agencies.

The process of adjusting the assumptions underlying the choice of exogenous variables should be viewed as a positive aspect of the model. However, this process may lead to the temptation of manipulating the data so that the model generates results compatible with preconceived ideas. Leif Johansen was aware of, and concerned about, this possible turn of events. He feared that model users, if they did not "trust" the model, would be tempted to "explain away" surprising results rather than taking them seriously.

4.2 Characteristics of the projections

Even with a facility for interchanging exogenous and endogenous variables, the MSG-model would not be a planning or decision model, since neither political or economic instruments are specified. It is not a true forecasting model either as there is no income generating mechanism. Total private consumption is determined so that all production factors are employed. The model does not tell what will happen, but rather what ought to happen if the development is to satisfy the particular constraints of the model. This interpretation of the information derived from the model is not always easy to convey.

The relationship between the medium-term projections based on MODIS and the long-term projections based on MSG may illustrate this.

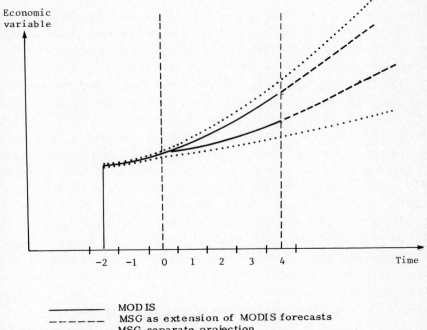

Figure 1. Connection between MSG and MODIS projections

The computations on both the MSG-model and the MODIS-model start out from a base year for which the national account figures are reasonably well established, usually one and two years back (see Figure 1). In the Long-Term Programmes, MSG is used to study longer term implications of medium-term projections prepared by MODIS. Great efforts have been made, therefore, to get the MSG results for the first years close to the results of the MODIS model, at least for some key macro variables.

This procedure is a cumbersome and time consuming trial-and-error process. Still it has been considered worthwhile for presentational purposes and to avoid futile discussions of the consistency between the medium-term and long-term projections based on minor discrepancies between the numbers. So far the long-term perspectives based on MSG are not so well established that they are taken as a reference to which the medium-term projections based on MODIS are adapted.

Until the latest Long-Term Programme only one medium-term development path was presented, as the government desired to make quite clear the programme content of the figures. With the help of the MSG-model, two to five extensions of this path were then projected by a simulation starting from the terminal year of the MODIS calculations. On account of the obvious and large uncertainties surrounding international economic developments, the Long-Term Programme 1982-1985 (see Ministry of Planning (1981)) contained several different projections for the ensuing four years based on the MODIS-mode, and each of these projections were then extended with MSG simulations.

The reports from the Ministry of Finance (1970) and NOU (1983c) contain a greater number of alternative paths than is usual in governmental reports; in these two reports the MSG-model was used alone to calculate the time paths, independent of existing medium-term forecasts. This can be seen as a move away from the simple extrapolation approach towards viewing the MSG computations as possible equilibrium paths around which actual development, e.g. medium-term forecasts, will vary.

Leif Johansen himself was outspoken on the MSG-model's limited applicability in predicting future development patterns. He emphasized that the uncertainty attached to the behaviour of the agents in the economy makes the MSG-model inappropriate for studying the problems of policy implementation. In his last written communication to the "Perspective group" preparing NOU 1983:27 (see Johansen (1983) and also Bjerkholt and Tveitereid in this volume), he wrote:

"A feature of recent developments in many countries is for instance the substantial uncertainty that exists regarding the savings/consumption behaviour of households, and investment behaviour of firms.... Such uncertainty creates considerable problems for the steering of the economy. However, MSG behaves as if the development of the total capital stock can be controlled, and as if it is always possible through the use of various instruments to affect private consumption behaviour in such a way that total aggregate demand ensures the full utilization of the labour supply and capital stock. To the extent that there exists uncertainty about those components of behaviour that determine the effects of policy instruments on savings/consumption and investment, the steering will be made more difficult, resulting in a less balanced development than assumed by MSG. The MSG calculations as such cannot shed any further light on these problems. But one may perhaps say that the MSG calculations illuminate the decision choices one is confronted with in economic policy making due to uncertainty about the exogenous variables. They are less appropriate in explaining the policy implementation problems encountered due to the uncertainty attached to various behavioural relations in the economy."

The "Perspective group" recommended that economic policy be based on a strategy, an idea often advocated by Leif Johansen. The future is basically uncertain and therefore one should not search for the most likely outcome, but rather develop a scheme of preparedness towards different possible outcomes. An interesting approach to these problems is presented in Aslaksen and Bjerkholt (in this volume).

The economic situation in the beginning of the 1980s, characterized by stagnation, unemployment, and excess capacity, differs markedly from the full-employment, steady growth situation that prevailed when the MSG-model was first developed and applied. Fundamental questions have been raised about the relevance and applicability of a general equilibrium model which assumes full employment or takes employment as exogenous to current economic conditions.

To these questions one may respond that MSG generates desirable, or in some sense optimal paths, and that presumably deviations from this path in the early years will not have a significant impact on the longer term solution. Furthermore, the paths generated by MSG are internally consistent and may serve as useful "checks" on the compatibility of independently formulated goals despite the uncertainty that may exist concerning the exogenous variables.

Professor Ragnar Frisch once objected to the MSG-model on the ground that it was a neoclassical equilibrium model, not a planning model. To this critique Leif Johansen adressed himself in the concluding remarks of his book on the MSG-model, (see Johansen (1960a)):

"In connection with the possible application of the model to a planned economy one very important problem arises. We have seen that for given changes in the exogenous variables the model produces a definite solution for the endogenous variables. Can this solution be interpreted as indicating an optimal solution? We shall not delve deeply into this problem, since it would require a reiteration of almost all theorems in the welfare theory. The main point is that our model (with a few exceptions) represents a formal analogy with the solution which in theory is obtained under perfect competition. This should secure the fulfilment of certain well known optimum conditions, and it suggests that our model might be interpreted as a normative model for the manner in which the sectoral composition of the economy should change under a growth process."

5. Some reflections on the future of the MSG-model and its applications

The use of large econometric models as analytical and administrative tools in the Norwegian political administrative system is well established and increasing. There is also a growing interest in framing short-term policy making within a medium and longer term context. Therefore, even if only for these reasons, the MSG-model will be a cornerstone in further model development in Norway. Furthermore, there is a concern that demand management policies may have received too much attention in economic policy making at the expense of general resource allocation questions and in particular questions related to the efficient use of productive resources (supply-side problems). Since the MSG-model is a multisectoral general equilibrium model with facilities for alternative specifications of the

production structure, it is clearly well suited as a basis for further
explorations in this direction (see Johansen (1982)).

Over the years, a number of analyses on special subjects have been
derived on the basis of projections from the MSG-model (cf. section 3). In
future work there will be a challenge to update and bring together these
special studies. This could increase the realism of the perspectives,
improving the feedback to the exogenous assumptions underlying the MSG
projections.

There is a long "want list" of improvements and extensions to the MSG-
model which goes well beyond any realistic development programme (see
Barker (1981) and Ministry of Finance (1983a)). This does not mean that
the model is inferior as it now stands, since a model is never complete or
perfect, and often the experience is that the more it is improved and
extended, the more one becomes aware of its potential.

Another lesson of experience is that research programmes for model
building ought not to be too rigid. Problems which may arise in establishing a theoretical or empirical support for new elements of the model must
be taken seriously. Introduction of elements which are not well established theoretically and/or empirically may spoil the quality of an otherwise well functioning model. The strategy in Norwegian model building has
been to build open models rather than to close them with dubious relations. But one of the drawbacks of this strategy is that the interpretation
of results can be tricky. Increased flexibility and falling prices for
computer systems have, however, allowed for more experimentation with
tentative equations.

In the strategy for further development and expansion of the MSG-
model some directions can be indicated:

-   Further extension of the general equilibrium character of the model by
    including the labour market (endogenizing labour supply, wage, and
    income formation), the capital market (explaining capital formation
    and capital mobility), and behaviour in industries which are exposed
    to competition from abroad (endogenizing exports and import shares);
-   introduction of vintage capital stocks and drawing upon Leif Johansen's
    contributions to putty-clay capital theory;
-   improving the model's dynamic properties, particularly to facilitate the
    merging of short-, medium- and long-term analyses;
-   inclusion of flows of funds between institutional sectors to check the

consistency between the real and nominal flows and the implied net
lending and borrowing by sector.

This strategy will not distort the MSG-model or change its general
character. To the contrary, the basic structure of the model will remain.
New elements will be brought in only where Leif Johansen had to make
simplified assumptions in accordance with his stated research programme:

"The model presented in this study is in many respects unsatisfactory
when judged from a purely theoretical point of view. It is, however,
constructed with an eye to the possibility of being implemented by existing statistics. Without this possibility the model would hardly be
very interesting." (Johansen (1960a)).

It is our view that Leif Johansen struck a very happy balance between
theory and practice when working according to this programme. From the
beginning, the MSG-model has yielded both new theoretical insights and
quantitative estimates of great interest. It seems to have the potential to
continue to do so also in the future.

References

Alstadheim, H. (1968), "En disaggregert vekstmodell for Norge med 1963
      som basisår", Memorandum of January 2 from Institute of Economics,
      University of Oslo.

Aslaksen, I. and O. Bjerkholt (1984), "Macroeconomic Planning Strategies
      for an Oil Exporting Country under Uncertainty of Future Oil Price",
      paper presented at the seminar "Macroeconomic prospects for a small
      oil exporting country", Ullensvang, 14-16 May 1984.

Aslaksen, I. and O. Bjerkholt (1985), "Certainty equivalence procedures
      in decision-making under uncertainty: An empirical application", this
      volume.

Aukrust, O. and P.J. Bjerve (1945), Hva krigen kostet Norge, Dreyers
      forlag, Oslo.

Barker, T. (1981), "A Review of Models and Data in the Norwegian System of Economic Planning", Articles from the Central Bureau of Statistics, No 131, Oslo.

Bjerkholt, O. and S. Longva (1980), Modis IV - A Model for Economic Analysis and National Planning, Social Economic Studies from the Central Bureau of Statistics, No 43, Oslo.

Bjerkholt, O., L. Lorentsen and S. Strøm (1981), "Using the Oil and Gas Revenues: The Norwegian Case", in Barker and Brailovsky (eds.), Oil or Industry?, Academic Press 1981, London.

Bjerkholt, O., S. Longva, Ø. Olsen and S. Strøm (eds.) (1983), Analysis of Supply and Demand or Electricity in the Norwegian Economy, Social Economic Studies from the Central Bureau of Statistics, No 53, Oslo.

Bjerkholt, O. and S. Tveitereid (1985), "The use of the MSG-model in preparing a "Perspective Analysis 1980-2000" for the Norwegian economy", this volume.

Bjerve, P.J. (1976), "Trends in Norwegian Planning 1945-1975", Articles from the Central Bureau of Statistics, No 84, Oslo.

Borg, A. (1979), Prognoser for norsk detaljomsetning fram til 1990. Tanum-Nordli, Oslo.

Borg, A. (1983), Norsk detaljhandel i 1980-årene. Tanum-Nordli, Oslo.

Colbjørnsen, T. and K.A. Larsen (1985), "Framtidens jobber. Spekulasjoner i grenselandet mellom sosiologi og makroøkonomi", Melding 1985:1, Institute for Studies in Research and higher Education, Oslo.

Directorate of Labour (1971), Framskrivning av den totale sysselsetting til 1990 for riket, de enkelte fylker, og arbeidskontordistrikter, Oslo.

Dale, E., K. Jervan, A. Midttun, J.E. Myhre og D. Namtvedt (1984), "Markedsøkonomisk ressursforvaltning - En konsekvensanalyse av

264   P. Schreiner and K.A. Larsen

likebehandling av naturressurser", GRS - 587, Resource Policy
Group, Oslo.

Dale, E., K. Kalgraf og M.H. Raaholt (1985), "Analyse av energiforbruket
ved hjelp av MSG-modellen", GRS - 598, Resource Policy Group,
Oslo.

Energiprognoseutvalget (Expert Group on Energy Forecast), Unprinted
Annex to the White Paper on Energy 1985.

Eriksen, K. (1978), "Beregnet etterspørsel etter utdannet arbeidskraft i
1990", Melding 1978:4, Institute for Studies in Research and higher
Education, Oslo.

Eriksen, K. and T. Kjølberg (1981), "Lønnsutvikling og etterspørsel etter
ulike typer arbeidskraft", Melding 1981:5, Institute for Studies in
Research and higher Education, Oslo.

Eriksen, T., T. Thonstad and J.F. Qvigstad (1978), "Arbeidsmiljø og
næringsstruktur. Et forsøk på å knytte arbeidsmiljøvariable til økonomiske planleggingsmodeller", Memorandum from Institute of Economics, University of Oslo, Oslo.

Foundation of Industrial Development (SIU) (1984), "Norge som Industri-
nasjon", Mimeograph, Oslo.

Førsund, F.R. and S. Strøm (1973), "Modeller for sammenheng mellom
produksjon og utslipp av spillprodukter", Kap. 10 i Spesialanalyse 1,
forurensninger, annex to Ministry of Finance (1973).

Førsund, F.R. and S. Strøm (1974), "Industrial Structure, Growth and
Residual flows", in J. Rothenberg and I.G. Heggie (eds.), The
Management of Water Quality and the Environment, The Macmillan
Press Ltd., London and Basingstoke.

Gjærum, P.I. og T. Holm (1982), "Omstillinger mellom næringer i fortid og
fremtid", Sosialøkonomen nr. 3.

Resource Policy Group (1984), "Om å stabilisere Norges Energiforbruk", Report No. 582, Oslo.

Institute for Studies in Research and Higher Education (1983), "Behovet for sivilingeniører fram til år 2010", Annex 1 to NOU (1983a).

Johansen, L. (1960a), A Multi-sectoral Study of Economic Growth, North-Holland Publishing Company, Amsterdam.

Johansen, L. (1960b), "Rules of Thumb for the Expansion of Industries in a Process of Economic Growth", Econometrica, vol. 28.

Johansen, L. (1968), "Explorations in Long-Term Projections for the Norwegian Economy", Economics of Planning, No. 1-2.

Johansen, L. (1974), A Multi-Sectoral Study of Economic Growth. Second Enlarged Edition, North-Holland Publishing Company, Amsterdam.

Johansen, L. (1982), "Economic Models and Economic Planning and Policy: Some Trends and Problems", in M. Hazewinkel and A.H.G. Rinnooy Kan (eds.), Current Developments in the Interface: Economics, Econometrics, Mathematics, D. Reidel Publ. Co., Dordrecht.

Johansen, L. (1983), "Notat om enkelte metodeproblemer ved bruk av MSG-beregninger", i NOU (1983c)

Johansen, K.E. and H. Strand (1981), "Macroeconomic Models for Medium and Long-Term Planning", Articles from the Central Bureau of Statistics, No. 128, Oslo.

Kobberstad, T. (1976), "Etterspørsel etter ulike typer arbeidskraft - metoder og modeller", Melding 1976:7.   Institute for Studies in Research and higher Education, Oslo.

Larsen, K.A. (1976), "The choice of growth rate, savings rate and foreign financing. Some social aspects of long-run macroeconomic investment policies", paper prepared for the UN-seminar, "On Factors of Growth and Investment Policies: an International Approach",

Budapest 13-18 December 1976, Oslo.

Larsen, K.A. (1981), "Sysselsetting og økonomisk utvikling mot år 2000", in Brunstad, R., Colbjørnsen, T. og Rødseth, T.(eds.), Sysselsettingen i søkelyset, Universitetsforlaget, Bergen.

Larsen, K.A. (1982), "Høyere utdanning og arbeidsmarkedet mot år 2000", in Skotheim, S. og Utne, E. (eds.), Forskning og høgre utdanning. Årbok 1982, Universitetsforlaget, Bergen.

Larsen, K.A. (1985), "RULETT - en modell for etterspørselsprognoser for ulike typer arbeidskraft," forthcoming, Institute for Studies in Research and higher Education, Oslo.

Longva, S., L. Lorentsen and Ø. Olsen (1980), "Energy in a Multisectoral Model", Reports No. 80/1 from the Central Bureau of Statistics, Oslo.

Longva, S., L. Lorentsen and Ø. Olsen (1985), "The Multi-Sectoral Growth Model MSG-4; Formal Structure and Empirical Characteristics", this volume.

Longva, S., Ø. Olsen and J. Rinde (1983), "Energy Price Sensitivity of the Norwegian economy", in Bjerkholt et al. (1983), Oslo.

Longva, S., L. Lorentsen, J. Rinde and S. Strøm (1983), "Use of the MSG model in Forecasting Electricity Demand", in Bjerholt et al. (1983), Oslo.

Lorentsen, L., S. Strøm and L.E. Østby (1979), "Virkningen på norsk økonomi av en pause i den videre kraftutbygging (Impacts on the Norwegian Economy of a Temporary Halt in the Growth of Electricity Supply)", Statsøkonomisk Tidsskrift, No. 1, 1979.

Ministry of Finance (1969), "Noen hovedtrekk i den økonomiske utviklingen fram til 1990", in Finans- og tolldepartementet: Perspektivanalyser for Norges økonomi. Skisser for utviklingen fram til 1990. Annex to Langtidsprogrammet 1970-1973, St.meld. nr. 55 (1969-70), Oslo.

Ministry of Finance (1970), "Perspektivanalyser for Norges økonomi. Bidrag fra en arbeidsgruppe", Mimeograph, Oslo.

Ministry of Finance (1973), "Langtidsprogrammet 1974-1977", St.meld. nr. 71 (1972-73), Oslo.

Ministry of Finance (1974), "The Petroleum Industry and the Norwegian Society", St.meld. nr. 25 (1973-74), Oslo.

Ministry of Finance (1975), "Natural Resources and Economic Development", St.meld. nr. 50 (1974-75), Oslo.

Ministry of Finance (1977), "Langtidsprogrammet 1978-1981", St.meld. nr. 75 (1976-77), Oslo.

Ministry of Finance (1983a), "Modellutvikling for makroøkonomisk planlegging - tilråding fra Modellutvalget", (Model Development Committee) Mimeograph PA/42, Oslo.

Ministry of Finance (1983b), "Nasjonalbudsjettet 1984", St.meld. nr. 88 (1983-84), Oslo.

Ministry of Finance (1984), "Modellsystemet for makroøkonomisk planlegging", Mimeograph PA/10, Oslo.

Ministry of Oil and Energy (1984), "On the Future of Petroleum Industry", St.meld. nr. 32 (1984-85), Oslo.

Ministry of Planning (1981), "Langtidsprogrammet 1982-1985", St.meld. nr. 79 (1980-81), Oslo.

NOU (1976), "Langtidsplanlegging og modeller", NOU 1976:8, Oslo.

NOU (1983a), "Petroleumsvirksomhetens framtid", NOU 1983:27, Oslo.

NOU (1983b), "Perspektivanalyse for bygg- og anleggsnæringene 1980-2000", NOU 1983:28, Oslo.

NOU (1983c), "Perspektivberegninger for norsk økonomi til år 2000", NOU
    1983:27, Oslo.

NOU (1984a), "Trygdefinansiering", NOU 1984:10, Oslo.

NOU (1984b), "Statlig næringsstøtte i distriktene", NOU 1984:21, Oslo.

Norwegian Research Institute of Commerce (1979), "Norsk engroshandel
    frem mot århundreskiftet, Hovedrapport", HFU-rapport nr. 3, Oslo.

Norwegian Research Institute of Commerce (1982), "Omsetningsprognoser
    og fremskriving av bedrifts- og sysselsettingstall i norsk engros-
    handel 1982-2000", HFU-rapport nr. 14, Oslo.

Schreiner, A. and T. Skoglund (1984a), "Virkninger av oljevirksomheten
    i Nord-Norge", Reports from the Central Bureau of Statistics, No.
    84/17, Oslo.

Schreiner, A. and T. Skoglund (1984b):" Regional impacts of activities i
    Norway", paper presented at the seminar "Macroeconomic prospects
    for a small oil exporting country", Ullensvang, 14.-16. May 1984.

Schreiner, P. (1972), "The Role of Input-Output in the Perspective
    Analyses of the Norwegian Economy", in Brody, A. and Carter, A.P.
    (eds.), Input-Output Techniques, North-Holland Publishing Com-
    pany, Amsterdam.

Sevaldson, P. (1964), "An Interindustry Model of Production and Con-
    sumption in Norway", Income and Wealth, series X, 23-50.

Skoglund, T. (1980), "REGION: En modell for regional kryssløpsanalyse",
    Articles from Central Bureau of Statistics, nr. 122, Oslo.

Statistisk Sentralbyrå (1980), "Fylkesvise elektrisitetsprognoser for 1985
    og 1990. En metodestudie", Reports from the Central Bureau of
    Statistics No 80/6, Oslo.

Thonstad, T. (1969), "Noen perspektiver for utdanning og arbeids-
marked", Perspektivanalyser. Skisser for utviklingen fram til 1990,
Annex to "Langtidsprogrammet 1970-1973", St.meld. nr. 55 (1968-69),
Oslo.

Transportøkonomisk Institutt (1983): "Langsiktige perspektiver for den
økonomiske utviklingen i fylkene. Resultater og erfaringer fra utprø-
vingen av modellen REGION", Prosjektrapport, Oslo.

Vannebo, O. (1981): De tjenesteytende næringer i 80-årene, Tanum-Norli,
Oslo.

Production, Multi-Sectoral Growth and Planning
F.R. Førsund, M. Hoel, and S. Longva (Editors)
© Elsevier Science Publishers B.V. (North-Holland), 1985

THE USE OF THE MSG-MODEL IN PREPARING A "PERSPECTIVE ANALYSIS 1980-2000" FOR THE NORWEGIAN ECONOMY

Olav Bjerkholt

Central Bureau of Statistics of Norway

Sigurd Tveitereid

Ministry of Finance

1. Introduction

The MSG-model was first used for national economic planning purposes in the preparation of a supplement to the Long-Term Programme 1970-1973, published in 1969. The supplement contained a projection of the Norwegian economy towards 1990. Since then every Long-Term Programme has included, in addition to its four-year programme, a more noncommittal long-term projection of the Norwegian economy elaborated by means of successive versions of the MSG-model, which has become a prominent part in the inventory of tools for long-term policy analysis. In addition, during the 1960's a committee of civil servants and academic experts was given the mandate to prepare a Perspective Analysis that would elaborate alternative paths of development for the Norwegian economy towards 2000, and also to advise on the use of models for long-term analysis (NOU (1983)). Leif Johansen was a member of this committee until his untimely death in December 1982.

Although the Perspective Analysis is somewhat different from the Long-Term Programme supplements, it shares with them the reliance upon the MSG-model as the basic tool of analysis. Below follows some reflections on the use of the MSG-model as a tool for analyzing long-run growth projects within the context of the committee's work on the Perspective Analysis. Many of the points discussed are directly inspired by verbal and written notes contributed by Leif Johansen to the committee.

2. Diminished perspectives for growth

The usefulness of a macroeconomic model in a long-term analysis is conditioned upon:

- the model representing a reasonable approximation of the technology, the patterns of behaviour, and the forces at work in the economy;

- the model being able to describe and analyze the relevant problems under consideration;

- the model being able to help clarify how policy choices influence the course of development, and how they enhance or restrict future possibilities.

While the overall development of an economy can be considered as the result of an interplay between economic, social, and political factors, available macroeconomic models seldom model more than the interrelations between a restricted set of economic variables. If a model is to be used meaningfully, it must at least represent the general framework of the economy by giving a structural description of economic flows in national accounting terms, by capturing the essential rules of the game for the economic agents, and by including indispensable institutional assumptions. Furthermore, precise numerical assumptions about the development of the model's "exogenous variables" are required so that the "endogenous variables" can be solved.

The basic idea of the MSG-model is to generate efficient allocations of production factors between industries by simulating competitive markets under full employment of labour and capital equipment throughout the economy (Johansen, 1960, pp. 18-23). The model itself does not describe or explain the institutional prerequisites - such as financial markets, incentive schemes, laws, regulations, etc. - necessary to secure a steady and balanced growth process with full employment. Thus the interpretation of the results derived from the model depends upon a corroboration that the institutional support for the policies needed to implement the solution exists. This is, in short, "the user's problem" in applying the model:

"... the formal model in the following analysis is to a great extent applicable to growth processes which take place within different frameworks. The real content and interpretations may, however, of course, be quite different under different systems" (Johansen, 1960, pp.19-20).

At one end of the scale the model can be used to represent a well-behaved laissez-faire economy; at the other as a tool for selecting economic programmes in a command economy.

The driving forces in the MSG picture of the economy are 1) the supply constraints - capital accumulation, growth in labour force, and technical progress - and 2) changes in exogenous demand, i.e. government expenditure and foreign trade. Growth in capital, labour force, and productivity enhance the productive power of the economy. Exogenous demand influences the industrial pattern of growth, but may also affect overall growth by causing movement of factors of production between industries with unequal marginal productivities.

From 1945 up to the beginning of the 1970's, the characterization of the Norwegian economy as a smooth and efficient machine seemed to fit well even as a positive description. Observed growth in production from World War II up to 1974 was close to the average for the OECD area, and remarkably smooth. The average growth rate from 1950 to 1974 was 4.1 per cent. Published in 1969, the Norwegian Long-Term Programme for 1970-1973 reflected the current optimism at the time by stating:

"It seems that the industrialized countries to a great extent has been able to master the big fluctuations in economic activity which in earlier times led to sustained periods with low utilization of productive resources. It is therefore possible that the technological development and the supply of resources gives the possibility for continued growth at the same pace as that experienced in the 1950's and the 1960's."

This optimism, which was fairly widespread within the OECD area, faded quickly after 1973. It is probably correct to say, however, that a belief in OECD's ability to recover from higher energy prices and other disturbances, and return to accustomed patterns of growth and employment level, was maintained more confidently and longer in Norway than in most countries. The country's own growth record in the 1970's shows - at

least on the surface - no drop from previous trends. From 1974 to 1980
the GDP growth rate was 4.7 per cent, highest within the OECD area.
Official long-term projections from the mid-1970's predicted continued high
prosperity.

But under the surface, growth was not as smooth as earlier. During
the 1970's contrary forces were at work. Oil had entered the Norwegian
economy, boosting investment industries and opening up new avenues of
expansion, and moreover reinforcing the general optimism as new oil and
gas finds were reported. On the other hand traditional export industries
stagnated, with the shipping industry falling into its deepest crisis since
the steamship wiped out the Norwegian merchant-sailship fleet. The manufacturing sector faced sluggish markets, sharply increasing costs, and
harsher competition. However, the government bolstered ailing industries
with ample subsidies and financial support, thus postponing the necessary
restructuring of the manufacturing sector. It also expanded domestic
consumption, which increased almost 20 per cent from 1974 to 1977. This
expansive anticyclical policy not only kept unemployment low, but induced
a rapid increase in the labour force which in number of employed persons
was 15 per cent higher in 1980 than in 1974 due to a swift increase in
female participation rates.

The heavy North Sea investment and the expansive demand policy
caused a fast deterioration in the balance of payments. Towards the end
of the 1970's the brakes were applied in an effort to gain better control
over cost conditions and to stabilize the balance of payments. Therefore,
relative manufacturing unit costs peaked in 1977, 35 per cent higher than
in 1970, but the current account deficit had reached 14 per cent of GDP
in the same year. Fortunately, oil and gas revenues increased sharply
after 1978 as more fields came into operation.

In the meantime the OPEC price shock of 1979 occurred. The OECD
area went into a prolonged recession, while Norway with more oil and gas
relative to the size of the economy than any other OECD country had an
increase in her real disposable income of about 11 per cent in 1980. The
current balance of payments again became positive and has remained so in
the ensuing years.

In April 1981 the Labour government presented the latest long-term
projections for the Norwegian economy only some months before stepping
down after eight years in office. The aggregate results for the development of gross domestic product and private consumption 1980-2000 in that

projection and the three preceding ones are put together in Table 1. The 1973 projection had "high" and "low" alternatives, while the ensuing projections had "high," "medium," and "low" alternatives. The figures given in the table for the year 2000 are percentage increases over 1980 and average annual growth rates. The 1980 figures are those implicit in the respective projections; for the last projection these are the preliminary national account figures available at the time of calculation (see note to Table 1).

Table 1 illustrates the uncertainty over the future prospects of the economy. It also conveys an impression of cyclical change in the assessments of the future: from the modest growth projections of 1973 to the peak of optimism in the mid-1970's, back down to the slow growth prediction of 1981. The use of high-low intervals has been the method chosen for revealing the uncertainty in these projections. Note, however, that the medium growth rate of GDP in the 1981 projection is outside the high-low interval for all the preceding projections! One may indeed wonder whether the fluctuations in estimated long-term growth rates, as revealed by Table 1, reflect short-term changes in the economic climate and mood more than any real change in the evaluation of growth factors.

Like the projections before it, the projection from the 1981-analysis was also quickly off the mark. While the lowest annual rate of growth in GDP through the 1970's was 3.3 per cent, the growth in 1981 turned out to be nearly zero, except for 1958 the lowest since the Second World War. Moreover, domestic prices increased more than in any year since the war. The 1981 projection was based on a long-term oil price development widely predicted by international forecasters at the time, i.e. an expected doubling of the real oil price from 1980 to 2000. In early 1982 the oil market faltered, prices fell and long-term price forecasts were duly corrected, perhaps again an overreaction to short-term movements. Anxious on account of the fall in oil prices in 1982, the new Norwegian government, a conservative coalition, stressed the necessity to restrict demand further. As a result unemployment started to rise. Signs indicated the Dutch Disease syndrome had reached Norway. Such was the background for the Perspective Analysis of 1983. The task was to provide new long-term growth perspectives, and also to suggest improved methods for elaborating long-term projections with particular reference to the use of the MSG-model.

The 1983 analysis was approached in a conventional supply side

Table 1. Official government projections for the Norwegian economy.
Gross Domestic Product and Private Consumption in 2000 as
percentage increase over 1980
(Average annual growth rates in parentheses)

Source	Year	Gross Domestic Product			Private Consumption		
		High	Medium	Low	High	Medium	Low
Long-Term Programme 1974–1977	1973	119.2 (4.0)		75.7 (2.9)	80.7 (3.0)		61.5 (2.4)
White Paper on Natural Resources and Economic Development	1975	132.1 (4.3)	106.8 (3.7)	67.2 (2.6)	136.6 (4.4)	119.1 (4.0)	60.7 (2.4)
Long-Term Programme 1978–1981	1977	99.8 (3.5)	92.5 (3.3)	85.6 (3.1)	100.2 (3.5)	85.9 (3.1)	85.9 (3.1)
Long-Term Programme 1982–1985	1981	83.1 (3.0)	59.3 (2.4)	38.3 (1.6)	92.4 (3.3)	71.7 (2.7)	49.7 (2.9)

Note: The figures are derived from published data in the following publications: St.meld.nr. 71 (1972-73), St.meld.nr. 50 (1974-75), St.meld.nr.
75 (1976-77) and St.meld.nr. 79 (1980-81). Some recalculations have been
necessary to achieve comparability because of changes in the base year
for volume figures and different periods of projection. The 1980 figures
used are those implicit in the respective projections. For the first three
projections the 1980 figures overestimated GDP in 1980 by 5, 9, and 6 per
cent and Private Consumption by 0.5 and 6.5 per cent. A comparison of
the absolute year 2000 figures would thus make the 1977 projection stand
out as even more optimistic compared with the 1981 projection. In the
latter projection the 1980 figures used were the preliminary national
accounts figures available at the time.

fashion by assessing the factors of growth: labour, capital, and technical
progress. The size of the labour force was assumed to be determined by
autonomous demographic development. Except for changes caused by
migration, the size and the composition of the population could be
predicted with almost certainty for the perspective year 2000, since every

member of the potential labour force had already been born except for
migration. Participation rates were much harder to estimate. Among the
most important factors are the structural change in participation rates of
married women, and the effects on the labour supply of higher unemployment. As mentioned above, some of the increase in the labour force
during the 1970's was due to the growth in the public sector. Such
considerations make traditional assumptions about a given labour force
difficult to maintain. By and large, the Perspective Analysis assumed
independence between the size of the labour force and activity in the rest
of the economy. Most of the alternatives assumed that the labour force is
fully employed and that the remaining unemployment is of the "natural"
kind, allowing only for frictions and normal search activity. A necessary
condition for this is a flexible real wage rate.

The following interactions between the labour supply and the economic
situation were also considered:

- increased domestic use of oil income inducing higher participation
  rates,

- a current account constraint limiting domestic demand and causing
  reduced supply and/or unemployment,

- reduced growth in government consumption temporarily reducing
  the expected growth in women's participation rates.

With regard to developments in production capital, MSG can be solved
two different ways. The first approach is to concentrate on the demand
for capital (investment), assuming that the supply of capital and the
implied funds of saving are equal to the ex ante supplied funds of saving.
The opposite approach is to assume a given supply of capital, determined
by savings. The supplied capital is assumed to be automatically used.
Both ways of reasoning were applied in the Perspective Analysis, reflecting
extremes of a model with simultanous determination of investment, saving,
and the rate of return on capital.

In the case of demand determined capital, the rate of return is forced
to fall continuously in order to allow for the decreasing marginal productivity of capital. This demand approach to capital development implies an
accelerator mechanism between investment and production with investment

generally sensitive to different assumptions about the growth in employment. The accelerator effect is predicted to be rather significant for
investment in housing, which varies considerably with the growth in
income (total consumption).

For example, in the baseline alternative of the 1983 analysis investment grows slowly in the 1990's coinciding with a falling rate of return.
This is due both to the zero growth of the labour force in that decade and
to the comparatively high initial level of investments. Accordingly, a
boost in investment in the 1990's would require a rate of return quite
close to zero.

In the MSG-model technical progress in each industry is assumed to
be of Hicks-neutral type. The 1983-analysis assumed that technical progress up to the year 2000 would be lower than the estimated rate for the
1950's and 1960's, but somewhat higher than the observed rate in the
weakest period of the 1970's. These assumptions about technical progress
are consistent with slow growth in the rest of the world combined with
expected structural inefficiencies in the economy. If the world economy
grows at a pace even slower than expected, the assumptions made about
technical progress are probably too optimistic.

Assumptions made about technical progress are assumptions about
largely unspecified residuals. No wonder these assumptions are without a
firm basis either in theory or in empirical analysis. Still, considering
there exist possibilities of a major breakthrough, for instance in the
application of telecommunications and computer technology, they might be
viewed as too pessimistic. It must be admitted that this is a weak point in
assessing the possibilities for growth.

Alternative assumptions about the rate of technical progress have been
tried. Minor changes were made in several alternatives to correct for the
possibility that higher activity could result in higher productivity, especially through embodied technical progress brought forward by higher
levels of investment.

When it comes to oil and gas, production is exogenously determined.
Unlike other prices in the model, the prices of oil and gas are determined
in the world market and not by Norwegian long-run production costs.

Oil income is important to the Norwegian economy, and neither prices,
production, nor costs are easy to predict. In the Perspective Analysis of
1983 it is assumed that the real price of oil will increase over time. In the
baseline scenario the real price grows by 2 per cent p.a. from 1985 to

2000. In the high-price alternative growth is assumed to be 3 per cent p.a. in the same period. While the production of oil is assumed to grow, the expected increase in production costs imply a more modest growth in value added. It is assumed that gas production will become increasingly important, and that gas prices will rise from their present relatively low level per energy unit and increase even faster than oil prices.

Over a long time span the continuing terms-of-trade improvement caused by rising oil prices imply a marked difference between growth in production (measured in fixed prices) and the growth in real income. Summarizing on an aggregate level the "causes of wealth" in the Norwegian economy, it may therefore be natural to suggest that oil income be added to the three more conventional factors: labour, capital, and technical progress.

The growth path for 1980-2000 drawn up in the Perspective Analysis of 1983 continues the trend of downward adjustments as seen in Table 1: a GDP growth of 43 per cent or 1.8 per cent p.a., and a growth in Private Consumption of 60.7 per cent or 2.4 per cent p.a.

3. Medium-term problems and long-run efficiency

An important aspect of interpretating the results from a general equilibrium model is in relating the long-term path depicted by the model with the short- and medium-term projections on which current policy is based. Long-term projections run the risk of never becoming operative in the sense of shaping policies. The underlying logic of a long-term equilibrium path is that medium-term policy should be transitory and directed towards reaching the long-term path even though unforeseen events may ultimately prevent the economy from ever attaining this path. This guidance role of long-term projections is perhaps their most important function within a political-institutional context, but at least in Norway, experience indicates that the coordination between medium- and long-term planning is hard to achieve. As a surrogate solution the long-term path is sometimes forced through either the current base year or through the last year of the current medium-term projection.

The main results explained by the MSG-model are the allocation of investment and employment between industries, the sectoral distribution of production, and changes in relative prices or terms of trade between the sectors. All of this is most valuable information concerning the future development of the economy, and should to be used as a basis for long-term decisions within enterprises and households. However, for the various branches of government, and those responsible for macroeconomic policy decisions in particular, a projection by the model does not provide the same kind of information that it provides enterprises and households. Rather the realization of the projection becomes the target of government decision. For example, what are the implicit constraints on fiscal policy, monetary policy, exchange rate policy, etc., necessary to promote the development depicted in the projection. While some clues as to what are the constraints can be derived from the model solution, to answer in detail MSG must be supported by auxiliary models that can calculate financial consequences, implications for balance of payments, etc., without feeding-back into the MSG-solution. Such calculations are quite necessary to corroborate and evaluate the results from model exercises. The rationale for using the model in this way is, of course, the assumption that the inventory of policy tools is rich enough to implement the solution in the possibility space depicted by the general equilibrium model.

In an open economy like Norway, where exports and imports each equal about 40 per cent of GNP, the structure and development of foreign trade is of great importance for the industrial composition of the economy. Since the solution of a general equilibrium model for a constant-returns-to-scale competitive economy suggests that the number of industries with world-market determined prices should be equal to the number of primary factors, the actual determination of foreign trade in MSG is incomplete. This leaves open to the user's discretion such important questions as the industrial composition of the "tradeables" sector. Usually the volume of exports for the individual industries is exogenously determined, while prices are endogenously determined as long-run marginal costs. Price determination is based on the assumption that production costs in Norway will develop similarly to production costs in competitor countries. This is a reasonable assumption for a small open economy if its technical progress and relative factor supplies develop in step with other countries. Whether this applies to Norway in her current situation is more problematic, and even if applicable, leaves unanswered the question of how exports should be spread over the individual industries. Norway differs from most of her competitor countries by having a large primary commodity export sector, i.e. crude oil and natural gas, whose export value now approaches half of all other commodity exports and which may be expected to be at least as large for an extended period of time. This fact is undoubtedly the key to explaining the stagnation in the manufacturing sector since 1974 when the petroleum sector was in its infancy. It may also indicate that manufacturing and other export industries must be assigned a different role in the future than would have been the case otherwise.

The composition of Norwegian exports could be approached by modelling the world market demand for Norwegian products as a function of, inter alia, Norwegian and foreign prices. Such relations could then be added to the model, which would mean that the exogenous assumptions about export volumes would be replaced by corresponding assumptions concerning foreign prices and other export market indicators. Alternatively, a set of such relations could be used iteratively in conjunction with MSG. One problem with this approach is the weak price response that a model like MSG generates when exogenous export demand shifts. In the model most export oriented sectors exhibit constant returns to scale while the input from sectors with decreasing returns to scale is so modest that the effect on prices are quite limited. On the other hand, the quantitative effect on export volumes may be unrealistically sharp.

With respect to its treatment of foreign trade MSG touches upon another problematic difficulty for a general equilibrium model, namely, the actual appearance of differentials in remunerations to labour and capital in different industries. In reality, such differentials are statistically quite significant with large annual variations especially observed for the remuneration of capital. The differentials embedded in the MSG-model are based on estimated averages over a period of about 15 years and are as a rule held constant in projections. The optimal allocation of investment in the model is directly dependent upon these differentials. Unless they can be accounted for, such differentials are at variance with the model's assumption of perfect mobility of labour and capital. Several explanations for the observed differentials are possible. Wage and salary differentials may, for instance, reflect differences in skill, education, conditions of work, regional labour market conditions, or safety associated with specific industries or occupations. It is an obvious weakness of the model that labour is considered as a homogeneous factor not broken down by skill and education. The differentials may also reflect "social standing" or limited entry. In the remuneration of capital, differentials may depend on differences in risk, traditional differences in profit requirements, the degree of concentration, the occurrence of intangible assets such as research and development, monopolization, financial convenience between multinationals and daughter companies, etc. Although some of these reasons are consistent with the free mobility assumption, foremost risk, others are at variance with it. The problem is that differentials in the remuneration to capital are higher than can be accounted for by differences in risk (and risk here should mean "social" risk).

All the reasons mentioned above may apply in an equilibrium situation, however, differentials may also arise in or as a result of disequilibrium situations. Fluctuations in world market prices or unfulfilled expectations may cause deviations which can be eliminated by using averages over longer periods. A more tricky problem is that in a real world with more friction in the movement of factors of production than assumed in the model, observed differentials in the remuneration to labour as well as to capital may be explained partly by the long-term movements themselves.

The problem described above in linking MSG with export demand relations when there are large discrepancies between foreign prices and Norwegian costs could be approached by partly endogenizing the determination of the differentials in remuneration. Some part of the price impulses from abroad could be absorbed by adjustments to the differentials in remuneration for the industries concerned.

MSG assumes substitution in production between labour, capital, energy, and other materials, but substitution possibilities vary between industries. The substitution properties are of great importance both for the long-run development of the economy and for medium-term adjustments. The neoclassical assumptions made in MSG are more apt to reflect long-run possibilities than model "structural problems" in a medium-term context. Leif Johansen expressed this by saying that MSG can calculate a structural development, but the production theoretic assumptions in the model imply that one cannot directly represent structural problems.

A formalized quantitative approach for dealing with such problems requires production theoretic assumptions that can account for the rigidity and inflexibility in existing production capacities, i.e. a putty-clay approach along the lines of Johansen (1972). A development of MSG in this direction may well be feasible, but a complete putty-clay vintage representation of the production structure in all industries at the current level of disaggregation in the model seems to be beyond reach (see

Førsund and Jansen in this volume).

A close scrutiny of the results from the model may, however, indicate warning signals of structural problems, and may indicate modifications and adjustments that could be made to take into account some of the effects tha. would have been more clearly observed within a putty-clay approach. One such effect is the link between gross investment and technical progress. In expanding industries with high investment, technical progress should be adjusted upwards and vice versa for stagnating industries. These adjustments could be included as ad hoc additional relations in MSG or taken care of outside the model by repeated runs.

Another such effect takes place when production increases sharply. MSG may then underestimate the amount of investment required since it exaggerates the substitution possibilities of existing production equipment. In the rare case of a production decrease, MSG assumes that capital equipment can be transferred to other industries, which normally is wholly unrealistic. Sharp increases in energy prices, as happened after the OPEC shock of 1973, may similarly lead to obsolescence of energy-inefficient production equipment. In this case MSG will overstate the amount of capital in place. Abrupt changes in demand or relative prices may thus require a more detailed evaluation of the results obtained from MSG.

4.   Uncertainty and strategies

One of the more difficult tasks in the preparation and presentation of a perspective analysis is to properly account for the many inherent aspects of uncertainty surrounding future development paths. With a projection horizon of twenty years there are always large uncertainties with regard to many of the exogenous assumptions on which the analysis is based. Greater efforts at gathering information could reduce this uncertainty to some degree, but probably not very much. Traditionally such uncertainty has been handled by either presenting alternative broad scenarios or by deriving sensitivity calculations with varying exogenous assumptions.

These methods can give interesting illustrations of the uncertainties, but in a planning context the important question is what conclusions can

be drawn for current and future planning decisions from these uncertainties. Uncertainty as it propagates from the exogenous assumptions via the
model to the endogenous results must be evaluated with respect to what
can be governed or influenced by means of economic policy.

A direct or "naive" interpretation of the MSG-calculations may underestimate the policy problems connected with uncertainty. MSG appears to
give a general equilibrium solution for any given set of exogenous
assumptions. But some of the exogenous variables such as exports from
individual industries are in fact partially and indirectly influenced by
policy measures. Incentives may have to be provided to channel investments in the right direction for the equilibrium path to materialize. If the
economy is disturbed for instance via foreign trade, then according to
MSG, factors of production will be reallocated and relative prices adjusted
smoothly. However, changes will not be as smooth or as swift in real life,
and may incur losses and expenses of different kinds.

Uncertainty is also inherent in the relations embodied in the model.
Even when the stochastic properties of the individual estimates are determined in a reliable way, it is hardly possible to properly account for the
influence on the model's exogenous variables of the joint uncertainty in
the many econometrically estimated coefficients. But some coefficients may
have particular significance and deserve special consideration. Among
these are the coefficients for technical progress. The interrelation between
technological progress, rate of capital accumulation, and returns to
capital can lead to unreasonable results if prior assumptions are used
uncritically. When the rates of technical progress are low, a high rate of
capital accumulation may become unreasonably costly, and quite the
opposite when technical progress is high. (In addition there is the
relation between investment and technological progress within the individual industries. No attempt has been made to model this within MSG, as it
seems to require a more micro-oriented description of the production
structure.)

In view of the uncertainty surrounding technical progress it may seem
better to adopt a strategy with regard to capital accumulation, i.e. a
planned adaptation to future observations of productivity. The benefits of
a strategic approach have been particularly stressed by Leif Johansen in
some earlier works and in his contribution to the Perspective Analysis.

The results actually presented in the Perspective Analysis only
slightly embodied this concept of strategy. But it was doubtlessly of value

during the preparing of scenarios to think in terms of strategies rather than fixed policies. The main purpose of the Perspective Analysis and similar exercises is not to provide guidelines for policy and policy evaluation throughout the period under consideration, but rather to support the decisions made at the initial period. The exercises will probably be repeated after some years based on newer data, other assumptions, and possibly a newer or revised model. Nevertheless, initial decisions may be different when they are thought of as the first decision point in a strategy. Sensitivity calculations will give different results when policies can be adjusted according to a strategy rather than a fixed policy. An excellent exemplification of this can be seen with the important impact international crude oil prices have on the Norwegian economy. The perceived uncertainty in the future oil prices (to which the price of natural gas is linked) is so large that likely variations in the oil price may make any "fixed policy" seem rather silly. However, to make full use of the strategy concept in the MSG-model requires more powerful algorithms for "controlling" the solution than presently are available.

The petroleum sector accounted for 18 per cent of GDP in 1983, not counting the indirect effects via deliveries of platforms, equipment, services, etc. In the future it will loom even larger; under most reasonable scenarios it reaches 25-30 per cent of GDP. The uncertainty connected with the petroleum sector is foremost uncertainty of the future price of oil and gas, but the uncertainties of the future costs, resource base, and other aspects are also quite substantial. In the context of the Perspective Analysis uncertainty related to the petroleum sector implies that macro-economic decisions must be considered as decisions under uncertainty.

The Perspective Analysis approaches the strategic problem of how to use the oil and gas revenues while at the same time hedging against adverse price developments by considering the necessary conditions for optimal saving and optimal asset management (considering oil and gas still in the ground as an asset). This requires, inter alia, an assessment of the rates of return on various assets. The outline of one strategy sketched by the Perspective Analysis is as follows (see NOU (1983), pp. 66-69):

On the basis of the assumptions made about growth factors, rates of return, etc., select a stable path of consumption growth such that the total domestic use of goods and services is kept somewhat lower than the national income. This means that the tradeable sector should be maintained at a higher level than would suffice for a balanced current account, thus providing the margin of safety needed with respect to the use of oil and gas revenues. Lower than expected revenues should be countered by drawing on the accumulated balance of payments surplus rather than by shifts in final demand and activity levels.

To apply this strategy, however, requires that one is able to distinguish between transitory and permanent changes in oil and gas prices. A more elaborate approach in pursuing this line of thought is attempted by Aslaksen and Bjerkholt (in this volume).

Unfortunately MSG-calculations may give an exaggerated impression of the possibilities of finding "good strategies". One reason has been referred to above: the smooth substitution possibilities of the model compared to the higher rigidity of production equipment in place. Another reason is the genuine uncertainty about many behavioural relationships, for instance the saving/consumption behaviour of households and the investment behaviour of establishments. The instability of such relationships can themselves be caused by the uncertainty of other exogenous influences. Such uncertainty with regard to behavioural relationships cause considerable problems in governing the economy. For instance, MSG's vision of a functioning economy pretends that the development of the total stock of capital can be completely governed, and that private consumption can always be influenced such that full employment of labour and capital is maintained. When uncertainty is present the use of government instruments will not result in the expected balanced growth paths that MSG displays. The model can not shed much light on this problem. Leif Johansen expressed this fact by stating that MSG can illuminate the choices and possibilities available within an economy, but cannot to any great extent illuminate the problems of governing the economy.

Model analyses can often give an exaggerated impression of precision. In the construction of a model there is a considerable element of subjective assessment in the choice of relations and functional forms, as realism is weighed against transparency and simplicity. There is, furthermore, considerable uncertainty in the numerical estimates of coefficients. Often the historical period for which data is available has not been rich enough in variation of exogenous influences, disturbances, and unexpected events to provide adequate estimates of coefficients which may be of crucial importance for projecting the future development of the economy. The relations of the model, especially those depicting production, are intended to represent long-term possibilities; however, estimates based on time series may be unduly influenced by shifting short-term possibilities.

To use a large model like MSG for projections is a very sophisticated method compared to trend extrapolation. It may be true, nevertheless, that the analysis still carries with it too many implicit and explicit assumptions of similarity between the historical past and the prospective future than will be found in retrospect some time in the future.

References

Johansen, L. (1960), A Multi-Sectoral Study of Economic Growth, North-Holland Publishing Company, Amsterdam.

Johansen, L. (1972), Production Functions, North-Holland Publishing Company, Amsterdam.

NOU (1983), "Perspektivberegninger for norsk økonomi til år 2000", NOU 1983:37, Universitetsforlaget, Oslo.

Production, Multi-Sectoral Growth and Planning
F.R. Førsund, M. Hoel, and S. Longva (Editors)
© Elsevier Science Publishers B.V. (North-Holland), 1985

CERTAINTY EQUIVALENCE PROCEDURES IN DECISION-MAKING UNDER UNCERTAINTY: AN EMPIRICAL APPLICATION

Iulie Aslaksen

Central Bureau of Statistics of Norway

Olav Bjerkholt

Central Bureau of Statistics of Norway

1. The Johansen approach to certainty equivalence procedures in decision-making under uncertainty

The application of certainty equivalence procedures is a useful method for simplifying a decision problem involving uncertainty. In the theory of economic policy and planning certainty equivalence procedures have mainly been elaborated in the case of a quadratic objective function combined with a linear structural model. One of the many contributions of Leif Johansen in this field has been the generalization of the usual certainty equivalence procedure to the case of an objective function expressed in terms of combinations of exponential functions by the so-called "parametric certainty equivalence." The idea is to formulate a procedure for optimal decision-making under uncertainty which is similar to the one which would be valid in the case of full certainty by permitting an appropriate adjustment of the parameters of the objective function.

Following the notation of Johansen (1980), we consider a decision problem of the following general nature:

x = a variable or a vector of variables to which we attach preferences

a = an action or decision represented by a vector of instrument variables

Jens Stoltenberg has given very valuable assistance, in particular with the calculations.

A = a set of possible actions, i.e. we have a ε A

z = a vector of random variables.

The values obtained for x are determined by the action taken and the random variables in a reduced form system which we write as

(1.1) $x = f(a,z)$.

The objective function is written as

(1.2) $U = U(x;\alpha)$

where α is a vector of parameters characterizing the objective function, i.a., the degree of risk aversion.

The optimization problem is to choose a decision that maximizes the expected value of U. In making the decision we do not know the actual values of the random variables z, but only the probability distribution of z. The optimal decision is determined by

(1.3) $\max_{a \varepsilon A} E(U(x;\alpha)) = \max_{a \varepsilon A} E(U(f(a,z);\alpha))$.

A certainty equivalence procedure for solving the problem (1.3) will consist in replacing the stochastic variables by non-stochastic values $\tilde{z}$ and then solving the problem

(1.4) $\max_{a \varepsilon A} U(f(a,\tilde{z});\alpha)$.

Such a procedure is often followed in practice, for instance with $\tilde{z} = Ez$. More generally the certainty equivalent $\tilde{z}$ may be considered as derived from the probability distribution of z.

Apart from the well-known linear-quadratic case it is not easy to obtain certainty equivalence procedures for which (1.4) yields the same solution as (1.3). However, one may obtain "parametric certainty equivalence" where the parameters of the objective function are adjusted in a prescribed way in order to take uncertainty into account.

The parametric certainty equivalence procedure can be formulated as

(1.5) $\max\limits_{a \epsilon A} U(f(a,\hat{z});\tilde{\alpha})$

where $\tilde{\alpha}$ is a modified parameter vector derived from the original parameter vector α and the probability distribution of the stochastic variables
z. As above, $\hat{z}$ is a non-stochastic value representing z, for instance Ez.

The parametric certainty equivalence procedure as formulated by (1.5)
involves no more complexity than what originates from the form of the
objective function U, the structural form f, and the form of the feasible
set A, i.e. those elements which are present also in the case of certainty.
The usefulness of the certainty equivalence procedure depends on
whether or not we can establish a sufficiently simple transformation to
derive the modified parameter vector $\tilde{\alpha}$.

In the following, such a procedure will be derived for the case of an
objective function expressed in terms of exponential functions, when the
probability distribution is restricted to the class of multi-normal distributions.

Although the _procedure_ in the case of parametric certainty equivalence
is the same as under certainty once the modified parameter vector $\tilde{\alpha}$ has
been established, the decisions actually taken will now in general be
different under uncertainty than under certainty. This is because the
parameter value $\tilde{\alpha}$ will depend on the probability distribution, which
implies that the existence of uncertainty makes us change our decision as
compared to what we would do in the absence of uncertainty.

For a scalar x, the exponential objective function is

(1.6) $U(x) = -B\exp(-\beta x)$ $B > 0, \beta > 0.$

This form implies constant absolute risk aversion:

(1.7) $-U''(x)/U'(x) = \beta$ = coefficient of absolute risk aversion.

For a vector of variables $x = (x_1, \ldots, x_n)$ a sum of exponential functions will yield the objective function

(1.8) $U(x) = -\Sigma\ B_i\exp(-\beta_i x_i)$ $B_i > 0, \beta_i > 0.$

The certainty equivalence procedure is derived from the following observation:

If x is a stochastic variable, normally distributed with expected value Ex and standard deviation σ_x, then the expected value of the objective function (1.6) can be expressed as

$$(1.9) \qquad EU(x) = -B\exp(-\beta\hat{x})$$

where $\hat{x} = Ex - 1/2\,\beta\sigma_x^2$.

The certainty equivalent of the stochastic variable x is the expected value minus a correction term which is proportional to the variance and the risk aversion coefficient.

The expected value of (1.6) can also be written as

$$(1.10) \qquad EU(x) = -\tilde{B}\exp(-\beta\,Ex)$$

where $\tilde{B} = B\exp(1/2\,\beta^2\sigma_x^2)$.

This formulation is the link between the general parametric certainty equivalence approach and the sum-of-exponentials objective functions. The parameter vector α of (1.8) is

$$\alpha = (B_1,\ldots,B_n,\,\beta_1,\ldots,\beta_n).$$

If $x_1,\ldots,x_n$ are normally distributed with expected values Ex_i and standard deviations σ_i, the expected value of (1.8) can - using (1.10) - be written as

$$(1.11) \qquad EU(x;\alpha) = U(Ex;\tilde{\alpha})$$

where the modified parameter vector $\tilde{\alpha}$ is given by

$$(1.12) \qquad \tilde{\alpha} = (\tilde{B}_1,\ldots,\tilde{B}_n,\,\beta_1,\ldots,\beta_n)$$

$$= (B_1\exp(1/2\,\beta_1^2\sigma_1^2),\ldots,B_n\exp(1/2\,\beta_n^2\sigma_n^2),\,\beta_1,\ldots,\beta_n).$$

The modification of the parameters involved in this procedure affects only $B_1,\ldots,B_n$ and not $\beta_1,\ldots,\beta_n$.

2. An illustration of the parametric certainty equivalence procedure

In order to illustrate the parametric certainty equivalence procedure, we introduce the optimization problem which will be elaborated in the following sections.

We consider a long-term macroeconomic planning problem in which a substantial part of national income is accrued from investments in uncertain sources of income. The planning problem consists in determining the optimal trade-off between consumption throughout the planning period and national wealth by the end of the planning period. The concept of terminal wealth is intended to represent future consumption possibilities beyond the given planning horizon of length T.

As an illustration of the parametric certainty equivalence procedure we first consider a static analogy to this dynamic optimization problem. We assume that preferences are formulated in terms of consumption growth over the planning period (C) and total wealth by the end of the planning period (W).

$$(2.1) \quad U(C,W) = -B\exp(-bC) - G\exp(-gW).$$

If there was no uncertainty involved, we would choose from the feasible points so as to maximize (2.1). The indifference curves of (2.1) are characterized by the marginal rate of substitution between C and W given by

$$(2.2) \quad \frac{dW}{dC} = -\frac{bB}{gG}\exp(gW - bC).$$

Given the assumption of normal probability distributions, the parametric certainty equivalence procedure entails the following transformation of (2.1).

$$(2.3) \quad \tilde{U}(EX, EW) = -\tilde{B}\exp(-b\ EC) - \tilde{G}\exp(-g\ EW)$$

where $\tilde{B} = B\exp(1/2\ b^2\sigma_c^2)$ and $\tilde{G} = G\exp(1/2\ g^2\sigma_w^2)$.

The standard deviations of C and W are denoted by σ_c and σ_w, respectively. The certainty equivalence procedure consists in choosing EC and EW so as to maximize (2.3). The marginal rate of substitution is now expressed as

(2.4) $\dfrac{dEW}{dEC} = -\dfrac{bB}{gG}\exp(1/2(b^2\sigma_c^2 - g^2\sigma_w^2))\exp(gEW - bEC).$

First it can be noted that uncertainty has no effect on the actual decisions
in the case where

$$b\sigma_c = g\sigma_w.$$

If this is not the case, the indifference curves of (2.3) will be twisted as
a consequence of uncertainty. Furthermore, a partial increase in σ_w will
make the indifference curve flatter, while a partial increase in σ_c will
make the indifference curve steeper. This will in general mean that a
larger σ_c tends to induce a change in the decision towards the direction
of a larger value of EC, while a larger value of σ_w tends to induce a
change in the decision towards the direction of a larger value of EW.

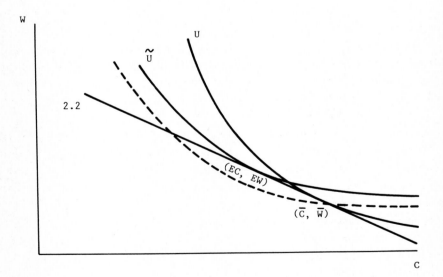

Figure 1. Consequences of uncertainty when $g\sigma_w > b\sigma_c$

In Figure 1 the consequences of uncertainty are illustrated in the case where the risk adjustment term of terminal wealth is the larger, which implies a flatter indifference curve compared to the case where uncertainty is disregarded.

The indifference curve U corresponds to the case where uncertainty is disregarded, and in this case ($\bar{C}, \bar{W}$) represent the optimal trade-off between consumption growth and terminal wealth. The dotted curve illustrates how the indifference curve is twisted due to the certainty equivalence transformation of the parameters. However, we assume that the feasible set of (C,W) combinations is not influenced by the uncertainty, and the relevant indifference curve is thus $\tilde{U}$. A flatter indifference curve thus entails a change in the decision in the direction of a larger expected value of terminal wealth and a small expected value of consumption growth. This is indicated by the point (EC,EW) in Figure 1, which represents the optimal trade-off between consumption growth and terminal wealth in terms of certainty equivalence. The parametric certainty equivalence procedure implies that the decision maker will tend to safeguard against uncertainty by taking a decision which implies a higher expected value of the variable which has the higher uncertainty, i.e. uncertainty as measured by the product of the standard deviation and the risk aversion coefficient.

The question we are addressing is what consequences should be inferred for current and future policy decisions from the uncertainty of national income. However, the conclusion suggested by the preceding analysis is partial in one important respect: Only the "substitution effect" of uncertainty was considered and not the "income effect." An implication of the static consideration is that the feasible set is given, i.e. expected income cannot be influenced by an appropriate reallocation of national wealth. Thus the larger uncertainty of terminal wealth induces an unambiguous substitution effect, since the planner safeguards against uncertainty by taking a decision which implies a higher expected value of terminal wealth and viz. a lower expected value of consumption growth.

On the other hand, in a dynamic context the appropriate problem is to search for guidelines on how national wealth should be reallocated in the light of uncertainty. An optimal composition of national wealth under uncertainty is obtained if risk-adjusted rates of return are equalized for all assets. That is, expected rates of return should be higher than the corresponding risk-free rate of return. In terms of expected values there is thus a potential gain from investment in uncertain assets; this is the source of the "income effect" with respect to uncertainty. In the following section the dynamic optimization problem will be outlined, and in Section 4 the complete income effect of uncertainty will be incorporated.

3.   Static and dynamic optimization in a two-period context

Consider the following macroeconomic planning problem. At the outset the accumulated national wealth $\bar{W}_o$ is given, and the planning horizon comprises two periods ("now" and "future"). The planning problem is to decide on consumption in two periods, C_1 and C_2, under uncertainty of income in both periods. The utility of current consumption is weighed against the amount of wealth remaining at the end of the second period, W_2. The optimization criterion is the expected value of a sum-of-exponentials preference functions given by

$$(3.1) \qquad F(C_1, C_2, W_2) = U(C_1) + U(C_2)/(1+\delta) + V(W_2)/(1+\delta)^2$$

where $U(C_i) = -B\exp(-\beta C_i)$, $V(W) = -G\exp(-\gamma W)$, and δ is the rate of time preference.

The budget constraint for the three alternative uses of total wealth can be written

$$(3.2) \qquad W_2 = (1+r)^2(\bar{W}_0 + R_1 - C_1) + (1+r)(R_2 - C_2)$$

where r is the certain rate of interest and R_i is income in period i. We shall assume that the R_is are independently normally distributed with expectation $\bar{R}_i$ and variance σ_i^2.

We now apply the certainty equivalence property of the preference function (3.1).

$$(3.3) \qquad \underset{C_1, C_2}{\text{Max}} \ E\big[F(C_1, C_2, W_2)\big] = \underset{C_1, C_2}{\text{Max}} \ F(C_1, C_2, \widetilde{W}_2)$$

where $\widetilde{W}_2 = EW_2 - 1/2\ \gamma\ \text{var}\,W_2 = (1+r)^2(\bar{W}_0 + \bar{R}_1 - C_1) + (1+r)(\bar{R}_2 - C_2)$

$$-1/2\ \gamma\ (1+r)^2((1+r)^2\sigma_1^2 + \sigma_2^2).$$

The stochastic optimization problem has been replaced by maximization of a non-stochastic function. The first-order conditions for a maximum are

$$(3.4a) \qquad U'(C_1) = ((1+r)/(1+\delta))^2 V'(\hat{w}_2)$$

$$(3.4b) \qquad U'(C_2) = ((1+r)/(1+\delta)) V'(\hat{w}_2)$$

from which the optimal values of C_1 and C_2 under <u>static optimization</u> can easily be derived. The solution is of the form

$$(3.5) \qquad C_i = b\bar{w}_0 + b(\bar{R}_1 - 1/2 \ \gamma(1+r)^2\sigma_1^2) + b(\bar{R}_2/(1+r) - 1/2 \ \gamma\sigma_2^2) + a_i \quad i=1,2$$

i.e. consumption – in both periods – is a linear function of initial wealth and risk-adjusted income in both periods.

The consumption propensity b depends upon the risk aversion parameters, β and γ, and the rate of interest. The constant term is dependent upon the parameters of the preference function, the rate of interest, and the rate of time preference. It can be seen directly from (3.4) that

$$(3.6) \qquad C_2 - C_1 = \ln((1+r)/(1+\delta))/\beta \approx (r-\delta)/\beta.$$

This growth formula for optimal consumption is in fact the same as under full certainty for the same preference function.

The static optimization problem as set out above pays no attention to the <u>strategic</u> problem faced by the long-term macroeconomic planner, which is the implications of taking sequential decisions under uncertainty of sequential events, rather than taking all decisions at the outset of the planning period as assumed above. The strategic problem has two important aspects. One is that the scope for possible action at a future point of time may, and normally will, be narrowed down as a consequence of earlier actions and external influences. This may be due to irreversibility, capacity constraints, sluggishness, etc. The other aspect is that future actions do not have to be taken until called for. This implies that future decisions can be based on more information than is available at the time of plan preparation; in particular, the realization of uncertain events in the period between the plan preparation and the decision point will be known. The problem is how to include this dynamic flexibility into an

integrated plan. The answer is to search for strategies, i.e. policy functions which are decision rules stating how policy decisions should be
determined in each period on the basis of information available at the
time. Perhaps the main purpose of long-term macroeconomic planning
exercises should be the search for strategies. Unfortunately, finding
solutions to strategic problems in the form of explicit policy functions is
almost impossible except in very simplified cases.

We shall illustrate the difference between static optimization and the
derivation of strategies by extending our very simple example set out
above into an optimal dynamic problem.

In the dynamic solution the decision about consumption in period 2 will
be postponed until the beginning of that period, that is to say, it will be
based on __known__ wealth after period 1, W_1. The constraint for the
remaining part of the planning period is

(3.7) $W_2 = (1+r)(W_1 + R_2 - C_2)$.

The second-period decision is thus the solution to

(3.8) $\underset{C_2}{\text{Max}}\ E[F(C_2, W_2)] = \underset{C_2}{\text{Max}}\ F(C_2, \tilde{W}_2)$

$$= \underset{C_2}{\text{Max}}\ \{U(C_2) + V(\tilde{W}_2)/(1+\delta)\}$$

where $\tilde{W}_2 = E_1 W_2 - 1/2\ \gamma\ \text{var}_1\ W_2$

$$= (1+r)(W_1 + \bar{R}_2 - C_2) - 1/2\ \gamma\ (1+r)^2 \sigma_2^2.$$

Note that $\tilde{W}_2$ here has a slightly different meaning than in (3.3): $E_1[\ ]$
and $\text{var}_1[\ ]$ are expectation and variance at the end of period 1. The
first-order condition for maximum of (3.8) is

(3.9) $U'(C_2) = ((1+r)/(1+\delta)) V'(\tilde{W}_2)$.

This equation determines C_2 as a linear function of W_1, $C_2^*(W_1)$,

(3.10) $C_2^* = b_2^* W_1 + b_2^*(\bar{R}_2 - 1/2\ \gamma(1+r)\sigma_2^2) + a_2^*$.

This is the strategy function for C_2. The optimal value of $\widetilde{W}_2$ can likewise be written as a strategy function of W_1, $\widetilde{W}_2^*(W_1)$, which follows directly from $C_2^*(W_1)$ and the expression for $\widetilde{W}_2$.

The optimal first-period decision can now in principle be found from (3.3) by replacing C_2 and $\widetilde{W}_2$ by their strategy functions, i.e. the following problem:

(3.11) $\underset{C_1}{\text{Max}}\ E\big[\,F(\,C_1\,,\,C_2^*(\,W_1\,)\,,\,\widetilde{W}_2(\,W_1\,)\,\big]$

where $W_1 = (1+r)(\,\overline{W}_o + R_1 - C_1\,).$

This way of proceeding leads, alas, to a problem we cannot solve explicitly. We must proceed by dynamic programming!

Let $J(W_1)$ be the optimal value of (3.8), i.e.,

(3.12) $J(\,W_1\,) = U(\,C_2^*(\,W_1\,)) + V(\,\widetilde{W}_2(\,W_1\,))/(1+\delta).$

From the first-order condition (3.9), it follows that $J(W_1)$ is proportional to $U(\,C_2^*(\,W_1\,))$. This implies that $J(\cdot)$ is an exponential function. The optimal C_1 can now be found by solving

(3.13) $\underset{C_1}{\text{Max}}\ \{U(\,C_1\,) + J(\,\widetilde{W}_1\,)/(1+\delta)\}$

where $\widetilde{W}_1$ is risk-adjusted W_1 with the risk aversion coefficient βb_2^* of $J(\cdot)$. The first-order condition of (3.13) is

(3.14) $U'(\,C_1\,) = ((1+r)/(1+\delta))J'(\,\widetilde{W}_1\,)$

from which the explicit solution of C_1 can be found to be

(3.15) $C_1^* = b\overline{W}_o + b(\,\overline{R}_1 - 1/2\ \gamma(1+r)^2\sigma_1^2\ \dfrac{\beta}{\beta+\gamma(1+r)}) +$

$\qquad\qquad b(\,\overline{R}_2/(1+r) - 1/2\ \gamma\ \sigma_2^2) + a_1.$

In the dynamic solution the consumption decision for period 1 is related to wealth at the beginning of period 1, $\overline{W}_1$, and the risk-adjusted expected values for income in both periods.

How does the solution to the dynamic optimization compare with the static solution? We see that the only difference between (3.15) and the expression for C_1 in (3.5) is that the risk-adjustment for R_1 has been reduced and the optimal consumption is accordingly higher. The intuitive explanation for this is that under dynamic optimization - which means sequential decisions - optimal consumption comes out higher in the first period because less emphasis is put on uncertainty of income in the first period. If this turns out to be different from expected income, it can to some extent be counteracted by the second period decision.

The answer given here is different from that which follows from the more widely known and applied assumption of a quadratic preference function. When combined with a linear model the answer in this case is given by the well-known certainty equivalence result of Theil (1964): the first period decision on C_1 is the same in both cases and entails no risk adjustment.

What then about the second-period consumption? In the strategy function for C_2, as given in (3.10), W_1 depends upon C_1 and realized income R_1. When C_1 is replaced by the right-hand side of (3.15) we arrive at the following expression for C_2

$$(3.16) \quad C_2 = b\bar{W}_0 + b\bar{R}_1 + b(\bar{R}_2/(1+r)-1/2\, \gamma\, \sigma_2^2) + \gamma(1+r)^2/(\beta+\gamma(1+r))$$

$$((R_1-\bar{R}_1) + b\, 1/2\, \gamma\, (1+r)^2\sigma_1^2\, \frac{\beta}{\beta+\gamma(1+r)}) + a_2.$$

The only difference between this expression and that of C_2 in the static solution (3.5) is the effect of first-period income. Since C_2 in (3.16) includes the stochastic variable R_1, it may turn out to be smaller than the static solution, but the expected value of (3.16) is obviously higher than C_2 in (3.5) for two reasons: (1) the risk adjustment of total wealth is smaller at a later date, and (2) by sequential decisions it is possible to consume from the "wealth reserve" that arises when the risk adjustment has been higher than the income loss. In short, by dynamic optimization the consumption decision in period 2 is based on more information: income in period 1 is not uncertain any longer. Thus it is worthwhile to search for strategies.

In the static optimization problem, (planned) consumption in the second period increases according to the same growth formula as under full

certainty, (cf. (3.6)). In the dynamic optimization problem, the increase
in expected consumption in the second period is somewhat higher. From
the solution given by (3.15) and (3.16) we obtain (using (3.6))

$$(3.17) \quad EC_2 - C_1 = (1/\beta)\ln((1+r)/(1+\delta)) +$$

$$(1/2)\beta\gamma^2(1+r)^4\sigma_1^2/(\beta+\gamma(1+r))^2.$$

The gain from elaborating strategies for optimal consumption is here
expressed by the risk-adjustment term of the growth formula. Using the
definition of certainty equivalence for consumption in the second period
we obtain

$$(3.18) \quad \tilde{C}_2 = EC_2 - (1/2)\beta\gamma^2(1+r)^4\sigma_1^2/(\beta+\gamma(1+r))^2$$

and

$$(3.19) \quad \tilde{C}_2 - C_1 = (1/\beta)\ln((1+r)/(1+\delta)) \approx (r-\sigma)/\beta.$$

In terms of certainty equivalent consumption, the dynamic optimization
solution yields the same growth formula for consumption as under full
certainty and in static optimization.

4.   A multi-period framework with stochastic rates of return

We assume that the national wealth is distributed over a number of
assets – physical and financial assets as well as natural resources. Assets
are measured in terms of the purchasing power of consumption goods. The
planning horizon is divided into periods of equal length. At the beginning
of each period the returns on the various assets are added up and distributed between consumption and accumulation in the same assets. For the
decisions to be taken at the beginning of each period we have the following
budget equation

$$(4.1) \quad R_t = C_t + \sum_{i=0}^{n} I_{it}$$

where I_{it} is the investment in asset no. i and C_t is consumption in period t. Consumption is defined as the sum total of private and government consumption. All income is assumed to be capital income, accruing from investment undertaken one period earlier, hence

$$R_t = \sum_{i=0}^{n} r_{it} W_{i,t-1}$$

where $W_{i,t-1}$ is the amount invested in asset no. i at the beginning of period t and r_{it} its rate of return. In asset terms the budget equation can be written

(4.2) $\qquad G_{t-1} = C_t + \sum_{i=0}^{n} W_{it}$

where $\qquad G_{t-1} = \sum_{i=0}^{n} W_{i,t-1} + R_t = W_{t-1} + R_t.$

Hence total wealth G_{t-1} at the beginning of period t consists of stocks of assets inherited from the past as well as capital income. The rates of return are stochastic variables. We assume that when decisions are to be made at the beginning of period t, the outcome of the stochastic rates of return dated t is known with certainty, whereas the uncertainty regarding future periods has to be taken into account. There is thus a minor difference here from the assumption made in the two-period model of the preceding section.

Oil reserves still in the ground can be considered as one type of asset although they are not usually counted as a part of national wealth. The value of the oil reserves can be measured as the product of the amount of reserves S_t and the price net of marginal extraction costs, $q_t = p_t - b_t$ where p_t is the current oil price and b_t is marginal extraction cost. We assume that marginal cost is constant with respect to the rate of extraction but is a hyperbolic function of the remaining reserves. The rate of return on the oil reserves is equal to the rate of growth of the net oil price.

Introducing oil as an additional asset in (4.2), and redefining total wealth G_t and total stock of assets W_t to include the oil reserves give

(4.3) $G_{t-1} = C_t + W_t$

where $G_{t-1} = \sum\limits_{i=0}^{n} W_{it-1} + R_t + q_t S_{t-1}$ and

           $W_t = \sum\limits_{i=0}^{n} W_{it} + q_t S_t$.

The planning problem is now defined as the maximization of the sum of discounted expected utility from consumption over a planning horizon of length T, taking into consideration the discounted utility of terminal wealth. The utility of terminal wealth must be interpreted as deriving from the consumption possibilities it represents beyond the planning horizon.

The objective function at the beginning of period t can thus be written as

(4.4) $\sum\limits_{\tau=t}^{T} U(C_\tau)(1+\delta)^{t-\tau} + V(G_T)(1+\delta)^{t-T-1}$ $t=1,2,\dots T.$

For $U(\cdot)$ and $V(\cdot)$ we use the utility functions for current consumption and terminal wealth, respectively, introduced in Section 3; δ is the rate of time preference.

The decision problem at the beginning of each period is deciding on the reinvestment of total wealth and the level of consumption to be maintained in the period. The results of earlier decision are represented in period t through the stock of assets inherited from the previous periods. We assume that total wealth can be frictionlessly reallocated between assets. The decisions to be taken in the following periods up to T have to be considered when deciding on consumption and investment at the beginning of period t. Decisions in all periods should reflect an appropriate trade-off between consumption and investment, as well as between consumption in the planning period and terminal wealth.

The optimization problem given by maximization of (4.4) under the budget constraint (4.3) with given initial values of oil stock and non-oil wealth can be solved by the method of stochastic dynamic programming which we applied in Section 3. For a planning horizon starting at t=1 and with given values of G_0 and S_0, the optimization problem is solved by beginning at the end of the planning horizon and solving the decision problem for each period recursively. At the beginning of period T the optimal W_{it}, S_T, and C_T are determined given the initial condition G_{T-1} and S_{T-1}. Having found the optimal solution for the last period contingent on any initial condition G_{T-1} and S_{T-1}, we solve the two-period problem for the last two periods by choosing the optimal $W_{i,t-1}$, S_{T-1}, and C_{T-1}, contingent on the initial condition G_{T-2} and S_{T-2}, and so on. In the last stage the optimal W_{i1}, S_1, and C_1 are determined given the initial values G_0 and S_0 available at the beginning of period 1. A crucial assumption for the optimality of this procedure is stochastic independence between rates of return, including the oil price, in different periods. Our approach follows Samuelson (1969) and Chow (1975, ch.8, 197-201).

In the notation of dynamic programming we denote the maximum expected value of (4.4) contingent on G_{t-1} by $J_t(G_{t-1})$. The decision problem at the beginning of period t can now be more precisely stated as

$$(4.5) \qquad J_t(G_{t-1}) = \text{Max } E\{U(C_t) + J_{t+1}(G_t)/(1+\delta)\}$$

where the maximization is with respect to the W_{it}s and S_t, and subject to (4.3). Before proceeding to the solution procedure, the stochastic assumptions must be specified.

The stochastic assumptions concerning future oil prices and rates of return are of considerable importance for the optimal solution. We shall assume that the rates of return of the various assets are multinormally distributed with expected values ρ_1 and variances and covariances σ_{ij}, i,j=0,...,n. This implies that the standard deviation of income is proportional to the amount of capital and not constant as assumed in Section 3. The oil price is assumed to be normally distributed with expected value π_t and variance τ^2. Covariances between the oil price and the rates of return on non-oil assets are given by τ_i, i=0,...,n. By the method of dynamic programming we start by solving the maximization problem given by (4.5) for t=T, i.e.,

$$(4.6) \qquad J_T(G_{T-1}) = \text{Max } E\{U(C_T) + V(G_T)/(1+\delta)\}$$

$$= \text{Max } \{U(G_T) + V(\hat{G}_T)/(1+\delta)\}$$

where $\quad \tilde{G}_T = EG_T - 1/2 \, \gamma \, \text{var} \, G_T$,

and $\quad EG_T = \sum_{i=0}^{n} W_{iT}(1+\rho_i) + (\pi_{T+1} - b_{T+1})S_T$,

$$\text{var} \, G_T = \sum_{i=0}^{n} \sum_{j=0}^{n} \sigma_{ij} W_{iT} W_{jT} + \tau^2 S_T^2 + 2 \sum_{j=0}^{n} \tau_j W_{jT} S_T;$$

subject to

$$G_{T-1} = G_T + \sum_{i=0}^{n} W_{iT},$$

where $\quad G_T = \sum_{i=0}^{n} W_{iT}(1+\rho_T).$

When evaluating the terminal value of the oil reserves, one should take into account the uncertainty of future oil prices beyond the planning horizon. The approach of measuring the terminal value by certainty equivalent net price at the beginning of period T does not capture this future uncertainty. However, the _marginal_ value of the terminal oil reserves is equal to the certainty equivalent net oil price, provided that the terminal level of oil reserves is optimally weighed against consumption throughout the planning period and against terminal stocks of non-oil assets.

The first-order conditions for the solution of (4.6) are

(4.7a) $\quad U'(C_T) = ((1+\tilde{r}_i)/(1+\delta)) \, V'(\tilde{G}_T) \qquad i=0,\ldots,n$ for non-oil assets

(4.7b) $\quad U'(C_T) = \tilde{q}_{T+1}/q_T V'(\tilde{G}_T)/(1+\delta) \qquad$ for the oil asset

where $\quad \tilde{r}_i = \dfrac{\partial \tilde{G}_T}{\partial W_{it}} - 1 = \rho_i - \gamma \sum_{j=0}^{n} \sigma_{ij} W_{jT} - \gamma \tau_i S_T \qquad i=0,\ldots,n$

and $\quad \tilde{q}_{T+1} = \dfrac{\partial \tilde{G}_T}{\partial S_T} = \pi_{T+1} - b_{T+1} - \gamma \tau^2 S_T - \gamma \sum_{j=0}^{N} \tau_j W_{jT} - b'_{T+1}(S_T)S_T.$

The certainty equivalent rate of return on asset no. i is $\tilde{r}_i$, i.e. the marginal increase in certainty equivalent wealth by a marginal increase

in asset no. i. The certainty equivalent net oil price in period T+1 is
$\tilde{q}_{T+1}$. The difference between the certainty equivalent net oil price and
the expected net oil price consists of the correction terms due to the uncertainty as well as a term due to the dependence of marginal cost on the
reserve level. With a hyperbolic marginal cost function, $b_t = m/S_{t-1}$,
cost function terms in $\tilde{q}_{T+1}$ cancel out, and $\tilde{q}_{T+1}$ appears as

$$\tilde{q}_{T+1} = \pi_{T+1} - \gamma\tau^2 S_T - \gamma \sum_{j=0}^{n} \tau_j W_j T.$$

To obtain an explicit solution for the optimal portfolio and consumption,
we make the crucial assumption that asset no. 0 is risk-free, yielding a
certain rate of return r_0. Hence, $\tilde{r}_0 = r_0$, and from the first-order conditions we obtain

(4.8a) $U'(C_T) = ((1+r_0)/(1+\delta))V'(\tilde{G}_T)$

(4.8b) $\tilde{r}_i = r_0$ $i=1,\ldots,n$

(4.8c) $\tilde{q}_{T+1}/q_T - 1 = r_0.$

Optimal accumulation in the uncertain assets is determined by the condition
that certainty equivalent rates of return should be equalized for all
assets. Oil extraction is determined by a modified Hotelling rule: certainty
equivalent net oil price should grow at a rate of return equal to the
certain rate of return.

Proceeding as in Section 3, we can solve the original problem recursively by starting at t=T and working backwards towards t=1. A more
complete presentation of the solution procedure is given in Aslaksen and
Bjerkholt (1984). The first-order condition at t with respect to asset no.
0 is

(4.9) $U'(C_t) = ((1+r_0)/(1+\delta))J'_{t+1}(\tilde{G}_t)$ $t=1,2,\ldots,T$

and we can show that

(4.10) $J'_t(G_{t-1}) = U'(C_t)$ $t=1,2,\ldots,T.$

Similar to what we found for the two-period model, we find that the general form of the solution can be written as

(4.11) $C_t = b_{T-t} G_{t-1} + a_{T-t}$

where $b_{T-t} = \gamma(1+r_0)^{T-t+1} / (\beta + \gamma \sum\limits_{\tau=}^{T-t+1} (1+r_0)^{\tau})$ $t=1,2,\ldots,T$

and $a_{T-t} = -\beta \dfrac{1+r_0}{r_0} \dfrac{\alpha}{r_0} + \dfrac{b_{T-t}}{(1+r_0)^t} \left[(\ln(\beta B/(\gamma(1+r_0)G)) + \chi)/\gamma(1+r_0) \right.$

$\left. - \dfrac{t}{1+r_0} (\dfrac{\beta}{\gamma} - \dfrac{1+r_0}{r_0})\alpha + \dfrac{1+r_0}{r_0} \dfrac{\alpha}{r_0} \right];$

where $\alpha = (\ln \dfrac{1+r_0}{1+\delta} - \chi)/\beta \approx (r_0 - \delta^*)/\beta$

$\delta^* = \delta + \chi$

and $\chi = 1/2 \sum\limits_{i=1}^{n} \sum\limits_{j=1}^{n} (\rho_i - r_0)(\rho_j - r_0)\hat{\sigma}_{ij} + (\dfrac{\bar{q}_{t+1}}{q_t} - 1 - r_0) \sum\limits_{j=0}^{n} (\rho_j - r_0)\hat{\tau}_j$

$+ 1/2(\dfrac{\bar{q}_{t+1}}{q_t} - 1 - r_0)^2 \hat{\tau}^2$

$\hat{\sigma}_{ij}$, $\hat{\tau}_j$, and $\hat{\tau}^2$ are the elements of the inverse of the variance-covariance matrix of σ_{ij}, τ_j and τ^2, and $\bar{q}_{t+1}$ is the expected net price (equal to $\pi_{t+1} - b_{t+1}$). The certainty equivalence procedure implying that the stochastic parameters appear only in the risk-adjusted time preference rate δ^*.

The marginal propensity to consume out of current wealth, b_{T-t}, is dependent upon the risk aversion coefficients γ and β as well as the interest rate r_0. It is in fact only the ratio between γ and β that matters. In the limiting case where $T-t \to \infty$, b_{T-t} approaches a constant given by

$b = r_0/(1+r_0)$.

In this case the marginal propensity to consume is independent of γ as well as β. However, γ and β appear in the constant term of the consumption function.

When the optimization problem has been solved step-by-step, optimal consumption is implemented by recording the actual development and inserting, period by period, the outcome of the stochastic rates of return, as expressed by G_{t-1}, in the consumption function (4.11). The optimal solution can thus be interpreted as a **strategy**; decision rules for optimal consumption are calculated initially, whereas actual consumption decisions are postponed until current wealth is known with certainty.

As in the two-period model, it is easily demonstrated that certainty equivalent consumption increases according to the same growth formula as under full certainty. From (4.9) and (4.10), it follows that

$$U'(C_t) = ((1+r_0)/(1+\delta))\, U'(\tilde{C}_{t+1});$$

hence,

(4.12) $\tilde{C}_{t+1} - C_t = \ln((1+r_0)/(1+\delta))/\beta \approx (r_0-\delta)/\beta.$

Given the optimal consumption, the accumulation in the uncertain assets is determined as a one-period portfolio problem

(4.13) $W_{it} = \dfrac{1}{\beta\, b_{T-t}} \{ \sum\limits_{j=1}^{n} (\rho_j - r_0)\hat{\sigma}_{ij} + \hat{\tau}_i (\pi_{t+1} - (1+r_0)q_t) \}$

(4.14) $S_t = \dfrac{1}{\beta\, b_{T-t}} \{ \sum\limits_{j=1}^{n} (\rho_j - r_0)\hat{\tau}_j + \hat{\tau}^2 (\pi_{t+1} - (1+r_0)q_t) \}.$

Hence, optimal oil extraction in period t is given by

(4.15) $X_t = S_{t-1} - S_t$

where S_t is determined by (4.14), and S_{t-1} is given from the previous period.

Due to the strong assumptions regarding the utility function and the stochastic parameters, as well as the production structure and the cost function for oil extraction, we have thus obtained explicit solutions with intuitive interpretations.

5. Preference functions derived from macroeconomic projections

An empirical application of the stochastic optimization framework requires an assessment of the risk aversion coefficients. In this context we have approached this problem by the method of deriving the underlying preferences from macroeconomic projections currently elaborated and presented.

In Norwegian economic planning long-term macroeconomic projections are usually elaborated in connection with the quadrennial government White Papers which present a four-year plan and a less detailed and less committing projection for the ensuing 20-30 years. The purpose of such projections is threefold. They serve

- as the basis for government policies over a wide range of issues
- as guidelines for the development of the national economy that can be linked to sectoral, regional, and other less comprehensive analyses
- as a general orientation about the economic prospects for the public at large.

In recent years such projections have been elaborated by means of successive versions of the MSG-model, originally constructed by Leif Johansen in 1960. The MSG-model is a large general equilibrium model which combines an overall macroeconomic framework with a considerable amount of details. The model has been extensively presented elsewhere in this book and will not be further discussed here.

One of the more difficult tasks in the elaboration of long-term projections is to account properly for the many aspects of inherent uncertainty in the preparation and presentation of future development paths. With a time span of twenty or more years ahead, there are large amounts of uncertainty with regard to many of the exogeneous assumptions on which the analysis is based. Greater efforts of gathering information could probably reduce this uncertainty to some degree, but much would still remain. For a small open economy much of the uncertainty stems from abroad, such as the growth in world trade and the future crude oil price.

The traditional ways of dealing with such uncertainty are either to present alternative broad scenarios or to use sensitivity calculations varying the assumptions about exogenous influences. Such methods can give interesting illustrations of the uncertainty. But in a planning context the important question is what conclusions can be drawn for current and future planning decisions from this uncertainty. The uncertainty as it propagates from the exogenous influences must be evaluated in view of what can be governed or influenced by means of economic policy.

The development of the oil sector in the Norwegian economy has entailed a considerable exposure to risk for the macroeconomy, and the need for an explicit consideration of uncertainty issues is thus more strongly felt today than earlier. With the increasing focus on petroleum extraction in the Norwegian economic and political debate, most of the attention given to uncertainty has been related to short- and medium-term consequences of a volatile oil price. Less attention has been given to uncertainty in the longer term perspective. However, two recent reports from government appointed committees have dealt with these perspectives (NOU 1983a, NOU 1983b).

Our work is related to that of these two committees and may be regarded as suggestions of how the analyses could be broadened further. We are well aware that the answers given are very tentative to say the least, both theoretically and empirically. Our own attitude can be well expressed by a quote from Leif Johansen (who in fact initiated our work on this topic). He wrote in the introduction to his book on the MSG-model: "...if I were required to make decisions and take actions in connection with relationships covered by this study I would (in the absence of more reliable results, and without doing more work) rely to a great extent on the data and the results presented in the following chapters." (Johansen, 1960)

The intended application of the stochastic optimization framework outlined above is mainly as a means for evaluating and corroborating long-term projections from the MSG-model. Although stochastic elements are not included in the MSG-model, the model is a valuable means for illustrating the wide range of possible long-term projections under alternative oil price assumptions. Model calculations are performed with alternative oil price scenarios and exogenously stipulated oil and gas production profiles. The consequences of alternative oil revenue scenarios are traced out by model calculations. These long-term projections illustrate the considerable impact on sectoral development and accumulated foreign reserves that alternative oil price assumptions have. A consistent evaluation of these long-term equilibrium growth paths under uncertainty requires a stochastic optimization framework.

Our emphasis is not on the treatment of uncertainty in macroeconomic projections in general, but rather on the implications of uncertainty for the selection of "optimal" or "good" paths.

Our analysis is based on projections in a report called the "Perspective Analysis" (NOU(1983b)), published in 1983 by an appointed committee of experts relying to a great extent on the model tools and data sources used by the government for its projections. The committee stated its view on the methodology of using macroeconomic models for long-term projections, as well as presenting its own projections in the form of a reference path and alternative scenarios reflecting uncertainty issues, policy alternatives, and policy performance. The methodological discussion included remarks on how to cope better with uncertainty in macroeconomic projections, but refrained from introducing new procedures for preparing and presenting projections.

Although the projections of the Perspective Analysis were elaborated without the political commitment that is usually given to the projections presented in, for example, the quadrennial medium-term programme, for our purposes it may not be totally misleading to interpret them as reflecting current political preferences. However, the projections of the Perspective Analysis do not readily avail themselves to an assessment of preferences. Little is said about the evaluation of the alternative projections, and no precise guidelines are given for the trade-off between consumption and wealth accumulation.

Although no explicit welfare function or preference indicator has been applied in the elaboration of the projections, the various statements given in the report can be interpreted as expressions of a set of underlying preferences. The discussion of the policy choices between domestic use of oil revenues versus increased current account surplus has been our starting point for deriving the preferences.

The present analysis is based on the reference path and the four alternative projections which are summarized in Table 1.

These alternative projections of the Norwegian economy towards the year 2000 result in different states of the economy by the end of the planning period. In the highly simplified representation of these alternatives that characterizes the following discussion, we ignore most structural and other aspects of the differences between these alternatives and focus on only two variables: consumption level (or rather consumption increase

Table 1. Selected results from the Perspective Analysis

Scenario	Total consumption (private and government) in year 2000 as increase over 1980. Percent	Net foreign reserves in year 2000 plus value of proven oil reserves in year 2000. Billion kroner
1. Reference path	62.2	1419.6
2. Higher petroleum income		
2.1 Increased domestic use	82.8	1575.4
2.2 Increased capital exports	62.2	1811.8
3. Sluggish world economy		
3.1 Tight policy	50.5	1379.4
3.2 Lax policy	70.6	1204.9

Note: The figures are derived from NOU(1983b), and unpublished material from the Ministry of Finance.   The reference path is based on full employment and an increase in the production of oil and gas reaching 80 mill. toe in year 2000.   In the reference path the crude oil price is assumed to grow 2 percent p.a. in real terms.   Non-oil exports grow less than 2 percent p.a.   In the two higher petroleum income scenarios the production of oil and gas is assumed to reach 90 mill. toe in the year 2000, while the crude oil price grows 3 percent p.a.   In 2.1 the increased income is used to promote growth in domestic demand with employment and the rate of technical progress increasing, while in 2.2 the increased income is accumulated as foreign assets.   The sluggish world economy scenarios depict developments where non-oil exports grow even less than in the reference path, only 1 percent p.a. In 3.1 the balance of payments is maintained by means of tight demand management. Employment falls off compared with the reference path. In 3.2 on the other hand priority is given to employment. Private and Government Consumption are increased with adverse consequences for the balance of payments. This table reveals, in fact, little about the differences between the alternatives. The Perspective Analysis also presented 3-4 other alternative scenarios.

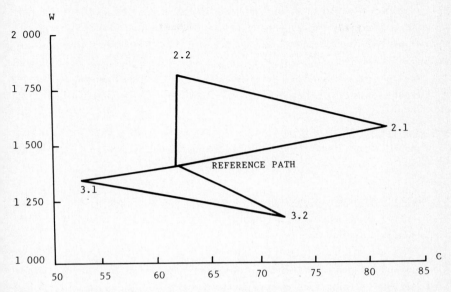

C = Total consumption (private and government) in the year 2000 as percentage increase over 1980.
W = Net foreign reserves in the year 2000 plus value of proven oil
   reserves in the year 2000 (see Table 1).

Figure 2. Selected projections from the Perspective Analysis: Percentage
          increase in total consumption in the year 2000 over 1980 (C) and
          accumulated wealth in the year 2000 (W)

over 1980) and wealth position. Figure 2 plots all five projections with
regard to these two characteristics.

These five projections illustrate a wide range of possibilities for the
choice between consumption and accumulation of foreign assets. The two
triangles in Figure 2 indicate the feasible sets under the assumptions of
either higher petroleum income (2.1 and 2.2) or sluggish world economy
(3.1 and 3.2). Little is said in the report about the choice between
increased domestic use and increased capital exports in the case of higher
petroleum income, and the choice between tight and lax policy in the case
of sluggish world economy.

    Based on the information provided in the report of the Perspective
Analysis we have, however, established the following crucial assumptions.
Consider the following stochastic experiment with two possible outcomes:

Either the outcome of higher petroleum income is realized with the feasible set is represented by the line segment between 2.1 and 2.2, or the outcome of a sluggish world economy is realized with the feasible set represented by the line segment between 3.1 and 3.2. These two outcomes are assumed to have an equal probability. The alternatives 2.1 or 2.2, and 3.1 or 3.2, thus represent extreme policies under each income scenario. To reveal the optimal policy we state the following assumptions:

a) Sluggish world economy: Given a feasible set of all points between 3.1 and 3.2, the best choice is to pursue a policy aiming at a result midway between the two extreme policies.

b) Higher petroleum income: Given a feasible set of all points between 2.1 2.2, the best choice is to pursue a policy aiming at a result slightly closer to 2.1 than the midpoint.

c) Reference path: The reference path is considered as the certainty equivalent of the stochastic experiment described above. Given the two optimal policies described in a)-b), the expected utility of these two outcomes is equal to the utility of the reference path.

These assumptions are formulated in view of a preference function given by

(5.1) $U(C,W) = -Bexp(-bC) - Gexp(-gW)$

C =   Total consumption (private and government) in the year 2000 as percentage increase over 1980.

W =   Net foreign reserves in the year 2000 plus value of proven oil reserves in the year 2000 (see Table 1).

To simplify the estimation of the risk aversion coefficients, the preference function (5.1) has been formulated as a static analogy to the multi-period preference function (4.4) of the dynamic optimization problem. The implications of a preference function like (5.1) are more extensively discussed in section 2. In (5.1) preferences are attached to the percentage increase in consumption over the planning horizon, rather than the sum of discounted utility of consumption in each period. However, this reformulation does not alter the main conclusions for the trade-off between consumption and terminal wealth under uncertainty. The numerical estimate for the risk aversion coefficient b will differ from the risk aversion coefficient β of the multi-period preference function. An appropriate estimate for β will be derived below.

The wealth concept W defined as net foreign reserves plus the value of the oil reserves is highly tentative, to say the least. It does not properly reflect the concept of national wealth as defined in the optimization model. According to the preference function (4.4), consumption should be weighed against total wealth at the end of the planning period, i.e. production capital, financial assets, and natural resources. The role of terminal wealth in the preference function is to represent the production and income potential for future consumption beyond the planning horizon. The discussion of the Perspective Analysis is however more explicitly related to the trade-off between consumption growth and net foreign reserves at the end of the planning period. The point of foreign reserves in this connection seems to be as a safeguard against the risk inherent in the oil reserves. In order to translate the views expressed in the report into a guideline for our estimation of the risk aversion coefficients, the value of petroleum reserves and net foreign reserves are included in our wealth concept here, while other assets are disregarded. This is perhaps a dubious interpretation and inclusion of real capital would have given different estimation results.

The assumptions a)-c) give three relationships to determine the parameters b, g, and G/B. The level of utility is arbitrarily chosen by setting B=1. Furthermore, the parameter values are adjusted to yield G=B=1. The following parameter values are thus obtained:

$$b = 0.1426$$
$$g = 0.00589 \ .$$

Figure 3 shows the estimated preference function as represented by three indifference curves implicitly referred to in assumptions a)-c). In order to apply the multi-period framework of Section 4, we have to establish the correspondance between the preference function (4.4) of the dynamic model and the static analogy given by (5.1). In the dynamic model, which is to be applied in Section 6, preferences are formulated in terms of the sum of discounted utility from consumption over the planning period,

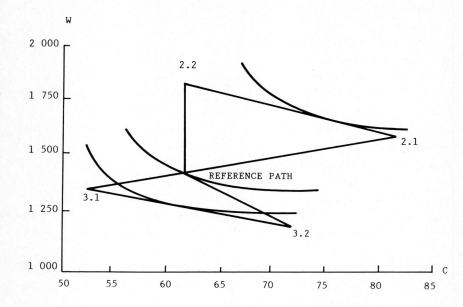

Figure 3. Indifference curves with b=0.1426 and g=0.00589

whereas in the static preference function (5.1), the relevant concept is percentage increase in consumption over the planning horizon. In order to find the appropriate risk aversion coefficient in a dynamic context, we make the assumption that the sum of discounted utility from consumption over the planning period is equal to the utility of the percentage increase of consumption. The annual growth rate of consumption in the reference path is 2.4 percent. We assume here that the rate of time preference is one percent. Given the estimate of b=0.1426, an estimate of β=0.0352 is thus obtained for the risk aversion coefficient of the dynamic model. The estimate of the risk aversion coefficient g=0.00589 is calibrated in order to include the production capital. An estimate of γ=0.0027 is thus obtained.

6. A strategy for optimal consumption under uncertainty: empirical applications

In the preceding section we looked at actual long-term projections of the Norwegian economy, and tried to estimate the risk aversion coefficients that seemed to be implicit in the considerations of the committee responsible for the projections. An application of certainty equivalence procedures in establishing long-term projections would, of course, imply an integration of the ideas set out in this article at a much earlier stage in the elaboration of projections. We shall nevertheless attempt a tentative application within the framework and scenarios of the Perspective Analysis.

The point of departure is the formal model framework of Section 4. First we shall define the composition of total wealth as required in the model. We shall distinguish between four assets apart from oil:

W_S = real capital in the sheltered sector (i.e. non-tradeable goods production, protected sectors, and government)

W_E = real capital in the export sector

W_H = real capital in the import-competing sector

W_U = foreign assets.

Table 2. Average rates of return: Estimation period
1962-1981

ρ_i	Percent
Sheltered sector (excluding government)	7.53
Import-competing sector	10.00
Export sector	5.45

Foreign assets are assumed to yield a risk-free rate of return of 3 percent. This is our r_0. The increase in expected net oil price, is assumed to be 2 percent p.a. throughout the whole period.

The variance-covariance matrix for the estimated rates of return in the

period 1962–1981 is given in Table 3 and the inverse variance-covariance
matrix is given in Table 4.

Table 3. Variance-covariance matrix: Estimation period 1962–1981

σ_{ij}, τ_i, τ^2	Sheltered sector	Import-competing sector	Export sector	Real oil price
Sheltered sector	1.65685	−0.088861	−1.84331	−1.28275
Import-competing sector		2.30443	1.93291	−0.897742
Export sector			13.8807	0.621457
Real oil price				16.789

Table 4. Inverse variance-covariance matrix

$\hat{\sigma}_{ij}$, $\hat{\tau}_i$, $\hat{\tau}^2$	Sheltered sector	Import-competing sector	Export sector	Real oil price
Sheltered sector	0.756811	−0.037254	0.102251	0.052005
Import-competing sector		0.507536	−0.076836	0.027137
Export sector			0.096458	0.000218
Real oil price				0.064979

The chosen breakdown of non-oil national wealth is – as the other
specifications of the model – rather tentative. A priori we would expect
capital in the non-tradeable sector to be a more certain asset (i.e. lower
rate of return, but also lower variance) than investment in the tradeable
sectors, while foreign reserves would be assumed to be a risk-free asset.

For a small oil exporting country like Norway the oil price is exogenous, independent of domestic reserves and rate of extraction. It may be
less obvious that the stochastic rates of return on assets other than oil
are independent of time and of the stocks of the respective assets, as
assumed in Section 4 above. In the following we assume that real capital

by sector has constant expected rates of return as set out above. This exceedingly simplified picture of a national economy can only be defended on the ground that it serves a broader purpose!

For the risk aversion coefficients we use those derived in Section 5. For the rate of time preference we assume $\delta = 0.01$.

From these estimates and assumptions we can calculate a reference scenario based on the stochastic optimization model. There are many reasons why this reference scenario will not coincide with the reference scenario of the Perspective Analysis as elaborated by means of the MSG-model. The stochastic optimization model has hardly any macroeconomic infrastructure. The labour market, production structure, and foreign trade are not explicitly dealt with. The asset composition can be changed in a frictionless way, thus we pay no attention to the transition problem of changing the asset composition from what is historically given. An additional problem is the more specific assumptions of the constancy of the parameters of the model estimated above. We have chosen, however, to interpret the scenario based on these assumptions as the appropriate scenario for the further analyses. In the reference scenario, consumption increases smoothly and reaches a level in the year 2000 which is 74.4 percent higher than in 1980. Investments in uncertain assets are declining throughout the planning horizon, whereas foreign debt is gradually reduced. Total wealth is increasing in early years and is decreasing thereafter. The development of total wealth is crucially dependent on the relationship between the risk aversion parameters and the risk-free rate of return. The parameters of our reference scenario give the condition

$$(6.1) \qquad \beta/\gamma < (1+r_0)/r_0$$

which entails the concave path of total wealth as shown in Figure 5. If the inequality sign of (6.1) is reversed, total wealth increases along a convex path.

Optimal oil reserves in 1980 turn out somewhat lower than the actual level of oil reserves in 1980. An initial jump in the oil production profile to 161 million toe is thus necessary in order to reach the optimal path which starts at 106 million toe in 1981 and increases gradually to 123 million toe in the year 2000.

The numerical results obtained by the stochastic optimization model are highly dependent on the choice of parameter values. Table 5 illustrates the effects on consumption, foreign reserves and terminal wealth of partial shifts in the parameters of the reference scenario.

A partial increase in β implies reduced consumption in all periods at least when the planning horizon is 20 years. In the optimal strategy for consumption, the marginal propensity to consume out of current wealth decreases with β (not shown in the table) in the two-period as well as in the multi-period context, and this wealth effect dominates any positive effect through the certainty equivalence correction terms. Lower consumption throughout the planning horizon entails higher total terminal wealth. Investments in uncertain assets decrease with β because the certainty equivalent rates of return are reduced and it is less profitable to invest in uncertain assets. However, in the last period of the planning horizon, the increase in β has no effect on the level of investment in the uncertain assets – in the last period it is γ which is the risk aversion parameter for deriving the certainty equivalent rates of return and hence optimal investments in the uncertain assets. The reduced accumulation in uncertain assets implies higher foreign reserves.

Table 5. Impact effects of shifts in parameters

		C		G	W_U	
		1980	2000	2000	1980	2000
Parameter shift:						
β	15 percent	−	−	+	+	+
γ	15 percent	+	+	−	+	+
τ	25 percent	≈0	+	+	+	+
π_{t+1}/π_t	0.01	≈0	+	−	−	−
ρ_S	0.01	≈0	+	+	−	+
ρ_{HK}	0.01	≈0	+	+	−	+
ρ_{UK}	0.01	≈0	+	+	−	−
r_o	0.01	+	−	−	+	−
δ	0.01	+	−	−	−	−

An increase in γ has the opposite effect on consumption in all periods and on terminal wealth as compared to an increase in β. This has a quite intuitive appeal in view of the dynamic programming solution of the model whereby the optimal trade-off between consumption and remaining wealth is established in each period recursively. However, increases in γ and β both tend to reduce investment in uncertain assets through the certainty equivalence correction terms. In order to maintain the higher consumption entailed by an increased γ, investment in foreign assets must increase towards the end of the planning horizon.

An increase in the variance of the oil price implies that investments in all uncertain assets are reduced because the increased uncertainty in the oil price makes it relatively less profitable to invest in uncertain assets; hence more wealth is converted into the risk-free asset. Moreover, consumption is higher throughout the planning period.

An increase in any of the expected rates of return, including the expected growth rate of net oil price, provides a positive income effect which increases consumption in all periods as well as terminal wealth. A higher expected rate of return naturally implies increased investment in the asset in question, and the effect on the other uncertain assets depends on the signs of the covariances. The effect on investing in foreign assets is initially negative; for later periods the sign varies.

The role of the risk-free rate of return r_0 is somewhat complicated. The potential gain from choosing uncertain alternatives in the allocation of national wealth lessens, the higher r_0 is in comparison to the expected rates of return. Investments in all uncertain assets are thus reduced when r_0 increases. This income loss gives less scope for investing in foreign assets, and it is therefore not true that an increase in the risk-free rate of return implies higher investment in the risk-free asset. Naturally, terminal wealth is reduced. Consumption is somewhat higher in the first periods and is later reduced due to the loss of the potential gain from uncertainty.

An increase in the rate of time preference δ implies that the consumption path shifts towards the beginning of the planning period. This early increase in consumption gives less scope for saving, and terminal wealth is reduced. Investments in uncertain assets are not affected by δ, since the allocation of total wealth between uncertain alternatives is determined as a static portfolio problem once the optimal trade-off between consumption and future wealth has been established in each period.

An important question in macroeconomic planning under uncertainty is to elucidate the implications for economic policy of given stochastic assumptions and an explicitly stated attitude towards risk. The scenarios of the Perspective Analysis to which we are referring illustrate the implications of a tight as compared to a lax economic policy under alternative scenarios for uncertain future income. These policy alternatives are established in the MSG-model by varying the exogenous variables and government instruments. It is not obvious how a corresponding simulation of policy alternatives can be performed in the stochastic optimization model. However, different assumptions about the risk aversion parameters result in a different propensity to pursue a tight or a lax economic policy. Consider a situation where the government is more concerned about future consumption possibilities and wants to pursue a policy for increasing the national wealth at the end of the planning period. Within a fully elaborated macroeconomic context this is aimed at by steering the exogenous variables so as to decrease current consumption and promote accumulation in foreign (and domestic) assets. In our model it is natural to express such a concern in terms of risk aversion: a policy which aims at reducing current consumption and increasing terminal wealth corresponds to a shift in the risk aversion parameters towards a higher β and lower γ.

In order to illustrate the effects of risk aversion, it is elucidating to express a specified change in economic policy by the corresponding variations in the risk aversion parameters. Within this empirical application we have interpreted the policy alternatives discussed in the Perspective Analysis in terms of risk aversion.

The alternatives 2.2 and 3.1 represent the tight policy alternative under each income scenario, whereas 2.1 and 3.2 represent the lax policy alternatives. By variations in β and γ we have established the scenarios of our model which correspond to these four policy alternatives. The results are presented in Table 6 and in Figure 4.

Since the reference scenario of the stochastic optimization model deviates from the reference scenario of the MSG-model, it has not been our intention to simulate the four alternatives (2.1, 2.2, 3.1, 3.2) exactly by appropriate adjustments of the risk aversion parameters. However, for establishing our alternatives we have applied the same criteria as those of the Perspective Analysis:

    –   Tight policy in the high expected income scenario (=2.2) and lax policy in the low expected income scenario (=3.2) should aim at the same increase in consumption as the reference scenario.

- Tight policy in the low expected income scenario (=3.1) and lax policy in the high expected income scenario (=2.1) should aim at the same terminal wealth position as the reference scenario.

Table 6. Selected results from the stochastic optimization model

Scenario	Total consumption in year 2000 as increase over 1980. Percent	Total wealth in year 2000 Billion kr.	Net foreign reserves in year 2000 Billion kr.
1. Reference path	74.4	5568	-1219
2. Higher petro-leum income			
2.1 Increased domestic use	118.2	5561	- 973
2.2 Increased capital exports	100.0	7846	- 878
3. Sluggish world economy			
3.1 Tight policy	56.3	5619	-1218
3.2 Lax policy	70.2	4904	-1911

These criteria have been our guidelines for the choice of appropriate variations of the risk aversion coefficients. The numerical results can be summarized as follows:

An increase in β of 15 percent corresponds to a tight policy whereby consumption is reduced according to this criterion. Since the terminal wealth position differs between the two income scenarios, it was further-more necessary to reduce γ by 10 percent to simulate 2.2 and to reduce γ by 5 percent to simulate 3.1. Terminal wealth varies inversely with γ. Since 2.2 has a higher expected income than 3.1, it was necessary to

reduce γ relatively more in the simulation of 2.2 to account for the large
terminal wealth of this alternative.

In the simulation of the lax policy alternatives 2.1 and 3.2, β was
decreased accordingly, i.e. by 15 percent. Since the terminal wealth position of 2.1 should reflect the higher expected income as compared to 3.2,
γ is increased by 20 percent in 2.1 and γ is decreased by 5 percent in
3.2.

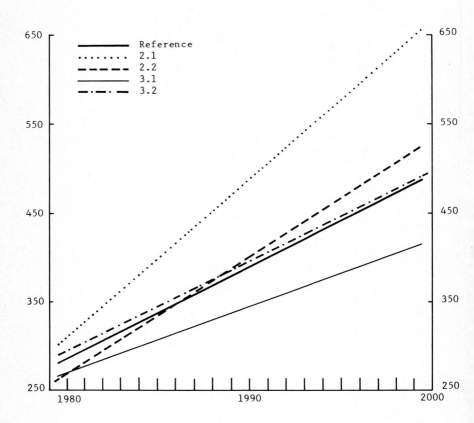

Figure 4. Consumption path 1980-2000 (In billion kroner)

The optimal consumption paths are illustrated in Figure 4. The simulations of the lax policy alternatives, 2.1 and 3.2, give consumption paths
which are higher than that of the reference scenario throughout the plan

ning horizon. The consumption path of the tight policy alternative 3.1 is accordingly lower. However, the consumption path of 2.2, which simulates tight policy in the high income scenario, intersects the consumption path of the reference scenario. The appropriate increase in risk aversion entails lower consumption in early years, but this effect is gradually reversed due to the wealth effect of the high income assumption.

The variations of the risk aversion coefficients β and γ in the simulation alternatives are all within the range given by (6.1), thus total wealth increases in the earlier years and declines thereafter (see Figure 5). In accordance with our criteria for establishing the simulation alternatives, terminal wealth in the scenarios of 2.1 and 3.1 turns out as in the reference path, while terminal wealth of 3.2 is lower and terminal wealth

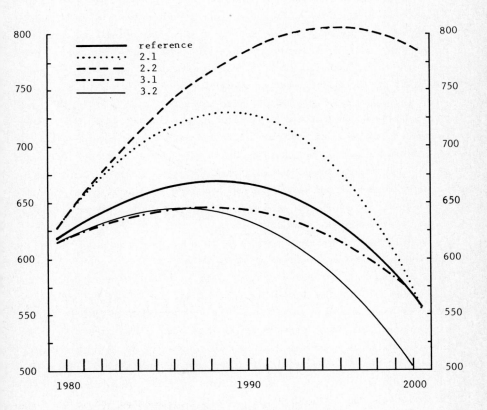

Figure 5. Total wealth 1980-2000 (in 10 billion kroner)

of 2.2 is higher. The initial decline in consumption in the high income
scenario 2.2 gives a considerable growth in total wealth, and the downward movement of total wealth occurs at a later stage than in the other
alternatives. Thus consumption in the year 2000 comes out somewhat
higher than in the reference scenario.

Investments in uncertain assets decline monotonically in all simulation
alternatives, since our assumptions about the risk aversion parameters
entail that a conversion from some uncertain assets into the risk-free
alternative must take place. Thus foreign debt is reduced throughout the
planning period in all alternatives. However, none of the alternatives
imply positive foreign reserves within a horizon of 20 years. The explanation is that initial optimal accumulation in the uncertain assets is substantially higher in all alternatives than the corresponding national account
figures for 1979, which have been used to determine the initial wealth
parameters of the model. In order to realize the optimal solutions for
consumption and investments in uncertain assets a substantial foreign
debt has to be incurred initially. Foreign wealth position is determined
residually in the model, and the initial levels of foreign debt entail that
positive foreign reserves cannot be obtained in a time span of 20 years.
This conclusion is crucially dependent on the constancy of all the other
parameters except the risk aversion coefficients. If, for example, the
standard deviation of the oil price is increased by 25 percent, there is a
decline in the accumulation of uncertain assets whereby foreign debt
starts at a more modest level than in the depicted alternatives. With this
assumption the reference scenario will in fact come out with positive
foreign reserves in the year 2000.

Within each alternative, oil production is fairly constant once the
optimal path has been reached (see Figure 6). In the lax policy alternatives 2.1 and 3.2, the initial optimal value of the oil reserves is substantially higher than the initial factual estimate for the value of the oil
reserves because of the reduction in the risk aversion coefficient β. As a
consequence, the model projects negative oil extraction in 1980. Similarly,
a substanital peak occurs in initial oil production in the tight policy alternatives 2.2 and 3.1 because the initial optimal value of the oil reserves is
reduced due to the higher degree of risk aversion. However, from 1981
the oil production paths show that optimal oil production is higher in the
lax policy alternatives and lower in the tight policy alternatives as compared to the reference scenario.

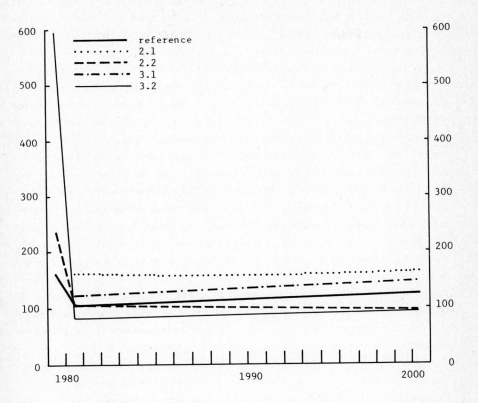

Notes: For scenario 2.1 and 3.2 the first-year depletion is negative, about
       -320 mtoe.

Figure 6. Oil depletion, 1980-2000 (mtoe.)

Although solutions with initial peaks in oil production or initial negative oil production are not exceptional in an optimization context, they can
not be implemented. In terms of policy guidelines, however, we can interpret the initial negative oil production as an indication that oil production
has been too high in the preceding periods, and that the remaining level
of oil reserves is too small in 1980 relative to the optimal oil reserves. If
oil production is temporarily postponed for some years, the value of the
oil reserves will gradually reach the optimal level and thereafter oil production can follow the optimal path.

Accordingly, a solution whose initial oil prodution is higher than existing capacity suggests that actual oil production should increase as quickly as practical above the optimal level until the optimal reallocation of uncertain assets has taken place.

As a consequence of uncertainty, oil production in all the alternatives is higher throughout the planning horizon than the projected oil production paths in the scenarios of the Perspective Analysis. However, in the alternatives of low risk aversion (2.1 and 3.2), optimal oil reserves are initially higher than the current estimate because it is more profitable to maintain uncertain assets. On the other hand, the optimal terminal oil reserves come out lower in all alternatives as compared to the projections of the Perspective Analysis. Thus we approach the conclusion that uncertainty provides an incentive to increase oil production and convert the oil reserves into more certain assets. This conclusion is in accordance with the present value calculations given in the report of the government appointed committee on the future extent of petroleum activities on the Norwegian continental shelf (NOU (1983a), annex 14). In that committee's present-value considerations uncertainty was not explicitly taken into account. However it must be kept in mind that although a lower risk aversion implies higher oil production, it also indicates that the initial oil reserves should be higher.

In terms of risk aversion, we have thus established alternatives for economic policy that are consistent with what is considered by the Perspective Analysis as a relevant feasible set. Starting from given stochastic assumptions and with a given degree of risk aversion, the stochastic optimization model yields guidelines for policy implementation under uncertainty which can be applied for evaluating long-term macroeconomic projections of the MSG-model.

The important lesson to be drawn is that moderate variations in the attitude towards risk may have fairly large impacts on the choice of economic policies.

References

Aslaksen, I. and O. Bjerkholt (1985), "Certainty equivalence procedures in the macroeconomic planning of an oil economy", Discussion paper no. 1, Central Bureau of Statistics, Oslo.

Chow, G.C. (1975), Analysis and Control of Dynamic Economic Systems, John Wiley & Sons, New York.

Johansen, L. (1960), A Multi-Sectoral Study of Economic Growth, North-Holland Publishing Company, Amsterdam.

Johansen, L. (1980), "Parametric Certainty Equivalence procedures in decision-making under uncertainty", Zeitschrift für Nationaløkonomie 40, No. 3-4, 257-279.

NOU (1983a), "The Future Extent of Petroleum Activities on the Norwegian Continental Shelf. Summary and conclusions of the Report from a Commision appointed by Royal Decree of 5 March 1982", NOU 1983:27, Universitetsforlaget, Oslo.

NOU (1983b), "Perspektivberegninger for norsk økonomi til år 2000", NOU 1983:37, Universitetsforlaget, Oslo.

Samuelson, P.A. (1969), "Lifetime portfolio selection by dynamic stochastic programming", Review of Economics and Statistics, 239-246.

Theil, H. (1964), Optimal Decision Rules for Government and Industry, North-Holland Publishing Company, Amsterdam.

AUTHOR INDEX

Abel, A., 106
Adelman, I., 137
Aitchison, J., 60
Albrecht, J., 106
Alstadheim, H., 6, 249
Andersson, Å., 163
Armington, P., 146, 194
Aslaksen, I., 259, 286, 306
Aukrust, O., 242

Barker, T., 261
Barten, A.P., 165
Bergan, R., 212
Bergman, L., 137-8, 141, 148
    151, 164-5, 189
Berndt, E.R., 203, 235
Bianchi, P., 12
Bischoff, C., 6
Bjerkholt, O., 109, 122, 191
    213, 235, 242, 251, 253,
    258-9, 286, 306
Bjerve, P.J., 242
Black, S.L., 137, 139, 143,
    145
Bolker, E., 70, 75-8
Brown, J.A.C., 60

Cappelen, Å., 109, 122, 191,
    215
Carlsson, B., 12
Chetham, R., 137, 139
Chow, G.C., 304
Christensen, L.R., 12, 203,
    235
Condon, T., 148
Cramer, H., 75

Denny, M., 12
Dervis, K., 137, 139, 143,
    151-2
de Jong, H.W., 12
de Melo, J., 137, 139, 143,
    146, 148, 151-2
Diewert, W.E., 202
Dixon, P.B., 137, 150-1

Feller, W., 78
Feltenstein, A., 140
Frenger, P., 187

Frisch, R., 3, 7, 99, 187-8,
    207, 242, 244, 246, 260
Fuss, M., 12, 107
Førsund, F.R., 16, 18, 26,
    50, 55, 60-1, 87, 110,
    115, 122, 283

Griliches, Z., 110

Haavelmo, T., 246
Hartman, R., 106
Hart, A., 106
Helgason, S., 75
Hicks, J., 90, 196, 203, 221,
    230
Hildenbrand, K., 16
Hildenbrand, W., 16, 43, 60,
    65, 67, 70, 75, 123
Hjalmarsson, L., 16, 18, 26,
    50, 55, 60-1, 115, 122, 163
Hoel, M., 187
Hogan, W., 192, 225
Holm, I., 215
Homberg, R., 12
Houthakker, H.S., 5, 65-7,
    70-1, 75
Hudson, E.A., 137, 140, 150

Isachsen, A.J., 109

Jansen, E., 110, 122, 283
Johansen, L., 1-3, 5-7, 11,
    14, 16-8, 43, 45, 65-6,
    70-1, 75, 87, 105-6, 109-11,
    113, 122-3, 127, 164-5,
    187-9, 194, 205-6, 271-87,
    289, 309-10
Johansson, B., 163
Jorgenson, D.W., 12, 137,
    140, 150, 187

Karlstrøm, U., 140
Kelley, A., 137, 139
Kon, Y., 106

Langsether, Å., 6
Larsen, K.A., 188-9
Levhari, D., 60, 123
Levy, P., 78

SUBJECT INDEX

absolute monotonicity, 70
activity, 195
    price indices, 202
    region, 17-9
algorithm, 16
annual plan, 244
Armington assumption, 147-8,
    194

backward linkages, 100
basic value, 201, 209
best practice, 27
beta distribution, 47-63
Borel
    function, 71
    measure, 70, 75-8
    sets, 84
break-even price, 91

Cambridge Growth Project, 191
capacity
    constrained, 92
    distribution, 4-5, 38,
    114-5, 120
    distribution,estimation
    of, 38
    distribution,invariance
    of, 45
    fluctuating utilization
    rates, 100
    utilization, 89, 112, 196
    utilization,degree of, 90
    utilization,full, 196, 235
    utilization,optimal
    strategy of, 91
    utilization rates, 211, 235
capital-intensive techniques,
    100
capital
    demand for, 277
    fixed commitments, 99
    intensive, 102
    supply of, 277
    vintages, 122
cement industry, 11-42
center of symmetry, 68
Central Bank of Norway, 246-7
Central Bureau of Statistics,
    7, 109, 188, 245-6, 249-51

central planning, 141
choice-of-technique function,
    89, 91
commodity-by-activity
    coefficients, 201
comparative advantages, 146
complete
    growth equation, 122
    scheme, 7, 207
    specialization, 146
computable general
    equilibrium model (CGE),
    128, 137-41, 146-7, 150
    of developing countries,
    139
concept of strategy, 284
coordination of investment,
    102

dairy industry, 50, 55
decision models, 246
demand constrained, 92
Department of Economics,
    245-6, 248-9
development of plans, 249
direct instruments, 241
disequilibrium, 191
distribution approach, 5
dual problem, 112
Dutch Disease, 275
Dutch Planning Bureau, 6
dynamic flexibility, 297
dynamic optimization problem,
    293

econometric models, 242-3
economic
    planning, 191, 241, 243
    policy, 241, 244, 246
    programme, 248
    triangle, 245
efficiency frontier, 121
elasticity
    of scale, 16
    of substitution, 16
endogenous foreign trade, 146
    sector, 143
Energy Modelling Forum, 226
envelope function, 115